Photo by Honey Lee Cottrell

Estelle B. Freedman received her doctorate in history from Columbia University
and is an assistant professor at Stanford
University. In addition to *Their Sisters'
Keepers*, she has authored a number of
journal articles dealing with women and
history.

D0983234

Their Sisters' Keepers

 Women and
Culture Series

The Women and Culture Series is dedicated to books that illuminate the lives, roles, achievements, and position of women, past or present.

La Partera: Story of a Midwife   Fran Leeper Buss

Harriet Martineau: The Woman and   Valerie Kossew Pichanick
  Her Work, 1802–76

Women and Politics: The   Sandra Baxter and
  Invisible Majority   Marjorie Lansing

Their Sisters' Keepers: Women's Prison   Estelle B. Freedman
  Reform in America, 1830–1930

ESTELLE B. FREEDMAN is a Hamilton Prize winner for 1978. The Alice and Edith Hamilton Prize is named for two outstanding women scholars: Alice Hamilton (educated at the University of Michigan Medical School), a pioneer in environmental medicine; and her sister Edith Hamilton, the renowned classicist. The Hamilton Prize Competition is supported by the University of Michigan Horace H. Rackham School of Graduate Studies and by private donors.

Their Sisters' Keepers

Women's Prison Reform in America, 1830–1930

Estelle B. Freedman

The University of Michigan Press
Ann Arbor

Library of Congress Cataloging in Publication Data

Freedman, Estelle B   1947–
   Their sisters' keepers.

   (Women and culture series)
   Based on the author's thesis, Columbia University.
   Bibliography: p.
   Includes index.
   1. Reformatories for women—United States—History.
2. Prison reformers—United States—History. I. Title.
II. Series.
HV9466.F73   365'.43'0973   80–24918
ISBN 0–472–10008–4

To the memory of my grandparents

Acknowledgments

I began to study the history of women's prison reform in 1972, when women's history was not yet included in the graduate curriculum. No one I talked with then knew why separate women's prisons had originated in the nineteenth century, and I decided to find an answer. Thanks to the growth of women's history, and in turn to the feminist movement, I have been able to ask many more questions about this topic and to begin to answer them in this book. I am grateful to the students and teachers of women's history for making this study possible, and to the Horace H. Rackham Graduate School of the University of Michigan for recognizing the importance of women's studies by establishing the Hamilton Prize.

I have many friends and co-workers to thank for their help. First, I would like to acknowledge the research funds provided by the departments of history at Stanford and Princeton universities and the Criminal Justice Program at Princeton. The librarians at these universities, and at the Schlesinger Library at Radcliffe College; the Massachusetts Correctional Institution at Framingham; the archives of Earlham College in Richmond, Indiana; the state libraries of Indiana, Massachusetts, and New York; and the volunteers' office at the New York Reformatory for Women at Bedford Hills all helped me locate obscure sources. My dissertation advisor at Columbia University, Kenneth T. Jackson, offered both encouragement and useful criticism from the outset of the project. I benefited greatly from comments on my thesis by John D'Emilio, Michael Hindus, Louise Knauer, Judith Johnston, Elaine Tyler May, Rosalind Rosenberg, and Nancy Weiss, and from close readings of the revised manuscript by David Kennedy, Carolyn Lougee, Elizabeth Pleck, Carroll Smith-Rosenberg, Louise Tilly, and the anonymous referees on the Hamilton Prize committee. In addition, criticisms of individual chapters by Carl Degler, Irene Diamond, Yolaida Durán, Mary Felstiner, Gary Sue Goodman, Gail Hershatter, Paul Robinson, and Michelle Rosaldo influenced my thinking and my writing. I am especially grateful to John D'Emilio for suggesting improvements on successive drafts of each chapter, for typing the manuscript speedily and skillfully, and for providing consistent moral support. I appreciate as well the careful research assistance and friendships of Yolaida Durán, Cindy Fritz, Sue Macy, and Joanne Meyerowitz. While each of these individuals helped improve the book, I am solely responsible for its final contents.

Members of several women's groups offered intellectual stimulation and personal support as I researched and wrote this study. The Center for Research on Women group at Stanford helped me clarify my ideas about women's prison reform. Feminist study groups in Princeton, Palo Alto, and San Francisco have contributed to my personal and political appreciation of the issues raised by this topic. I want to thank all of my friends in the East and in California, my parents, and my sister and her family for both their interest in my work and the diversions they provided from it over the years. Above all, my best friends, Ilene Levitt and John D'Emilio, deserve special credit for helping me in every way they could.

Contents

Introduction

From the mid-nineteenth century to the present, the woman prisoner has aroused strong sympathies from feminists and social reformers. When under the control of male keepers, she represents an extreme case of sexual powerlessness. Her imprisonment symbolizes as well the constraints placed on all women by authoritarian institutions. Nineteenth-century reformers first proclaimed a sisterhood with the imprisoned woman, and contemporary feminists explicitly identify with her plight. As Bernice Reagon explains in her song about Joann Little, the black prisoner who fought back when raped by her jailer: "Joann is you and Joann is me / Our Prison is the whole society."[1]

Their Sisters' Keepers explores the origins of women's concerns for female inmates in the United States. Its subjects are reformers, their ideas, and the institutions they created. Although female criminals are not the focus of this study, the meaning of women's crime, the impact of prisons on female inmates, and the changing relationship between reformers and criminals are important elements of this history. The first section of the book analyzes white, middle-class women's response to the problems of female prisoners in the nineteenth century. The central chapters provide a composite history of the first state prisons run by and for women, from approximately 1870 to 1910. The third section investigates the work of women criminologists and penologists during the Progressive era. An epilogue suggests the legacy of women's prison reform since 1920.

The growing literature on the history of women in the nineteenth century provides the major framework for this study. In the past decade two approaches have dominated this field. The first asks whether women as a group lost or gained status as America changed from an agricultural to an industrial society. Many scholars argue that middle-class women's economic and political rights declined after the Revolutionary era as a result of the gradual separation of paid work in the public sphere and unpaid work in the home.[2] Other writers stress the improvements industrialization brought to these women's lives and the ways they gained power within the family.³ The second approach explores the separate female sphere of the nineteenth century. Although the cultural ideal of the "true woman"⁴ confined to her home has long influenced historians' critique of woman's sphere, recent studies have shown that some women created a personally supportive sisterhood from this model. Furthermore, separate female networks and religious or social organizations provided a base from which women could expand their influence far beyond the domestic sphere.⁵

Both of these themes—the changing status of women and the function of the female sphere—help explain the tensions that run throughout the history of women's prison reform. The movement to aid female prisoners had roots in the antebellum, domestic, female sphere, yet it facilitated white middle-class women's entry into public and professional work by the end of the century. Throughout this period, however, prison reformers clung to a definition of woman's separate nature that limited their own power and often stifled the inmates they sought to aid. Why reformers in the nineteenth century used this argument of sexual difference, and women in the Progressive era began to question it, is one of the problems addressed in this book.

Women's prison reform has a complicated relationship to the history of American feminism. Prison reformers had important feminist insights; that is, they recognized sexual inequalities and at times spoke out against them. In contrast to women in the temperance and abolitionist movements, however, they only rarely became women's rights activists. Rather, prison reformers in the nineteenth century adopted a "separate but equal" political strategy that derived, in part, from the nature of their work. Abolitionists wanted to emancipate individuals from an oppressive institution, slavery; women who applied this principle to their own sex often demanded freedom from legal restraints.⁶ Prison reformers, however, did not reject the institution that controlled criminals. Instead, they wanted to improve penal treatment of women, and to do so they eventually became keepers in their own prisons. Arguments about individual liberty were unlikely to develop in this setting, while arguments about sexual differences flourished in support of their cause.

Although women's history provides the central context for this study, the history of prisons offers another important perspective. The fact that Americans increasingly turned to state institutions to house the poor, insane, and criminal in the nineteenth century helps explain why women sought to establish their own prisons during this period. In addition, the histories of these institutions often ran parallel, and at times women's prisons followed their patterns. But because they reflected the different contours of women's historical experience, the separate prisons had unique origins and functions that raise questions about both prisons as institutions and the sexual categories they supported.

The historical literature on prisons raises as well the difficult problem of evaluating institutional reforms. One school of thought measures change in comparison to past abuses. As prison historian O. F. Lewis wrote in 1922: "A reform is to be judged, of course, not by what to-day would be considered adequate . . . but in the light of its relative progressiveness as a substitute for existing conditions, in an existing state of public opinion and of prevailing customs."[7] Revisionist historians, in contrast, are often critical of the failures of past reforms in comparison to radical alternatives. David Rothman, for instance, evaluated the founders of prisons and insane asylums from this perspective in 1971: "By incarcerating the deviant and dependent, and defending the step with hyperbolic rhetoric, they discouraged—really eliminated—the search for other solutions that might have been less susceptible to abuse."[8]

Both of these perspectives can be applied to the history of women's prison reform. The activists deserve credit for their progressive and feminist insights and for the benefits they procured for female inmates. At the same time, an historical analysis of the limitations of their institutions may contribute to new solutions to the problems of women prisoners. In the final chapter I have evaluated the women's prisons in these terms. Throughout the book, however, I have tried to concentrate on a series of broader historical questions: Why did reformers think and act as they did? What internal and external forces influenced the history of their institutions? How, and why, did their movement change from the nineteenth to the early twentieth centuries? And why has the legacy of "their sisters' keepers" remained so powerful?

Part 1

The Origins of Women's Prison Reform

Chapter 1

The Problem of the Woman Prisoner, 1820–70

In 1819 the male managers of the New York Society for the Prevention of Pauperism described the women's quarters at the Bellevue Penitentiary as "one great school of vice and desperation," replete with "prostitutes, vagrants, lunatics, thieves, and those of a less heinous character." What shocked them as much as the indiscriminate mixing of "every kind of female convict" was the lack of attention paid to these outcasts by the more fortunate of their sex:

> Why this melancholy spectacle of female wretchedness has claimed no more attention, and excited no more sympathy, in a city like ours, where scenes of exalted benevolence and acts of religious devotion are continually displayed, we cannot say. Why no female messengers have entered this gloomy abode of guilt and despair, like angels of mercy, and seraphs of peace and consolation, is a matter of deep reflection and regret.

After citing the example of British reformer Elizabeth Fry, the managers expressed their hopes that a similar "benevolent spirit will take root in our own country."[1]

This plea for "female messengers" rested on two assumptions that would eventually provide a foundation for American women's prison reform: first, that women constituted a special category of prisoners, and second, that women more than men had a responsibility to come to their aid. In 1819 these ideas were not yet widely shared and the angels invoked by the managers did not materialize. But soon three historical preconditions for a movement to aid women prisoners occurred. First, most northern states adopted the prison as a primary means of punishing and reducing criminal activity. Second, a small but significant number of women became inmates of these prisons, especially after 1840. Finally, middle-class American women, motivated by both religious benevolence and their growing consciousness as a sex, became active in reform movements that brought them into contact with their imprisoned sisters. To understand why reformers would view

7

women as a special group of prisoners in need of their care requires an examination of woman's place in nineteenth-century prisons.

The Use of the Prison

In the beginning of the nineteenth century, Americans engaged in the restructuring of their economic, political, and social institutions. Commerce and later industry gradually replaced agriculture as the base of the economy. National political parties superseded local deference politics. Public educational institutions supplemented familial and religious training. At the same time, new legal and penal systems, partly adapted from European models, reorganized criminal justice and punishment.

Systems of criminal justice in Europe and the colonies had begun to change rapidly during the period of the American and French revolutions. Formerly, capital punishment had predominated as the ultimate deterrent to crimes ranging from murder to adultery. Lesser punishments were still severe, corporal, and usually executed in public. In the American colonies, for instance, both men and women who broke the law were publicly hanged, whipped, ducked, or placed in stocks or pillories, thus adding humiliation to their physical discomfort. Local jails served mainly to detain those awaiting trial or punishment.[2] In the late eighteenth century, Enlightenment thinkers on both sides of the Atlantic began to reject the widespread use of capital punishment. They argued that carefully designed criminal codes provided a more rational and humane deterrent to crime. Soon after criminal law reform began, however, the concept of prison reform seized the imaginations of many Americans.[3]

The term "prison reform" has come to refer to efforts to improve prison conditions, but it has a more basic meaning as well: the use of prisons to re-form, rather than merely to detain, criminals. Advocates of prison reform in the early nineteenth century favored the establishment of prisons which, through their influence on prisoners' behavior, would encourage repentance. The penitentiary, they believed, best combined the goals of punishing criminals and re-forming their characters so that they would not break the law again. The penitentiary ideal consisted of extreme isolation of criminals from society, extensive supervision over their daily lives, and compulsory productive labor.

Although it originated in eighteenth-century England and France, the penitentiary had its most enthusiastic reception in the United States. After 1815 dozens of American states, counties, and municipalities constructed penitentiarylike institutions. American advocates of prison reform, men like Louis Dwight, Matthew Carey, and John Griscom, elaborated the penitentiary ideal into two competing models. One, the Pennsylvania system, used by Quakers in Philadelphia since the turn of the century, isolated each prisoner in a separate cell and required total silence, both day and night. Left alone, except when the Bible was read to him, the prisoner might repent his crimes and even achieve religious conversion. The alternative Auburn plan, named for the congregate-style prison that opened in Auburn, New York, in 1817, introduced a variation of the silent system. After 1825 Auburn's inmates, though isolated in separate cells at night, worked together during the day in silence under an elaborate system of regimentation and surveillance which included the lockstep, striped uniforms, and extensive corporal punishment. Less concerned with spiritual redemption, the Auburn system attempted to remold inmates through "prison discipline."[4]

Historians have speculated widely about the rise of the penitentiary, its appeal to nineteenth-century Europeans and Americans, and its effect on both prisoners and the society as a whole. One set of scholars has debated the motivations of the middle- to upper-class men who founded American institutions for the "deviant and dependent." Gerald Grob has emphasized the humanitarian impulses of the institutional founders, while David Rothman has insisted that the reformers were responding to fears of social disorder and acting from their need for social control.[5] Other writers have assessed the penitentiary within the context of the nineteenth-century capitalist political economy. As the wage-labor system enlarged the dependent, unproductive classes, Michael Katz has explained, transients and criminals had to be retrained as productive laborers. The factorylike penal institutions served this purpose.[6] Transcending questions of individual motivation and economic function, French historian Michel Foucault has approached the penitentiary as an expression of the "political anatomy." According to Foucault, the distinguishing feature of the penitentiary—surveillance, or discipline—reproduced the power mechanism of the larger social body, the "disciplinary society" of the nineteenth century.[7]

Whether the isolation and regimentation of the penitentiary was intended to convert, control, or retrain prisoners, the institution ultimately failed to achieve its founders' goals. Most writers agree that prisons, like other nineteenth-century asylums, deteriorated rapidly into purely custodial institutions. They then provided a convenient storage system for individuals who were no longer defined as members of the body politic.

This approach meshed well with the new perception of criminals. No longer seen as individual sinners who remained integral members of the community, those who committed crimes now acquired new identities as members of a separate criminal subculture. The "dangerous class" of anonymous vagrants, thieves, and prostitutes who were increasingly noticed on European and American city streets after 1815 were seen as a threat to property and public order.[8] Since the traditional community sanctions of public humiliation, excommunication, or banishment were ineffective in a mobile, heterogeneous, urban society, new forms of control evolved that included professional police forces and prison systems. Arrest and incarceration helped to seal the identities of criminals and segregate them further from the society.

Although historians of prison reform have concentrated largely on male criminals and reformers, women also entered the new penal institutions as inmates and eventually as keepers. Some European reformers expected women to serve in the penitentiary,[9] but Americans rarely mentioned female prisoners as a special group. In fact, very few women served in the earliest American prisons, and women were not at first considered a significant part of America's dangerous classes.

The initial infrequency of women's incarceration can be explained by their different historical relationship to institutions of social control. As several historians have noted, imprisonment developed simultaneously with the growth of "republicanism," the extension of political liberties and economic rights to men.[10] The punishment for abusing these privileges was the denial of political and economic liberties through imprisonment. Women, however, had fewer liberties to abuse. Because their place in the republican society remained in the home, they had less opportunity to commit crimes. More importantly, women remained under the traditional controls of family and church longer than did men. Because women's behavior was more closely regulated by these private institutions, they were less likely to become the subjects of new public agencies of punishment, at least for the reasons that men were. Only after certain categories of female crime emerged within a sexual ideology of female purity were more women punished in jails and prisons.

Although the fragmentary evidence left by prison reformers and state officials does not reveal how often women committed crimes, it does show the limited use of imprisonment for women up to 1840 and the types of crimes for which women were convicted. In four state penitentiaries observed by Gustave de Beaumont and Alexis de Tocqueville in 1831, an average of only one in twelve prisoners was female, ranging from one in nineteen in New York to one in six in Maryland.[11] In 1850 women constituted only 3.6 percent of the total inmates in thirty-four state and county prisons. New York's penitentiaries received the highest proportion of women, 5.6 percent; the Massachusetts state prison, on the other hand, held no women because women convicts were sentenced to local institutions. In 1850 women represented 19.5 percent of the inmates of the Massachusetts county jails and houses of correction.[12]

The small number of women in state prisons as opposed to local jails was due in part to the different types of crimes for which men and women were convicted. Of the three major categories of crimes—against person, property, and public order—only the last included a significant number of women. In New York state, for instance, men's convictions outnumbered women's by fifteen to one in the Courts of Record, which tried person and property crimes. In the Courts of Special Session, however, which tried drunkenness, vagrancy, streetwalking, and petty larceny, the ratio of male to female convictions narrowed to five to one for county courts and four to one for city courts[13] (see table 1). When convicted for murder, manslaughter, arson, or burglary, women did serve in penitentiaries. The most frequent women's crimes, however—the petty street crimes and those governed by moral and sexual codes—usually led to jail terms.

American officials and foreign observers commented on the small number of women convicted of "serious" crimes in the United States. New York Secretary of State John Dix noted in 1838 that while in England the ratio of male to female criminals was five to one, in New York it was sixteen to one, a comparison he found "very highly in favor of the morals of the female sex in the State." Dix also cited Belgian criminologist Adolphe Quetelet's theory that the strict sexual division of labor in America, which kept women closer to the home than in Europe, provided fewer opportunities for female crime.[14] Another New York secretary of state elaborated on the lower incidence of female crime when he reported in 1842 that women accounted for only 1/114th of the state's criminal convictions, even though they constituted almost half of the population. "This is a very remarkable disproportion," Secretary Samuel Young noted, "which may be accounted for partly by the reluctance to prosecute females, partly by their domestic life and habits, leaving them less exposed to temptation, and partly by the unavoidable inference that they are superior to men in moral honesty."[15]

Whatever protection from temptation or prosecution women enjoyed soon proved to be temporary, for the criminal statistics began to reveal a startling trend. New York and Massachusetts records show that after 1840 women joined the ranks of the criminal class in America, though in smaller numbers and for different crimes than men. In New York courts, convictions of women increased between 1847 and 1860 at a much higher rate than that of men's convictions (appendix A). Consequently, the ratio of male to female crime fell from over six to one in 1840 to under two to one in 1860 (table 1). The ratio gradually rose at the end of the century

TABLE 1. New York Sex-Crime Ratios, 1833–92 (Males: 1 Female)

	Courts of Record	Courts of Special Sessions		Sum of All Criminal Courts
		County	City	
1833–37	n.a.	n.a.	n.a.	6.02
1838–42	14.14	6.40	4.01	6.40
1843–47	13.89	5.79	3.83	5.90
1848–52	17.80	6.76	3.92	3.46
1853–57	14.85	4.50	1.70	2.01
1858–62	9.41	3.04	1.69	1.94
1863–67	11.62	4.14	1.56	2.32
1868–72	15.71	4.97	1.90	2.89
1873–77	16.78	4.54	2.27	2.99
1878–82	20.00	5.88	2.51	3.27
1883–87	n.a.	n.a.	n.a.	3.85
1888–92	21.00	8.06	0.27	4.21
Average	15.52	5.40	2.37	3.77

Source: New York Secretary of State, Convictions for Criminal Offenses, 1830–1899.

Note: The figures from which the ratios are derived represent male convictions per 100,000 adult males/female convictions per 100,000 adult females.

but it never returned to the earlier extreme disparity. Imprisonment rates in Massachusetts revealed a similar trend. Shortly after 1840 the incidence of incarceration rose for both sexes, but after 1860 the female rate continued to climb despite a drop in the total rate. The ratio of all women committed to Massachusetts jails (per 100,000 women in the state) increased from under 300 in the 1840s to over 400 in the 1860s. The proportion of women among the total commitments to jails and houses of correction rose in Massachusetts from 20 percent in 1842 to a high of 37.2 percent in 1864.[16]

The most dramatic increase in women's criminal convictions and imprisonments occurred during the 1860s. In New York City, Buffalo, Boston, and Detroit, female crime rates soared during the Civil War years. During this period the female populations of Massachusetts and New York prisons increased by a third while the number of male prisoners declined by almost half. As the warden of the Eastern State Penitentiary in Pennsylvania noted, "while the number of male prisoners has been diminished by the civil war now raging, the number of female prisoners has been increased."[17]

In addition to the relative shift attributable to men's absence during wartime, the 1860s witnessed an independent rise in criminal convictions of women. The traditional offenses against public order accounted for part of this trend, with a probable increase in the visibility of prostitution during the war as one factor. But contemporary observers expressed more alarm over the frequency of women's serious crimes. In New York the number of women convicted for crimes against the person more than tripled between the 1850s and 1860s, although comparable male convictions declined. Women's conviction rates for crimes against property also rose during the 1860s—ten times as fast as men's.[18] Some commentators blamed women's increasing practice of abortion for the rise in crimes against the person, although stricter statutes and enforcement may have been equally responsible.[19]

The conviction and imprisonment of women resulted from many of the social changes that fostered a general increase in European and American crime rates between 1815 and 1860. Movement from rural to urban areas, or across the Atlantic, as well as the gradual transformation from a family to a market economy, disrupted the lives of migrant, immigrant, and working-class men and women. A growing number of individuals lived outside of the traditional institutions of church, family, and community. Many led economically marginal and geographically mobile lives.

Especially in the rapidly growing cities, they came into conflict with new agents of social control, such as urban police forces and moral reformers. Not serious crimes against person or property, but unlawful personal behavior—drunkenness, idle and disorderly conduct, and vagrancy—brought the majority of criminals of both sexes into courts and prisons.

Women's crimes, however, had additional economic and sexual origins. The limited opportunities for wage earning and the lower salaries paid working women placed them in the most marginal economic position in the society. Prostitution provided a temporary source of income for poor women throughout the century. At times of stress, as when the Civil War removed male wage earners from many families, women may have had greater need to resort to crimes, whether theft or prostitution.[20] Equally important, though, was the sexual definition of women's offenses. A subcategory of public order offenses, sometimes called crimes against chastity or decency, applied almost exclusively to women. Although laws against sexual misconduct had regulated both women and men in colonial America, a stricter code of female morality in the nineteenth century led to the overrepresentation of women in this category of crimes. A wide range of behavior, including lewd and lascivious carriage, stubbornness, idle and disorderly conduct, drunkenness, and vagrancy, as well as fornication and adultery, brought women, more often than men, into conflict with law enforcers.

Arrest, conviction, or imprisonment for offenses against chastity, decency, or public order carried a unique penalty for the nineteenth-century female criminal—the label of "fallen woman." In the past a woman convicted of even a sexual offense might repent, accept her punishment, and return to society.[21] Now, however, a new moral standard helped create a permanent category of female criminals. No longer the perpetrator of a single immoral act, those who crossed the boundary of chastity gained a lifetime identity as a "fallen woman."

A nineteenth-century fallen woman experienced a greater stigma than did contemporary male criminals or than had women criminals in the past. Many women and men refused to associate with or employ even a suspected fallen woman. Thus outcast, the first offender often entered a vicious cycle which led her directly into the criminal class, often as a prostitute, as case histories illustrate. A respectable young widow left penniless, for example, became the mistress of a man who later abandoned her. "The poor woman had sinned away her right to return to her friends at home—men despised her—*decent* women here could not speak to her! She had recourse to the Lethe of our Christian age, and after a series of miseries was found . . . in the Tombs."[22]

The penitentiary had not been designed with the fallen woman in mind. Yet female inmates who carried this special stigma did enter state and local penal institutions in antebellum America. Their increasing numbers and their special status posed unique problems for both prisons and reformers.

The Treatment of the Fallen Woman

The women who served in penal institutions between 1820 and 1870 were not subject to the prison reform experienced by male inmates. Officials employed isolation, silence, and hard labor to rehabilitate male prisoners. The lack of accommodations for female inmates made isolation and silence impossible for them, and productive labor was not considered an important part of their routine. The neglect of female prisoners, however, was rarely benevolent. Rather, a pattern of overcrowding, harsh treatment, and sexual abuse recurred throughout prison histories.

The Auburn, New York, penitentiary combined most of these features. In the 1820s the prison had no separate cells designated for the twenty to thirty women who served there at any one time, some of them for sentences of up to fourteen years. Lodged together, unattended, in a one room attic, the windows sealed to prevent communication with men, the female prisoners were overcrowded, immobilized, and neglected.[23] Although they escaped the isolation and regimentation imposed on male inmates, their quarters, as a member of the Board of Inspection reported in 1832, presented "a specimen of the most disgusting and appalling features of the old system of prison management at the worst period of its history."[24]

In 1826, despite the attempt to keep women segregated, prisoner Rachel Welch became pregnant while serving a punishment sentence in a solitary cell. As a result of a flogging by a prison officer, Welch died after childbirth. A grand jury investigating the flogging seemed unconcerned about her pregnancy or the condition of other women at Auburn. The public scandal, however, may have influenced the passage of a law in 1828 requiring county prisons to separate male and female inmates. In 1832 Auburn hired a matron for the women's quarters.[25]

Neither public attention nor the presence of a female guard alleviated the plight of Auburn's women. Both overcrowding and disinterest in women's rehabilitation continued to bring harsh treatment. As English visitor Harriet Martineau observed after touring Auburn in 1838:

> The arrangements for the women were extremely bad. . . . There was an engine in sight which made me doubt the evidence of my own eyes: stocks, of a terrible construction; a chair, with a fastening for the head and all the limbs. . . . The [warden] liked it no better than we. He pleaded that it was the only means of keeping his refractory prisoners quiet with only one room to put them in.[26]

Little wonder that the prison chaplain once proclaimed of Auburn: "To be a male convict in this prison would be quite tolerable; but to be a female convict, for any protracted period, would be worse than death."[27]

In jails, prisons, and penitentiaries established throughout the East and Midwest, the difficulty of housing and supervising women prisoners in institutions that had not been designed for them produced wretched conditions. In 1838 the New York City Tombs had only forty-two cells to hold up to seventy women inmates, while in the Albany, New York, jail, "fifteen females were in one room with bed, so far as they had beds, on the floor."[28] In Michigan in the 1850s, ten women—three of them pregnant—were confined in two small, poorly ventilated rooms, where only male keepers entered. An 1859 newspaper account described an overcrowded Michigan prison ward as "hot and putrid." The inmates, it reported, "dwell as in Pandemonium."[29] Although almost every account of prisons and jails mention illegitimate births by female prisoners,[30] in one state, Indiana, the sexual exploitation of inmates was overt and systematic. A corrupt administration at the Indiana state prison operated a prostitution service for male guards, using the forced labor of female prisoners.[31] The Illinois state penitentiary opened a separate women's building during the 1860s, but in 1870 the twenty-two female inmates were removed to the fifth floor of the warden's house. They remained in this so-called Chicken Coop for the rest of their sentences, sitting all day in rows of chairs, mending the male prisoners' stockings. A warden later described their annual outing: "They were allowed a holiday stroll in the yard—to the accompaniment of the whistles and cries from the locked-in and eagerly watching male prisoners."[32]

Although the women's quarters of nineteenth-century penal institutions contrasted markedly with prison reformers' ideals of order, discipline, and silence, only rarely did male officials address the problem of women prisoners. When they did, little came of it. In 1828 New York Governor DeWitt Clinton recommended the establishment of a separate penitentiary for women, but the legislature decided against it because the women's washing, ironing, and sewing saved the Auburn prison money.[33] Massachusetts Governor Emory Washburn in 1854 commissioned a survey of women in the county jails. Although the report revealed poor physical conditions, few matrons, and little work for inmates, it recommended only that matrons be hired under the authority of jail keepers and that women nursing infants be transferred to the poorhouse.[34] A report on whether to establish an institution "for the punishment and reform of abandoned women," made to the Connecticut legislature in 1860, resulted in the founding of a home for delinquent girls, but adult women criminals remained in mixed jails and prisons.[35]

Why did male reformers and state officials so neglect the state of women prisoners at a time when they were occupied with methods for curing or controlling men's criminality? One historian of prisons, W. David Lewis, has suggested a relationship between the sexual double standard and the treatment of women prisoners. "Especially if she had been sexually promiscuous," he wrote, "the female convict was a veritable pariah" who was viewed with "a special degree of aversion and despair." He summarized her treatment in New York prisons as "The Ordeal of the Unredeemable." Or, as a nineteenth-century prison official explained: "The opinion seems to have been entertained that the female convicts were beyond the reach of reformations, and it seems to have been regarded as a sufficient performance of the object of punishment to turn them loose within the pen of the prison and there leave them to feed upon and destroy each other."[36]

The statements of other male prison reformers support the view that the fallen woman was considered beyond hope. They suggest that the condemnation of women criminals derived in part from the pressures placed on women to maintain a morality superior to men's. Francis Lieber, for example, argued that men's crime was more "rational" than women's, for men were made for an "agitated life." Because she had denied her own pure nature, the female criminal was more depraved than her male counterpart. Therefore the fallen woman, Lieber believed, was more likely to reach the depths of sinfulness and commit the most heinous crimes.[37] Or, as the Reverend James B. Finley, the chaplain of the Ohio state penitentiary, wrote in 1851, "No one, without experience, can tell the obduracy of the female heart when hardened and lost in sin. As woman falls from a higher point of perfection, so she sinks to a profounder depth of misery than man."[38]

Instead of sympathy for her plight, however, most men expressed outright hostility to the fallen woman and blamed her for men's crimes as well. Her defiance of the law, they reasoned, had more serious social consequences than a man's, for by removing her influence as a virtuous wife and mother she undoubtedly encouraged male criminality. Dr. Lieber pointed to "a worthless mother who poisons by her corrupt examples the souls of her children—or a slothful intemperate wife who disgusts her husband with her home" as the cause of men's crimes.[39] Another male reformer lamented: "Worse than outer darkness ensues when the light of a household has gone out in the one most essential particular . . . the pure mother's influence has no equal; for its loss there is no earthly substitute and for criminal default the world tolerates no expiation."[40]

Not only by default, but through direct assault the fallen woman disrupted society when she, like Eve, tempted men to sin. The Prison Association of New York cited an incident at the Connecticut State Prison to illustrate "the influence of licentiousness on the production of crime." A chaplain explained that although born virtuous, when "a woman had once fallen she desired to revenge herself not only on her seducer, but on all his sex." One woman whose case the association detailed had caused the "downfall" of thirty-two erstwhile innocent young men.[41] Henry Lord warned charity workers in the 1870s of the young courtesan who "goes forth to prey upon mankind" and of the "wanton women" who could make life "dangerous for your sons in their necessary walks and journeys."[42]

Although not all officials shared this extreme hostility toward the fallen woman, the attitudes expressed by these influential men do help explain the neglect of women in American prisons. They also raise an important question for nineteenth-century women's history: Why was the fallen woman so feared and despised? Part of the answer lies in the dominant sexual ideology of the Victorian era.

The nineteenth-century sexual system has often been described in terms of the ideology of the separate sexual spheres. White, middle-class men and women inhabited sexually differentiated social spaces with distinct values and manners. The model of the self-made man who was adventuresome, mobile, aggressive, and competitive predominated in Jacksonian America. These men entered the public spheres of paid labor, the professions, or politics. Women, in contrast, were supposed to remain in the home where they cultivated the virtues of piety, purity, and submissiveness.[43]

Although this ideology limited women to unpaid labor in the domestic sphere, it placed a high cultural value on the tasks they performed there. Because women reared children, managed the household, and maintained spiritual and moral values, men could specialize in wage-earning tasks. As men entered the impersonal world of the marketplace, moreover, they knew they could return to the domestic sanctuary, where a pure woman waited inside to refresh them. As novelist James Fenimore Cooper explained, in order to ease, console, and correct her husband's "sordid struggles with the world," woman had to be "placed beyond their influence."[44] The idea of women's superior morality thus provided a foundation and justification for the sexual division of labor.

Interestingly enough, nineteenth-century sexual ideology began to suggest that purity came naturally to women, in contrast to men, who had to struggle to control their innate lust. Influential Victorian authorities argued that women had little or no sensual appetite and that they submitted to sexual intercourse solely for the purpose of procreation.[45] Born innocent, woman had a natural self-control which could counterbalance man's lust. Female sexual desire seemed pathological to many medical and moral authorities; unchaste behavior signalled deep depravity. According to one popular novelist, "even as woman is supremely virtuous, [she] becomes, when once fallen, the vilest of her sex."[46]

The impure woman presented a serious threat to a society that relied on women's chastity for important symbolic functions. Female purity, historian Ben Barker-Benfield has argued, upheld the "spermatic economy" by channeling men's energies away from sex and into the economically productive tasks required during this period of capital accumulation.[47] Whether or not there was a direct relationship between economic change and sexual ideals, the social changes accompanying the early phases of American capitalism did influence sexual ideology. Carroll Smith-Rosenberg has characterized the concentration on sexual purity among Jacksonian male reformers as the result of a deep fear of social disorder, for which sexual pollution functioned as a central symbol. The men who helped establish purity as a cultural ideal, she argues, were experiencing "psychosocial tensions" as their familial and economic relations were transformed by commercial and urban growth. Uncontrolled sexuality represented for them potential chaos. Women had to be pure to enforce male continence; and this emphasis on their purity gave women enormous power. The impure woman had the capacity to unleash not just male sperm, but more importantly, the social disintegration that sexuality symbolized.[48]

Within the context of this ideology of sexual purity it becomes clear why responses to the impure or fallen woman were so emotionally charged. She represented, on a basic level, a symbol of women's resistance to the ideal of purity and their misuse of the sexual power granted them. In addition, as male prison reformers pointed out, an impure woman had not only sinned, she had also removed the constraints on men's virtue—both those on the men in her family and, potentially, those on men in the streets.

Although the fallen woman lost her usefulness as a check on male behavior, she could become an example to other women of the high cost of resistance. The social stigma attached to fallen women, the belief in their total depravity, and the treatment they received in penal institutions thus helped control the behavior of all women.

By the 1840s a significant number of women served in prison, and their neglect, if not abuse, set them apart as a special category of prisoners. Nineteenth-century penitentiaries were never intended to rehabilitate women. In practice they rarely reformed criminals of either sex and probably served to confirm a prisoner's membership in the criminal class. Male reformers had several reasons for ignoring women prisoners: the small number of women in penitentiaries, the logistical and economic problems of caring for them, the disdain they felt for the fallen woman. But the question posed by New York reformers in 1819—why no female "angels of mercy" cared for women prisoners—remains to be answered.

Pure women had to surmount an ideological barrier before they reached out to female prisoners. The line that separated the pure woman from the fallen demarcated privilege on one side and degradation on the other. By not crossing that line, pure women could retain their class privilege at the expense of their outcast fallen sisters. However, these two groups of women remained separated only if pure women agreed that the boundary dividing the pure and the fallen, a class division, was stronger than the sexual division between women and men. Both the ideology of the separate sexual spheres and women's personal experiences over the course of the century supported a definition of women as a sexual class, an identity that contradicted and potentially weakened the purity boundary. Eventually some women would find the concept of a common womanhood stronger than the boundary of moral purity. A few would cross the line and cautiously enter the "gloomy abode" of women prisoners.

Chapter 2

"The Helping Hand": The Origins and Ideas of Women's Prison Reform, 1840–1900

Between 1840 and 1900 small groups of women, concentrated in New York, Massachusetts, and Indiana, took up the cause of women prisoners as their special mission. At first individuals merely visited penal institutions. Then, gradually, women formed associations to aid released female prisoners. In the decades after the Civil War, women prison reformers demanded greater authority over public institutions that housed women. And by the end of the century women had joined men as professionals in the growing field of charities and corrections.

In the course of their encounters with prisoners, middle-class women found that the fallen were not as depraved as they had expected. As early as the 1840s some reformers questioned the condemnation of the fallen woman. By the last quarter of the century women had elaborated a new interpretation of female crime that reversed the earlier view. One reformer's comment reveals the change in public opinion that women sought. "Much is said about the depths to which women may fall," Rhoda Coffin stated in 1885. "While we always have claimed that women are equal to men, we have never yet admitted the point that she was superior to him in ability to sin or to entangle others."[1]

The Origins of Benevolent Reform, 1820–60

Looking back over the women's prison reform movement at the end of the century, Susan Barney offered a simplistic but useful explanation of its origins: "When Elizabeth Fry, in 1815, rapped at the prison doors in England, she not only summoned the turnkey, but sounded a call to women in other lands to enter upon a most Christlike mission."[2] Elizabeth Fry did provide both a personal example and a set of theories for American women. Although the movement outgrew her voluntary, benevolent methods by the 1860s, it also fulfilled her vision of women's prison reform. Fry's career provides a fitting introduction to the questions of why and how nineteenth-century women reached out "the helping hand" to their imprisoned sisters.

Like many of the American reformers who would follow in her path, Elizabeth Gurney Fry (1780–1845) came from a Quaker family with deep commitments to both religion and antislavery. In 1811, after marriage and a conversion experience, Fry became a minister, a position open to her because the Society of Friends believed in the spiritual equality of the sexes. Following a long tradition of prison visiting by Quaker women, Fry entered London's Newgate Gaol in 1813. There she encountered starving, drunken, partially clothed women, often accompanied in prison by their young children. Although her original mission was religious conversion through prayer, she recognized that alleviating the physical misery of prisoners was necessary for their salvation. Thus she first offered clothing and comfort, and only later, prayer.[3]

In 1816, when Fry returned to Newgate after bearing and burying several of her children, she found conditions as appalling as before. This jail, one of her biographers has written, "offered an extreme example of how badly the dominant masculine upper class could design and administer a prison."[4] Determined to improve it, Fry and her companions obtained permission to experiment with prison reform for women. They established a Ladies Association for the Improvement of the Female Prisoners at Newgate which organized workshops, Bible classes, and a system of discipline monitored by inmates. They also hired a matron and attempted to aid female prisoners after their release.

Fry's 1827 treatise, *Observations in Visiting, Superintendence and Government of Female Prisoners*, furnished the principles that would later dominate American women's prison reform. She argued that female prisoners could be reformed, elaborated on the methods for doing so, and emphasized women's responsibility to come to the aid of their fallen sisters. Combining the themes of sisterhood and female superiority, Fry wrote, "May the attention of *women* be more and more directed to these labors of love; and may the time quickly arrive, when there shall not exist, in this realm, a single public institution [where women] . . . shall not enjoy the *efficacious superintendence* of the pious and benevolent of THEIR OWN SEX!"[5]

Perhaps it was the strength with which Fry argued for women's superintendence of female inmates that brought her into disfavor with English authorities, who rescinded her reforms in 1835 for allegedly making prison life too soft. Perhaps it was simply her loss of status following her husband's bankruptcy in the late 1820s. Biographer John Kent suggests that Fry lost influence because she had exceeded the limitations society placed on her sex.[6]

However short-lived her personal involvement, Fry's followers in England and America benefited from her experience and writings. Americans learned of Fry's work in the 1820s both from her book and from newspaper and travelers' accounts.[7] Like Fry, Quaker women in American cities, along with evangelical reformers from other denominations, were beginning to visit penal institutions to comfort or proselytize inmates.

The American women who followed in Fry's path had many individual motives for reaching out to women prisoners. As a group, however, they did share certain historical experiences as well as many social characteristics. Of thirty women active in some type of women's prison reform in America during the nineteenth century, a majority came from middle- and upper-middle-class Protestant families in the northeastern United States (see table 2). A disproportionate number belonged to liberal sects; almost a third were Quakers and many others were Unitarians. In all of these respects, the prison reformers resembled women abolitionists and feminists.[8] Indeed, some women participated in all three movements as well as a variety of other reforms, including temperance, social purity, and pacifism. Abby Hopper Gibbons, Josephine Shaw Lowell, and Elizabeth Buffum Chace, for instance, were each raised in antislavery families and each led two or three reform movements during her life.

Growing up in such families influenced young daughters' views of themselves as women. Since most of their families could afford to send them to school, many reformers had attended a Female or Friends' Academy. At school, as at home, they were exposed to the ideology of "true womanhood" which was directed especially at young women of their class. Those who attended all-female institutions or who later joined women's missionary, benevolent, or antislavery associations experienced the full implications of the separate sexual spheres. As historian Nancy Cott has shown for New England women, these educational and religious "sisterhoods" intensified both female identity and women's sense of their own mission.[9]

The work histories of these reformers suggest how they acquired further skills necessary for the type of prison reform Elizabeth Fry recommended. Although trained for domestic tasks, their socialization as moral guardians influenced many middle-class women to seek suitable work until marriage.[10] The reformers had most frequently been occupied as teachers, and many had been engaged in church-related work as missionaries or Sunday school instructors. A few single women in this group had careers as writers, doctors, or nurses. During the Civil War many of the reformers served as nurses, aides, and administrators in field hospitals and on the home front.

Like most nineteenth-century women, the majority of the prison reformers married, gave birth to an average of four to five children, and experienced the death of one or more children.[11] Several women, including Fry, Gibbons, and Chace, returned to reform shortly after mourning, while others became active when widowed. Traditional women in many ways, only a few actively supported the women's rights movement when it emerged at midcentury. Most, however, publicly expressed their respect for women's contributions to the society and their opposition to the degradation of women in any sphere, but particularly in prisons.

Stressing only common experiences, however, provides too static and homogeneous a profile of the reformers. Women entered prison reform during different decades, during different times in their life cycles, and at different stages in the movement they were creating. From the small steps taken by a few religious women in the 1820s to the opening of the third state reformatory prison for women in the 1890s, women's prison reform changed from private, voluntary benevolence to public, professional work for women. In the process, reformers revised their ideas about fallen women and attempted to transform penal policies toward them.

American women first discovered the plight of female prisoners during a period of religious revival and social reform. The Second Great Awakening of the 1820s and 1830s popularized a new, perfectionist theology that held out the possibility of individual and social salvation. As a result, movements for the redemption of sinners, including temperance, prison reform, and moral reform, proliferated in the Jacksonian period.[12]

Although Quaker women had begun to engage in benevolent reforms in the late eighteenth century, large numbers of other Protestant women experienced religious conversion during the Awakening and joined the ranks of social reformers. Religious benevolence offered women an excellent opportunity to fulfill their tasks of moral guardianship. Many believed that through their efforts the

TABLE 2. Personal Backgrounds of Women Prison Reformers

	Nineteenth Century (n = 30)		Twentieth Century (n = 20)	
	%	n	%	n
Place of Birth				
Foreign	6.66	(2)	11.11	(2)
Northeast	76.67	(22)	50.00	(9)
Midwest	6.66	(2)	33.33	(6)
South	10.00	(3)	5.55	(1)
West		(0)		(0)
Unknown		(1)		(2)
Primary Religious Affiliation				
Quaker	32.15	(9)	9.09	(1)
Unitarian or Universalist	25.00	(7)		(0)
Methodist	10.71	(3)		(0)
Presbyterian or Congregational	10.71	(3)	9.09	(1)
Episcopal or Anglican	3.57	(1)	36.36	(4)
Other Protestant denominations	17.86	(5)	9.09	(1)
Catholic		(0)	27.27	(3)
Jewish		(0)	9.09	(1)
Unknown		(2)		(9)
Highest Educational Level				
Some education	30.00	(6)	4.76	(1)
High school or academy	40.00	(8)	33.33	(7)
College or normal school	15.00	(3)	9.52	(2)
Graduate or professional	15.00	(3)	52.38	(11)
Unknown (or none)		(10)		(0)
Prison Reform				
Private, voluntary	43.33	(13)	15.00	(3)
Public, professional	20.00	(6)	70.00	(14)
Both	36.67	(11)	15.00	(3)
Paid Work				
Some	66.67	(16)	89.47	(17)
None	33.33	(8)	10.53	(2)
Unknown		(6)		(1)
Primary Type of Paid Work				
Writer		(4)		(3)
Teacher		(11)		(4)

TABLE 2 —*Continued*

	Nineteenth Century (n = 30)		Twentieth Century (n = 20)	
	%	n	%	n
Primary Type of Paid Work (*continued*)				
Doctor or lawyer		(3)		(5)
Social work (and research)		(0)		(10)
Other		(3)		(2)
Other Reform Activity				
Civil War nurse or aide		(9)		(0)
Missionary or Sunday school		(8)		(2)
Women's rights and suffrage		(5)		(8)
Temperance		(7)		(2)
Antislavery		(7)		(0)
Antisuffrage		(3)		(0)
Social purity/social hygiene		(3)		(1)
Pacifism		(3)		(1)
Politics		(1)		(5)
Women's clubs		(1)		(5)
Settlement houses		(0)		(4)
Labor organization		(0)		(2)
Family				
Ever married	73.33	(22)	63.16	(12)
separated/divorced	3.33	(1)	31.58	(6)
Single	26.67	(7)	36.84	(7)
Age at first marriage				
median	21		22.5	
mean	25.4		24.8	
Number of children born				
median	4.5		2	
mean	4.64		2.8	
Number of children surviving				
median	3		2	
mean	2.64		2.5	
Age first widowed/ divorced				
median	49		45	
mean	42.56		44	

Note: See appendix B for individual data and biographical sources.

most hardened sinners—drunkards, adulterers, slave owners, and even prostitutes—could be saved.[13]

Like the men who earlier became "their brothers' keepers" when they proselytized the unconverted through Bible, tract, and temperance societies, middle-class women formed associations to aid the indigent or dissolute. Both the ideology of the separate spheres and women's personal experiences in various sisterhoods encouraged these reformers to aid dependents of their own sex. In the 1820s and 1830s, for instance, female urban missionaries considered widows, orphans, and homeless women to be their special charges, while the female moral reformers dedicated themselves to the unpopular task of uplifting prostitutes.[14]

Philadelphia Quakers were the first Americans to attend to imprisoned women. Inspired by Elizabeth Fry, they began to visit women inmates at the Arch Street Prison in 1823. A women's prison visiting committee later expanded Fry's work by offering "individual and systematic instruction" to female prisoners to aid their spiritual redemption. The visitors also provided a library, and sewing and writing classes. For inmates who seemed truly penitent they sought "to procure suitable situations . . . in families or institutions."[15]

In the 1840s Protestant missionaries to New York City's charitable institutions encountered female prisoners during their rounds. Phoebe Palmer, a popular evangelical preacher, and Sarah Platt Doremus, a member of the Tract and Mission societies, found the women incarcerated in the New York City Tombs most in need of their services. Palmer helped organize the Methodist Five Points Mission while Doremus helped found a house of industry for poor women, a women's hospital, a women's missionary society, and a women's old age home. During the same period, members of the New York Female Moral Reform Society tried to convert and uplift young prostitutes both within prison and after their release.[16]

These scattered efforts at individual moral regeneration took on greater urgency when, in the 1840s, women's crime became the subject of concern to the men who had recently formed the Prison Association of New York (PANY). The male reformers visited the city's penal institutions and, confronted with the "contamination of evil communication" between male and female inmates, wondered whether any reformation could take place of women confined there. In 1845 they reported that "it is a matter of great doubt whether it would not be better for an innocent female to be consigned at once to a brothel . . . [where] she would at least enjoy the advantage of being able to fly from the approach of corruption at her pleasure."[17]

Although the men were indignant about sexual license in city prisons, their willingness, even in jest, to commit the fallen woman to a brothel reflected the popular view that she was beyond redemption. In contrast, the women whom the Prison Association asked to form a ladies' auxiliary began to question not only prison conditions, but also the underlying attitudes toward female criminals that perpetuated them. Could reform ever take place, they wondered, given the greater condemnation of the fallen woman?

The New York women who raised this question joined the auxiliary to the Prison Association, called the Female Department, in the same spirit that initially motivated Elizabeth Fry—to encourage religious feelings among female prisoners. In the course of their benevolent activities, they encountered the increasing numbers of immigrant and working women sentenced to city jails. The meeting of these pure women with those the society deemed fallen affected a number of benevolent reformers who began to reconsider the prevailing view, as the early history of the Female Department illustrates.

The leader of the Female Department of the prison association, Abby Hopper Gibbons, came from a Quaker family of very modest means. Her mother was a Quaker minister and her father, Isaac Hopper, devoted himself to abolitionism and prison reform. Abby Hopper had operated a Friends' school in Philadelphia and had taught in New York before marrying James Gibbons in 1833. She belonged to a predominantly black female antislavery society and resigned from the Society of Friends in part because it had disowned her father and husband for their abolitionism.

In 1846 Isaac Hopper encouraged his daughter to join the work of the Prison Association of New York which he had helped found. In its ladies' auxiliary Abby Hopper Gibbons met Sarah Doremus, local authors Catherine Sedgewick and Caroline Kirkland, and a number of women from prominent New York families. These women's lives conformed in many ways to the cultural ideal of true womanhood. Most were married, had large families, and were active in benevolent organizations like the Tract and Mission societies. Even the self-supporting among them maintained the ideal; for example authors Sedgewick, who was single, and Kirkland, a widow, wrote on domestic themes.[18]

The Female Department decided to open a home for discharged

women prisoners, a halfway house providing shelter, prayer, and training in order to prevent recidivism among drunken, vagrant, and immoral women. A fitting extension of the reformers' domestic sphere, the home provided a means of expanding these women's moral guardianship beyond their own families and to the fallen women whom they would receive and nurture.

The campaign for a home for discharged women prisoners had the support of one of the country's outstanding feminists, Margaret Fuller, then an editor of the New York *Tribune*. Her insights into the problems of women inmates represented a more radical approach than the New York auxiliary had yet assumed. Fuller provided one of the earliest feminist perspectives on women's crime when she introduced the theme of women's victimization by social forces.

Fuller had visited the women's department at Sing Sing prison in October 1844 when she spoke with the "so-called worst" (whom she compared favorably with the proper women in her Boston classes!). Returning to address the inmates on Christmas Day, she defended the fallen woman. According to William Channing's memoir of her talk, Fuller explained that "the conduct of some now here was such that the world said:—'Women once lost are far worse than abandoned men, and cannot be restored.' But no! It is not so! I know my sex better." The inmates, she suggested, were victims who needed help to overcome the circumstances which had led them to crime: "Born of unfortunate marriages, inheriting dangerous inclinations, neglected in childhood, with bad habits and associates, as certainly must be the case with some of you, how terrible will be the struggle when you leave this shelter!"[19]

Fuller's views reached the public in a series of articles which appeared in the *Tribune* in the spring of 1845, coinciding with the campaign for a home for discharged women prisoners. The author reported that the city almshouses and penitentiaries contained shocking sights of mothers with newborn infants, "exposed to the careless scrutiny of male visitors" and to dreary, daily routines without even the pretense of training. At the "gloomiest" institution, the penitentiary, she decried "the want of proper matrons, or any matrons, to take the care so necessary for the bodily or mental improvement or even decent conditions of the seven hundred women assembled here." Most importantly, she questioned the predominant view that these women were hopelessly fallen. The Transcendentalist and feminist was struck by "how many there are in whom the feelings of innocent childhood are not dead, who need only good influences and steady aid to raise them from the pit of infamy into which they have fallen." Following closely the advice of Elizabeth Fry's *Observations*, she suggested that the first principles of the institution should be inmate classification and instruction, and a good sanitary system. "We trust," she wrote, "that interest on this subject will not slumber."[20]

A few months later, when the Female Department of the prison association opened its home for discharged women prisoners, Fuller published an appeal to New York citizens to support the endeavor with money and furnishings. Once again, she rejected the condemnation of fallen women. She addressed her article to "men, to atone for the wrongs inflicted by men on that 'weaker sex,' who should, they say, be soft, confiding, dependent on them for protection. [And] to women, to feel for those who have not been guarded either by social influence or inward strength from that first mistake which the opinion of the world makes irrevocable for women alone." Then, in a twist on the concept of women's greater fall, she added: "Since their danger is so great, their fall so terrible, let mercies be multiplied when there is a chance of that partial restoration which society at present permits." Fuller admonished "people of leisure" to see at first hand the sick and ruined women at Blackwell's Island penitentiary and hospital, and to recognize social responsibility for them. Her article concluded with Thomas Hood's poem, "The Bridge of Sighs," a moral tale narrating the plight of a fallen woman who, when rejected by family and society, plunged into a river. The sins of those who had refused to help her, it preached, were as great as those of the victim.[21]

Gibbons, Sedgewick, and their colleagues who operated the home for discharged prisoners had, in general, more traditional views than the feminist advocate Margaret Fuller. They also were far more actively involved in providing practical services to prisoners. Through the home they hoped to prevent the immediate rearrest of released prisoners who had no family or friends.

The Isaac Hopper Home, named after Gibbons's father, provided a refuge for inmates who would forsake smoking, drinking, and cursing in favor of the domestic pursuits of sewing, laundry, and religious study. After a month or more of residence, about half of the inmates were placed in domestic positions, ideally in homes like Catherine Sedgewick's, which offered the "favorable circumstances and kindness [which] were the means best adapted to save them from an evil life."[22]

From 1845 to 1864, the home sheltered 2,961 women, found

placements for 1,083 of them, and deemed only 480 "unworthy or without hope of being reclaimed." The case of one inmate, as told by Caroline Kirkland, expresses the attitudes that reformers often repeated about the influence of the home:

> S.C. was considered a hopeless case; but after she had been several months at the Home—too bad to be recommended to a place, yet show-ing occasionally such encouraging signs that we did not dare reject her—she began to improve so evidently that the records of the House speak of it as an "astonishing change." From having been very violent in her temper, she became, under the influence of kind words and good offices, docile and pleasant. The religious exercises of the Home exerted an influence over her, and the Chaplain at Blackwell's Island expressed his surprise that he had not seen her there *for more than a year*—a re-markable thing in his experience.[23]

Kind words, prayers, and a full schedule of domestic tasks trans-formed thousands of New York City's female prisoners into docile and pleasant women who, no longer resisting the standards of feminine behavior, would be spared the harsh penalties of prison life.

In the course of effecting these transformations, members of the Female Department adopted new attitudes toward women pris-oners. In contrast to most prison officials and male reformers, who condemned the fallen woman as a social outcast, these women in-sisted on removing the stigma that separated them from their fallen sisters. As one of their reports explained, "we would ap-proach the fallen woman, and when all the world turns away with loathing from her misery, we would take her by the hand, lift her from her degradation, whisper hope to her amid her despair, teach her lessons of self-control, instill into her ideas of purity and in-dustry, and send her forth to work her own way upward to her final destiny."[24]

Once reformers had proclaimed that the fallen could be redi-rected toward purity, they took issue with the analysis of women's crime that had condemned female prisoners. The women they aided, their reports noted, had not been designing temptresses very often. Rather, many were innocent victims of male seduction. Women drifted astray, they argued, not simply from lust or greed, but through the deception of others. Although "they seem to be what they are . . . by their own perverse choice," reformers asked, "has there in truth been any such deliberate choice—any such in-sane election!"

Our experience has shown us conclusively that in nine cases out of ten, no choice was ever made, for none was ever offered. Hereditary tendencies have their share, evil associations theirs, temptations, . . . lack of any kindly aid after the first offense, . . . the hard trials of poverty— . . . the passion for drinking.

Given the lives these women had led, the reformers concluded, "How, then, can we be pitiless toward the transgressions of the untaught, the unwarned, the neglected!" As long as the fallen woman retained "a hope of redeeming the past," reformers would treat her "as a woman and as a sister."[25]

The use of sisterhood to describe the relationship of women prisoners and reformers suggests the influence of the ideology of women's separate sphere. Reformers attempted to dismiss class difference and emphasized the common bond of an innate womanly spirit. Moreover, case histories in their annual reports stressed the leveling influence of the home. In 1849, for example, an upper-class woman and an Irish servant, both seduced and abandoned by upper-class men, were given shelter. The former was "placed on an equal footing" with other inmates, all of whom achieved redemption through penitence and docility.[26]

Underlying the rhetoric of sisterhood was also the criticism of male behavior and attitudes which would contribute to the formation of the Women's Prison Association (WPA). Annual reports of the Female Department included attacks on the double standard, asking why "so unequal a measure of retribution should be meted out to the man and the woman?" In private correspondence members such as Abby Hopper Gibbons and Catherine Sedgewick occasionally expressed anger toward men's treatment of women.[27] Their own experiences working in a male organization may have further influenced the reformers' emphasis on sisterhood. Like women in the temperance and antislavery movements, some members of the Female Department of the PANY chafed against the limitations men placed on their work.

An explicit conflict with men's authority in the 1850s eventually brought New York reformers to assert their independence. Catherine Sedgewick recorded that when the women were discussing the management of their home, a "committee from the men's society appeared" at the meeting "to remind the women that they were but a department." Some of the women "were disposed to stand upon their reserved rights," Sedgewick wrote, and "some modestly hinted that they had privileges as well as responsibilities."[28] In response to these tensions several women left the PANY and in 1854 formed the autonomous Women's Prison Association and Home. They raised private funds to support the home and, beginning in 1861, they received a financial contribution from the city, acknowledging the home as a quasi-public institution.[29] Prison visiting continued, both at city jails and state penitentiaries.

Although their reports made no mention of the political movement for women's rights which had begun at Seneca Falls, New York, in 1848, the new organization did draw upon its rhetoric. Caroline Kirkland's fund-raising tract, *The Helping Hand*, asked privileged women to overcome the gulf between themselves and the fallen of their sex in the following terms:

> Among the most precious of Women's Rights is the right to do good to her own sex; . . . Sad it is that [the] fallen woman hopes less from her sisters than from her brothers; . . . women should consider themselves as a community, having special common needs and common obligations, which it is a shame to turn aside from under the plea of inability or distaste. *Every woman in misfortune is the proper object of care to the happier and safer part of her sex.* Not to stretch forth to her the helping hand—not to defend her against wrong and shield her from temptation—is to consent to her degradation and to become, in some sense, party to her ruin.[30]

An important distinction must be drawn between the prison reformers' appeal to sisterhood and the demand of the women's rights movement for political equality. Most antebellum prison reformers did not support women's rights. Like more vehement opponents, such as Catharine Beecher or the vocal antisuffragists of the late nineteenth century, benevolent reformers assumed that women's power emanated from the moral influence of their separate sphere. In contrast to radical feminists, they did not seek equality in the public sphere; many even prided themselves on remaining outside of politics.[31] These reformers did insist, however, that their feminine values should have equal weight in the society. Neither radical feminists nor antifeminists, their prison reform activities had led them to several prefeminist insights, including a critique of the double standard, a call for solidarity between women, and a commitment to establishing autonomous women's institutions.

The antebellum women reformers had set the precedent that the fallen woman need not be an outcast, that she could be uplifted, and that women had the right to direct this work. But, as they were the first to admit, the cause was not yet a popular one. "To solicit public assistance for the prisoner, and especially for the female prisoner," the WPA lamented in 1855, "is to row against wind and tide."[32] Their own activities, moreover, remained limited to voluntary measures aimed at individual moral regeneration through prison visiting and a halfway house for released prisoners. Only after the Civil War, with the expansion of women's prison reform, would their sympathies for fallen women lead to alternatives to the neglect of women in prison.

Professional Reformers, 1860–1900

In the decades after 1860 the scattered voluntary efforts to uplift women prisoners expanded into a movement to achieve public authority and professional status for women prison reformers. Building upon the precedents of the antebellum period, particularly the home for discharged women prisoners, postwar activists adopted new methods and added new responsibilities to their reform agenda, including authority on state correctional boards and institutions. By the end of the century they had attained legitimacy for women as professionals in public agencies which cared for female clients.

The Civil War influenced older prison reformers and helped bring more women into the movement. Abby Hopper Gibbons, who had served as a battlefield nurse, continued to work with the WPA but also became receptive to women's rights and a leader of the social purity movement. In the 1870s she joined forces with Josephine Shaw Lowell to campaign for the establishment of separate women's prisons in New York, to be run by women.[33]

Lowell had grown up in one of Boston's oldest families, surrounded by Transcendentalist and abolitionist luminaries. The widow of war hero Charles Russell Lowell, she helped direct the Women's Central Association of Relief for the Army and Navy and became an advocate of "scientific philanthropy." In addition to leading the postwar-charity organization movement in New York, Lowell investigated the conditions of women in jails, served on the state charities board, and argued for women's control over public institutions. She also supported woman suffrage, the Women's Municipal League, and the New York Consumers' League.[34]

In Massachusetts a group of women had similar experiences during and after the war. Ellen Cheney Johnson, a temperance advocate who had taught domestic skills to women in the slums, founded the New England Women's Auxiliary Association and raised funds for the U.S. Sanitary Commission. In the process of searching for veterans' dependents and survivors, she discovered many women virtually unattended in local jails and workhouses. In trying to assist them she met Hannah Chickering, who had become a prison visitor in order to be useful during the war. Chickering founded the Dedham Asylum for Discharged Female Prisoners, a home supported by prominent Boston women, including former WPA member Mary Pierce Poor. In the 1870s both Chickering and Poor served on the Massachusetts Prison Commission and, along with Ellen Cheney Johnson, led a statewide campaign for a separate women's prison.[35] Johnson later became the superintendent of the institution they succeeded in establishing.

Both wartime social service and religious benevolence motivated a group of midwestern Quakers to enter prison reform during the 1860s. The most active reformer in the Friends community was Rhoda Coffin of Richmond, Indiana. From yet another antislavery family, Coffin had originally learned about prison visiting during a trip East in 1858, when she and her husband, Charles, were impressed by the reforms their Quaker acquaintances had undertaken in New York and Philadelphia jails. During the war, influenced in part by a religious revival among Indiana Friends, the Coffins began visiting soldiers' families and prisoners. Quaker minister Sarah Smith and Chicago prison visitor Elizabeth Comstock, both of whom attended to soldiers and prisoners during the war, inspired the Coffins to launch a prison reform committee in the Indiana Yearly Meeting. Sarah Smith and Rhoda Coffin, like reformers in New York and Massachusetts, first aided women prisoners by establishing the Home for the Friendless in Richmond, Indiana. They also visited state penal institutions and, appalled at the treatment of women, campaigned for the creation of a separate state women's prison.[36] Like other reformers, after 1870 the Indiana women served as state officials.

These personal experiences of wartime social service and postwar prison reform suggest some of the ways the Civil War influenced American women. During the 1860s thousands of women worked for the state in some capacity—as nurses, charity workers, and clerks, on the battlefield, or in offices. They learned that women could serve competently in the absence of, or alongside, men. After the war many nurses, administrators, and volunteers were committed to a life of social service, but they did not want to accept subordinate rank or menial tasks.[37] Like the prison reformers, they sought public and professional roles in which to utilize their skills.

While wartime social service drew some women into prison reform, others entered the public charities movement that resulted from the centralization of social services during the war. Organizations like the U.S. Sanitary Commission facilitated the move away from benevolent, private reform and toward secular, "scientific philanthropy" modeled on the British charity organization movement.[38] The creation of state boards of charities and corrections provided new opportunities for women reformers to assume public, professional roles.

The entry of Elizabeth Buffum Chace into women's prison reform provides a notable example of how women began to demand official status in the new state agencies that directed correctional institutions. Like other prison reformers, she came from a Quaker, abolitionist family. The Buffum home in Providence, Rhode Island, had been a way station on the Underground Railroad and a meeting place for antislavery proponents. In 1835, several years after her marriage to cotton manufacturer Samuel Chace, Elizabeth Buffum Chace formed the Female Anti-Slavery Society and from 1868 to 1870 was vice-president of the American Anti-Slavery Society.[39]

The deaths of several of her children left Chace longing for activity, and the women's rights movement influenced her decision to enter public life. Chace had attended the 1850 women's rights convention in Massachusetts and, at the close of the Civil War, her feminist friend Lucy Stone urged her to accept the social responsibilities incumbent on her as an economically secure wife and mother. In response to Chace's doubts about entering public life, Stone advised that she "let the housekeeping take care of itself while you take care of the Republic."[40] Chace heeded the challenge. In addition to supporting Negro rights, woman suffrage, and higher education for women, she began to visit penal institutions in Rhode Island and to call attention to the problems of female inmates.

At the time, no woman sat on the official state board of control nor on the boards of management which directed most state institutions. Through the Rhode Island Woman Suffrage Association, of which she was president, Chace sent a memorial to the governor requesting that state charity boards include both sexes.[41] As a result of her effort, an 1870 Rhode Island act provided for a Board of Lady Visitors to inspect institutions which housed women; the board was not given power to enforce its recommendations. Chace was "rather scornful of the Legislative sop," but served on the new board for several years. In 1876, however, she resigned to protest women's lack of power on the board. "When the State of Rhode Island shall call its best women to an equal participation with men in the direction of its penal and reformatory institutions," she explained, "I have no doubt they will gladly assume the duties and responsibilities of such positions."[42]

By the time of her resignation, several states had established positions for women in directing charities and corrections. In Connecticut the newly created State Board of Charities (1876) formed a department with female members to supervise state institutions. In New York Josephine Shaw Lowell, who became a member of the State Board of Charities in 1876, began to inspect jails, penitentiaries, and almshouses, with particular attention to methods of caring for young women delinquents. The Massachusetts Prison Commission, established in 1870, legally required female members and was well advanced toward giving women complete control of their own reformatory. By 1888 the Department of Franchise of the Women's Christian Temperance Union recommended that women become directors and visitors for state institutions as one means of taking advantage of any local political power they could achieve en route to suffrage.[43]

Women's participation in two new national organizations provides another measure of the change from private to public, and from voluntary to professional, prison reform. Through the National Prison Congress (later called the American Prison Association) and the National Conference on Charities and Corrections (NCCC), new middle-class professionals in penal and charitable agencies sought to standardize their methods and to increase both their prestige and their influence on social policy. In each organization women eventually shared in these tasks.

The American Prison Association (APA) was formed in 1870 as a meeting place for reformers, public officials, and prison administrators. Originally called the National Prison Congress, it recommended penal reforms, including the indeterminate sentence, industrial and academic training for inmates, and the creation of specialized institutions for misdemeanants, first offenders, and women.[44] At its founding meeting, the APA adopted as the last of thirty-seven principles for a better correctional system that "both in official administration of such a system and in the voluntary co-operation of citizens therein, the agency of women may be employed with excellent effect." In 1875 Rhoda Coffin delivered the first paper by a female member and in 1896 Ellen Cheney Johnson became the first woman on a standing committee.[45]

A similar process occurred within the National Conference on Charities and Corrections, the social workers' professional organization. Between its founding in 1874 and the turn of the century women increased their participation at conferences, offering papers in those branches of the profession that seemed most open to their participation. Among these areas was penology, and women in the NCCC insisted that they were particularly suited for the tasks of preventing female crime and aiding women prisoners. By 1890 the organization officially recognized women's achievements, citing female membership on almost half of the existing state boards of charities and the increased use of female professional staff in state institutions that cared for women.[46]

The expansion of women's prison reform into public and professional life had been fostered by several events of the 1860s. Public officials, faced with the increase in the number of women arrested, convicted, and imprisoned during that decade may have been more willing to entertain women's ideas about female inmates. Women's wartime public service contributed to their interest in postwar charities and corrections. Furthermore, although the war had a dampening effect on most reform movements, for women the political aftermath of the war inspired feminist organization. The failure to include woman suffrage in the Fifteenth Amendment resulted in the establishment of two national suffrage associations that publicly questioned restrictions on women's rights over the next decades. After the war, female prison reformers became more sympathetic to the women's suffrage movement.

While the political feminists may have had a limited audience between 1870 and 1910, other women, since termed "social feminists," enjoyed growing support for their efforts to expand female moral guardianship from the home to the society.[47] Like temperance advocates, social purity leaders, and settlement house founders, the postwar prison reformers believed in women's separate sphere and superior morality. Even as they entered the public sphere and gained valuable skills by building separate women's organizations, social feminists continued to argue that women had unique, feminine virtues that should be embodied in social policy.

These principles strongly influenced prison reformers' attitudes toward fallen women and their growing interest in creating separate women's prisons.

The Fallen Woman Reconsidered

Ever since Elizabeth Fry first entered Newgate Gaol, women prison reformers had expressed sympathy for the fallen woman and a belief in her capacity for redemption. As nineteenth-century American women argued for a greater degree of public responsibility for women prisoners, they articulated these views more frequently and more publicly. Those who held official positions had a wider forum for their ideas, while others continued to volunteer their criticism of prevailing attitudes toward fallen women.

In speeches and writings, late nineteenth-century prison reformers elaborated on earlier observations that the fallen woman should not be held solely responsible for her crimes. Increasingly, women stressed that societal forces created the problem of woman's fall. This tendency toward a social, rather than individual, analysis of crime derived in part from the women's new vantage point as public reformers. In addition, two streams of late nineteenth-century social thought—determinist theories of crime and social feminist views of the relations of the sexes—influenced women's ideas and gave them credence among both professional colleagues and feminist allies.

A more sympathetic portrait of female criminals first reached the wider public through novels written between 1860 and 1890, when "fictional sympathy for the fallen and interest in their rehabilitation . . . generally shifted attention from the harlot as temptress of men and befouler of society to the harlot as victim of economic distress and the vice rackets." Stories by Rebecca Harding Davis, Elizabeth Stuart Phelps, Bayard Taylor, and Harriet Beecher Stowe, for instance, suggested that women were driven to crime by urban and industrial life, or by men. Moreover, the fictional fallen women were often rescued by other women, who helped them find Christian redemption and an honest means of support. By 1890 novelists had adopted the theme that fallen women could achieve almost total rehabilitation.[48]

Women who had participated in antebellum prison reform and those who entered charity and correctional work in the postwar decades shared these new attitudes about fallen women. What is especially interesting about these women's explanations of prostitution and other crimes is the way they singled out their own sex as a subculture of the dangerous class. Reversing the older view of women's greater fall, they argued that women were more victimized and even more capable of reformation than were male criminals.

A number of women prison reformers viewed the fallen woman through the dual perspectives of hereditarian thought and feminist sympathies. Josephine Shaw Lowell argued that since criminal tendencies could be inherited, women offenders were not entirely at fault for their sins; furthermore, environmental conditions, if properly manipulated, might subdue them. Thus Lowell told the 1879 meeting of the NCCC that "the community itself is responsible for the existence of such miserable, wrecked specimens of humanity" as the women and children who filled state almshouses. "Circumstances make the criminal," Ellen Cheney Johnson repeatedly contended, while Indiana reformers told their legislators that young women traveled the "path of ruin . . . not so much because of any predisposing fault of their own, as because parents, church and State have failed to give them sympathy, and to inspire them to seek a better and higher life."[49]

Dozens of other statements by women prison reformers over the next years reiterated the point that unique circumstances led to women's crimes. Although they realized that unhappy homes and immoral literature could create male as well as female criminals, the reformers singled out women as the victims of two particular social forces: economic and sexual exploitation. The economic explanation predominated in women's rights movement literature; it constituted a minor theme for prison reformers, who launched their major attack on the sexual victimization of women by men.

Radical feminist Susan B. Anthony provided the strongest expression of the economic origins of women's fall in her 1875 address on "Social Purity." Anthony distinguished between the causes of crime in men and women, claiming that the former acted from "love of vice," while the latter acted "from absolute want of the necessaries of life." Historical forces had created this want, she explained. Women who once engaged in profitable household manufacturing had been displaced by men and machines. When "thrust into the world's outer market," they found exhausting labor and little recompense. The working woman, Anthony wrote, "weary and worn from her day's toil . . . sees on every side and at every turn the gilded hand of vice and crime outstretched, . . . Can we wonder that so many poor girls fall, . . . Should we not wonder, rather, that so many escape the sad fate?"[50] Her solution was economic self-sufficiency: "Clearly, then, the first step toward solving this problem is to lift this vast army of poverty-stricken women who now crowd our cities, above the temptation, the necessity, to sell themselves in marriage or out, for bread and shelter."[51]

Although some antebellum writers, both male and female, had made similar points, limited economic opportunities for working women became a central focus of feminist analysis after 1870. Like Anthony, writers in the suffragist *Woman's Journal* anticipated the feminist economics of Charlotte Perkins Gilman. They too argued that financial need, not innate sexual depravity, sent women to the streets, largely because respectable work for women offered inadequate wages. "Society says to all women, 'Go sew' . . . and schools . . . train them chiefly to sew," but in an overcrowded market, the *Journal* lamented, they starved from low wages and were tempted to prostitution. The harlot would disappear only if women became "educated to self support" in various industries. Or, as one former prostitute from Indiana stated, "It was not knowing how to work that made me bad; now I can get my own living, married or single."[52] The Women's Prison Association began to agree with the economic argument in the postwar years. As long as working women received only "their pittance, just so long will they eke it out by the wages of sin," the WPA explained.[53]

Reformers' concerns about working women reflected changes in women's work experiences. Despite the persistent ideology of domesticity, many unmarried, working-class and immigrant women were entering the paid labor force in the decades after 1870. They earned meager salaries for tedious work as domestic servants, laundresses, and unskilled factory workers. A generation later women's low wages and poor working conditions would become a major concern of the Progressive movement. In the late nineteenth century, reformers often suspected the relationship between class and crime, but they did not extend their insight into a full-fledged analysis.

Most women prison reformers pointed to another social force which was unique to the etiology of female crime: sexual exploitation and the double standard of morality. Men, they held, demanded fallen women, but women alone paid the moral and legal price for prostitution. Like the female moral reformers of antebellum New England and New York, the women prison reformers increasingly claimed that men were the root of the social evil.

Elizabeth Buffum Chace came to this conclusion early in her

career when she wrote that only uplift work among men could check the demand for fallen women. Similarly, the WPA reported that "If disreputable men were not to be found upon our streets, disreputable women would not go there to seek them." In the *Woman's Journal*, Ellen Batelle Dietrick placed this cause above all others. Criticizing a group of clergymen she explained that "They are only dealing with half of the problem so long as they utterly ignore the fact that the chief cause for 'fallen women' is fallen men."[54]

Even more annoying was the double standard which, Dietrick held, served to deny the ideal of female superiority. When woman alone bore the blame for sexual infidelity she suffered a loss of status from which men were immune. "Every such [fallen] woman," she wrote, "was once an innocent girl born into a civilization which considers men her superior, supporter and protector. Every boy in our civilization knows that society will excuse in him, the superior, what it will relentlessly condemn in her, his inferior."[55]

That men established the demand for prostitutes, and that they usually escaped without punishment, constituted only part of the indictment. Case histories, written by reformers, blamed men for actively initiating women's fall. Women's crimes, ranging from drunkenness to lewdness to larceny, were attributed to the experiences of being "dragged down by a worthless husband"; accused by "a brutal husband"; "seduced by a coachman"; prostituted by a "bad, intemperate man"; "ruined by the wickedness" of men; or of having fallen "victim to masculine wills." Cruel stepfathers, dishonest lovers, or ruthless employers seemed to plague women at every turn. Other case histories pitied those who had "married a base man"; or been ruined by a promise of marriage that led to a house of prostitution; or been "led off by a married man."[56] One inmate's friends wrote to a women's prison that it was "better to leave her in jail where she has home and food" than to let her return to her drunken husband. So too did prison commissioners often note the woman of "more than usual capacity" who had "been dragged down by a worthless husband." As one case read, "if she had married a better man [she] might have turned out differently."[57]

The reconsideration of the fallen woman was encouraged in part by the deterministic thought which had begun to influence American criminology in general. Both experts in the newly founded social sciences and popular writers who attempted to explain the origins of crime and poverty rejected individual moral responsibility in favor of theories of hereditary and environmental causes. Despite the influence of Darwinian ideas in popularizing biological interpretations of crime, Americans displayed a deeply ingrained environmentalism that continued to hold out hope for the regeneration of the criminal, the insane, and the poor. The rise of a medical profession with a vested interest in "curing" not only disease but also deviancy tempered biological determinism, as did the emergence of a social service profession committed to eliminating poverty and vice.[58]

In addition to the influence of environmental determinism, the specifically antimale content of women's writings suggests other sources for new interpretations. The reformers approached the problem of the fallen woman as one rooted in the social relations of the sexes, rather than as simply the result of heredity or environment. Although they joined contemporaries in speculating on inherited vice and even pointed to the relationship between wages, working conditions, and crime, they repeatedly returned to the theme of woman's sexual vulnerability. Reformers' adoption of a sexual interpretation of crime is not surprising, given that the world of nineteenth-century women was so clearly defined as one in which their sex was supposed to inhabit its own separate sphere—one which had a morality superior to men's. The ideology of women's purity that had earlier condemned the fallen woman now could be used to condemn instead the impure men who, reformers claimed, were at the root of women's crimes.

This sexual interpretation illustrated an important strain of social feminist thought at the end of the century. Many feminists argued that men's intemperate drinking habits and their sexual indulgence led to the exploitation of women, whether as abused wives or as prostitutes. Therefore, the WCTU and the social purity movement attempted to control men's drinking and sexual behavior through personal moral force or through legislation outlawing liquor and vice districts. Some historians view these efforts as part of a symbolic struggle waged to increase women's power in the family and the society.[59] The attacks on men's behavior may have been more defensive, however. Women attempted to protect their personal interests by minimizing their physical vulnerability. Sexual activity carried heavy risks for Victorian women, including the dangers of venereal infection, the strain of repeated childbirth, and a life of constant child rearing.[60] Within this personal framework some women perceived chastity as a liberating experience and saw all institutions that fostered sexual activity as contributing to women's oppression. Thus, social feminists often condemned men's sexual freedom and women prison reformers attacked men's sexual victimization of women as a cause of female crime.

Women's prison visiting had begun as a suitable female auxiliary to men's antebellum reforms. Led by Quakers, charity workers, and social feminists, women's prison reform grew into an independent movement by the late nineteenth century. From their experiences visiting women in jails, operating homes for discharged women prisoners, and participating in the postwar charities and social feminist movements, women reformers developed a unique perspective on the fallen woman. They challenged the view of her total depravity and substituted an indictment of society and particularly of men for causing her fall.

Underlying both women's entry into prison reform and their reinterpretation of the fallen woman was a firm belief that women constituted a separate sexual class. Despite their social analysis of women's crimes, reformers accepted biological categories that separated them from men but bound them to their sisters in prison. Although they acknowledged economic sources of crime, they discounted class differences between themselves and the objects of their concern. In the WPA, and later in state charity and corrections boards, women claimed that, if given a chance to bring their feminine influence to bear, the fallen could be redeemed and made into true women. This commitment to female moral superiority ultimately led to demands for separate women's prisons.

Chapter 3

Feminist or Feminine? The Establishment of Separate Women's Prisons, 1870–1900

Sympathy for the fallen woman as victim and faith in her capacity for redemption characterized the nineteenth-century feminist approach to women prisoners. When women who shared these sentiments approached local and state correctional institutions, they found the American prison system severely deficient. Ameliorative efforts such as prison visiting and homes for discharged women prisoners seemed inadequate to correct the problems exposed by postwar reformers. After the 1860s, women who now had a foothold in public charities and corrections demanded changes in state policies. During the last third of the century they articulated an alternative model of feminine prison reform to replace the neglect of women in men's prisons. Three principles guided them: the separation of women prisoners from men; the provision of differential, feminine care; and control over women's prisons by female staff and management.

By the end of the nineteenth century reformers had succeeded in incorporating these principles into separate women's prisons in the three states in which they were most active—Indiana, Massachusetts, and New York. The Indiana Woman's Prison opened in Indianapolis in 1874. In the same year the Massachusetts legislature established a Reformatory Prison for Women that began to admit inmates in 1877. The first New York House of Refuge for women opened at Hudson in 1887, followed by the opening of the Western House of Refuge at Albion in 1893. A third New York institution, the Bedford Hills Reformatory, was completed in 1901.

The establishment of separate women's prisons contributed to the larger process of female institution-building in the late nineteenth century. Prison reformers and other social feminists drew upon the ideology of women's separate sphere and gradually expanded its boundaries from the private to the public realm. By creating extradomestic female institutions—colleges, clubs, reform organizations, and even prisons—middle-class American

46

women gained both valuable personal skills and greater public authority.[1]

Like the "separate but equal" racial ideology, however, social feminist strategy rested on a contradictory definition of equality. The nineteenth-century prison reformers did seek to expand women's rights when they argued for greater authority over public policy and improved treatment for women prisoners. But at the heart of their program was the principle of innate sexual difference, not sexual equality. Their femininity, reformers asserted, qualified them to control women's prisons. Moreover, they acted on a faith that simply strengthening the feminine elements in institutions would improve them. Thus, in their three major arguments for separate women's prisons, reformers combined feminist goals of preventing men's exploitation of women with feminine methods of extending women's sphere to encompass correctional institutions.

Separation of Female Prisoners

Since their first visits to prisons, reformers of both sexes had objected to the intermingling of male and female inmates. As early as 1826 the "promiscuous and unrestricted intercourse" and "universal riot and debauchery" in the Philadelphia jails inspired the separation of the sexes there. Officials elsewhere decried communication between inmates and passed statutes requiring jail keepers to maintain separate areas for the women in their charge. These regulations prevented sexual contact, but at the same time they usually forced all female inmates into the most uncomfortable quarters within penal institutions.[2]

Elizabeth Fry first articulated the importance of separating female inmates for purposes other than merely preventing sexual contact. In her *Observations*, the British prison reformer expressed fears that sexually mixed quarters undermined women's rehabilitation. Separate facilities, she argued, would allow the classification of women into categories by age and offense, rather than simply by sex, and would facilitate instruction and training in feminine pursuits.[3]

New impetus for separating women prisoners came from nineteenth-century penologists who favored the classification of inmates into age, sex, and offender groups. Both male and female reformers, notably Dorothea Dix, urged separate housing of the insane, juvenile criminals, and first offenders. By mid-century most states had provided facilities for the first two of these groups, and over the next fifty years they established specialized adult reformatories, asylums for alcoholics, and institutions for the mentally ill. These facilities were often designed with separate departments or buildings for female inmates that were an improvement over women's earlier, makeshift quarters.[4]

The first separate women's prison building opened at the Sing Sing, New York, state penitentiary in June 1839. Male staff administered the women's department but matrons served in it. Before long, overcrowding, inadequate hospital and nursery facilities, and disciplinary problems, which culminated in an 1843 riot, plagued the institution. A brief redemption occurred after 1844 with the appointment of Eliza W. Farnham—sometimes feminist, atheist, and phrenologist—as matron.[5]

Farnham believed in rehabilitation instead of punishment. She ended the silence rule, set up a library and a school, classified prisoners, offered incentives for good behavior, and used music, handicrafts, and entertainment to discourage criminal instincts. Instead of the Bible she read the women Dickens's *Oliver Twist*; Margaret Fuller came to speak to inmates at Farnham's request. Unfortunately, her secular methods provoked state officials. They complained that there was "nothing masculine" in the prison routine and forced her to retract her programs and impose silence, work, and strict discipline. Farnham left Sing Sing in 1848. Thereafter, although it remained the only separate state prison for women until the 1870s, it never really furthered the principles of women's prison reform.[6]

Several states continued to house female inmates apart from men within the same institutions, but no new women's prisons were constructed in the antebellum years. By the 1860s, however, when the mounting number of female commitments taxed existing facilities, several new women's quarters were constructed.[7] At the same time, women active in charities and corrections who visited sexually mixed institutions began criticizing the discriminatory treatment of female inmates and revived the issue of separate prisons. Elizabeth Chace, for instance, discovered in her visits to Rhode Island institutions that prisons held classes for men but not for women and that female inmates were offered neither exercise nor mental occupation while incarcerated.[8] Refusal to attempt the reformation of women bothered Josephine Shaw Lowell as well. She told the New York State Board of Charities in 1879 that the "visible links" in the chain of poverty and criminality were "women who from early girlhood have been tossed from poorhouse to jail, and from jail to poorhouse, until the last trace of woman-hood in them has been destroyed." Neither in "jail, poorhouse nor penitentiary," she charged, "will they find anything to help them turn back; on the contrary, all the surroundings will force them lower." Lowell concluded that only separate women's institutions would prevent this cycle.[9]

Women joined other critics of American prisons in calling for change. A revival of interest in prison reform, evidenced by the founding of the American Prison Association in 1870, led to re-newed debate about penal methods in general. By this date, American penitentiaries had declined into complacent, over-crowded, custodial institutions. Although many states continued to rely on penitentiaries, the newly organized charity and correc-tions workers brought several alternatives to public attention. They were particularly impressed by experiments in the British prison system and by the innovations of the reformatory prison.

The British system had instituted policies of commutation of sentences for good behavior, the merit marking-system, and pro-gressive reentry into society. Under the influence of American re-formers Enoch C. Wines, Zebulon Brockway, and Franklin San-born, these methods were incorporated into reformatory prisons for youthful, male first offenders at Elmira, New York (1876) and Concord, Massachusetts (1884). Brockway, the first superintendent of the Elmira Reformatory, instituted prison reforms that re-warded inmates for internalizing many of the controls formerly imposed by the external discipline of the penitentiary. Incentive systems offered greater privileges for good behavior and the inde-terminate sentence allowed prisoners' actions to influence their date of release.[10]

For women, the most significant innovation of the British sys-tem was demonstrated by the Mount Joy Female Convict prison in Ireland. In 1862 British prison reformer Mary Carpenter observed the separate women's reformatory at Mount Joy and became con-vinced of its efficacy in rehabilitating women criminals. Like her American counterparts, Carpenter explained that women only seemed unreformable because of the "injudicious treatment" they usually received as convicts. In her 1864 book, *Our Convicts*, Car-penter recommended that women prisoners should be gath-ered into one institution where a merit system would determine progression to various stages of treatment and privilege. Female staff would provide "considerable intellectual and cultural development" for inmates, while the use of male guards would be avoided.[11]

Americans were intrigued by the British plan of a separate, reformatory women's prison. As early as 1865 the Massachusetts Board of State Charities reported favorably on separation and the merit system for women in England. When the first International Penitentiary Congress convened in London in 1872, a session on women's work enabled Julia Ward Howe and Elizabeth Buffum Chace to meet Mary Carpenter and discuss the principle of separate female institutions.[12] Several male reformers were impressed by the fact that the superintendent, subordinate officers, and teachers at Mount Joy were all women.[13] Charles and Rhoda Coffin visited Mount Joy and praised its approximation of family life, the placement of released women in private homes, and particularly the self-respect engendered by the trust placed in upper-grade prisoners. All of these advantages had been unavailable to women dispersed throughout the predominantly male prisons.[14]

At the same time that Mount Joy presented a model for American reformers, the establishment of sexually segregated juvenile reformatories helped pave the way for separate adult prisons. Several reform schools for boys were founded after 1847 and the first State Industrial School for Girls, at Lancaster, Massachusetts, opened in 1856. In Connecticut legislators considered establishing a women's prison in the 1860s, but instead they chartered an industrial school for girls that classified inmates within a cottage system of residence and offered instruction, employment, indeterminate sentences, and conditional pardon and release.[15]

In 1867 a visit to the Lancaster, Massachusetts, girls' reform school inspired Zebulon Brockway, then superintendent of the Detroit House of Correction, to experiment with separate "reformatory" treatment for the women under his care. Brockway had been impressed with the methods of the girls' school, and so he helped establish a women's "House of Shelter." From 1869 to 1874, Emma Hall, a Detroit public school teacher, served as matron. Hall formed "a little society" with thirty female inmates living as a family in "commodious and well furnished" surroundings. She instituted a merit system, offered training for remunerative employment, and fostered "strong social bonds" among inmates. Although the House of Shelter was not technically a prison, it was the first penal institution where women had complete authority over female inmates. According to a historian of Michigan's prisons, "The House of Shelter was America's first women's reformatory."[16]

By 1870 other separate institutions were being established in Indiana. The Home for the Friendless in Richmond had just become the official city prison. Its female managers, deputized as sheriffs who "paroled" their prisoners to the home, attempted to achieve reformation through prayer, music, Bible study, and work. Meanwhile, Indiana Friends Sarah Smith and Rhoda Coffin led a campaign to end the sexual abuse of women in the state prison. Their lobbying efforts succeeded in 1869 when a bill creating a "Female Prison and Reformatory Institution for Girls and Women" passed the Indiana legislature. The prison, which opened in Indianapolis in 1874, was the first completely separate state women's penal institution in America.[17]

Even as the Indiana Woman's Prison was under construction, reformers in other states were adopting the model of sexually separate prisons. The three women and three men on the Massachusetts Prison Commission decided in 1870 that "a classification of the prisoners, according to sex, age, and degree of crime, was absolutely necessary before any satisfactory progress toward reformation could be expected."[18] In their first annual report they argued for sexual separation on several grounds. "In our county prisons, as a general rule, the poorest and most unfavorable quarters are assigned to women," they wrote. But separation would not help only one sex. "By separating the women from the men, both are benefitted," through the removal of sexual distractions and the possibility of improving the present system which, they felt, "does not tend to the reformation of men or women."[19]

Implementing the recommendation of sexual separation took a four-year campaign on the part of the commissioners and private reformers. First the commissioners tried to centralize all women prisoners into one county jail, but a hostile sheriff undermined that strategy by refusing to remove the male inmates.[20] The commissioners then decided that a new prison should be built. Two of them, Hannah Chickering of the Dedham Asylum for Discharged Female Prisoners and Clara Leonard of the Springfield Home for the Friendless, convened a public meeting in Boston and gathered hundreds of signatures on petitions to the legislature. When lawmakers, reluctant to appropriate money for a women's prison, rejected the bill in 1873, the prison commissioners argued that a women's prison would save money by reducing female crime.[21]

They insisted further that "for this State to say, by its Legislature, that it cannot afford to build a new prison . . . would be absurd. It did not say so last year when the necessity appeared for a new state prison for men."[22]

In June 1873 private reformers organized "a League to secure the establishment of a Separate Prison for the Female Convicts of Massachusetts." They publicized their cause in "secular and religious" newspapers and, borrowing a technique from the temperance movement, they asked for signatures to "The Pledge" of approval of a separate prison.[23] Drawing on local women's networks throughout the state, members held parlor meetings, wrote letters, and distributed new petitions. Over 7,000 signatures reached the Massachusetts legislature between January and March 1874. In June the legislation passed both House and Senate, and the second women's prison in America—the first statewide *reformatory* institution for adult women—was signed into law.[24]

By 1874, then, the principle of separating female convicts, not merely within existing prisons, but in specially constructed women's institutions, had been adopted in Indiana and Massachusetts. The logic of sexual separation was clear. First, it encouraged efficient management by collecting female inmates under one roof. Secondly, it expunged the malevolent male influences which had impeded women's reformation in mixed prisons. But in both states, and soon in New York as well, two additional arguments supported the reformers' commitment to separate institutions: the necessity for differential, feminine, treatment and the unique ability of women to supply that need.

Differential Treatment

Sexually mixed prison facilities in the nineteenth century, far from catering to uniquely feminine needs, usually stripped women inmates of the privileges normally extended to the "fairer sex" and gave them little or no hope of returning to society as restored women. Failure to provide feminine care was in no way egalitarian; rather, it rested on the belief that criminal women were more hardened than men.

Critics of American prisons in the 1870s took issue with the view that fallen women could not be reformed. They charged the correctional system with perpetuating a self-fulfilling prophecy of hopelessness for female offenders. Elizabeth Chace, for instance, complained of the discouraging treatment offered by male correctional officers, since even "good men regard a fallen woman as so much worse than a fallen man that they involuntarily shrink from association with her" and therefore do little toward her redemption. In a letter to the first national prison congress she amplified her argument:

> The public sentiment which condemns a woman to imprisonment and entire loss of reputation, and then pronounces her reformation hopeless, . . . fills our penal institutions with women of this class. . . . While men are constantly influenced by the expectation . . . [of becoming] virtuous and useful members of society, it is impossible to bring the influence of such a hope upon the women, when there is no belief in the possibility of such a change for *them*. The result is, the women go out hopeless for themselves.[25]

Similarly, the Massachusetts prison commissioners concluded that one evil of the existing system was having female prisoners under the "immediate and entire control of men" who had "little or no faith in the possibility of their reformation." Naturally, if "looked upon as incapable of reformation" in prison, the commissioners reasoned, inmates would lose heart and go back to "the life" after they were released.[26]

Thus the reformers argued that women would remain incurably criminal unless they received a new form of treatment within the correctional system. "We do not say or think more lenient," they pointed out, "but different. And at present the most prominent difference discernible is that they have for the most part poorer and less desirable quarters, and are employed virtually as servants for the men."[27] The alternative treatment reformers proposed represented an almost complete reversal of the patterns they were criticizing. Rather than differential treatment which condemned women, reformers called for greater help and better training to convert the fallen into respectable women.

Reformers wanted not only to alter the traditional belief that female criminals were more hardened than male offenders, they wanted to portray imprisoned women as untapped resources who had within them the cherished qualities of piety and purity. Only the chrysalis of a degrading environment concealed their natural womanhood. Healthier surroundings, both within and after prison, would permit the metamorphosis from depravity to "true womanhood." As the WPA wrote:

> We believe that woman in her deepest degradation
> Holds something sacred, something undefiled;
> And like the diamond in the dark, retains
> Some quenchless gleam of the celestial light.[28]

Their vision of training derived from the ideal of female behavior that had evolved during the nineteenth century. The virtues of "true womanhood"—purity, piety, domesticity, and submissiveness—appealed to middle-class reformers. Their own socialization had been accomplished by ladies' magazines, domestic guides, and academy or seminary courses in moral philosophy and domestic economy. But those who were not exposed to this curriculum, or who simply resisted it, were deviant women who required retraining. Instructing them for feminine roles meant treating women prisoners qua women, recognizing their innate femininity and then encouraging it to blossom under the influences of womanly sympathy and nurture. In essence, it meant extending the middle-class woman's socialization to fallen women.

Although male criminals might be reformed as well, their progress required a form of retraining suitable to masculine ideals of work and discipline, like that found in the factory or military model of penitentiaries. Consequently, even the new reformatories for young men prided themselves on industrial arts classes, physical culture, and military drill.

Women, like children with whom they were often compared, were more impressionable and called forth a special approach. Their innocence could be restored by appealing to intuition, to heart. "I think for women—I will not say for men—God's clear sunlight softens the human heart," one APA member remarked. Or, as Massachusetts officials wrote, "Women need different management from men; they are more emotional and more susceptible; they are far less likely to be influenced by general appeals or force of discipline, and are more open to personal treatment and the influence of kindness."[29]

One of the staunchest advocates of differential treatment, prison superintendent Ellen Cheney Johnson, recommended such "softening" influences on women prisoners as flowers, farm animals, music, and visits to the infant nursery. Johnson speculated that women's "different physical organization and consequent greater nervous sensitiveness" made them "as a class more difficult to deal with" and necessitated kinder treatment. Each woman retained "the germ of goodness in the heart" which Johnson hoped to "seek out and develop and establish."[30]

Once again, references to women criminals as a class apart from their male counterparts indicated the primacy of gender identity for nineteenth-century women. To reach the "true woman" within each fallen shell, reformers sought feminine methods of corrections. As Josephine Shaw Lowell and others saw their task, female criminals were "first of all, to be taught to be women." Hence, "they must be induced to love that which is good and pure, and to wish to resemble it." Not incidentally, "they must learn all household duties."[31] What better structure in which to carry out this task of socialization for womanhood than in the home, the center of the middle-class female sphere? Domesticity, then, provided a focal point for female corrections and a means of restoring femininity to the fallen.

The "home" had been an important response to female criminality since the 1840s when shelters were used as intermediate lodgings for released women prisoners. The Women's Prison Association of New York, for instance, employed domestic routines to regularize inmates' lives and to train them for proper womanly roles. "A Home," they explained, "is the very heart of the undertaking in behalf of female convicts."[32]

As the number of homes for released female convicts multiplied over the next decades, domestic structure became a requirement for women's reformation. In 1852 the Female Prison Association of Philadelphia sought a refuge for penitent women: " . . . we seem to want a stepping stone between the Prison, and the wide world. . . . —Yes! we want a *Home*; where they may begin anew to tread the path of life."[33] In Dedham and Springfield, Massachusetts, Richmond, Indiana, and other cities, dozens of homes opened between the 1870s and the 1890s.[34]

Not only as shelters, but also as retraining centers for fallen women, the homes catered to uniquely feminine needs. Through evangelical religion, education, and discipline, the matrons and managers offered courses to restore the womanhood of residents. Daily lessons in reading, writing, sewing, "and other feminine employments" supplemented the prayers, Bible study, and religious services, thus ensuring both domesticity and piety. Discipline included the banning of profanity, tobacco, alcohol, and coarse behavior, plus a routine of early rising, regular work (sewing, laundry, cleaning), and habits of neatness and industry at all times. In spite of the regimentation imposed, the managers of the homes insisted that the key to discipline lay in the familial patterns which they adopted. As the Crittenton Homes' regulations explained: "Inmates when admitted are adopted into the family and are expected to give the loving obedience of dutiful children towards their parents."[35]

The analogy with youth echoed another model upon which reformers of fallen women relied. In the mid-nineteenth century, juvenile reformatories adopted the "family system" to cure delinquency. Domestic training had been applied to female orphans and delinquents as early as 1800, but the introduction of the European cottage plan for juvenile institutions in the late 1850s further encouraged family-model care. In 1856 the Lancaster girls' school in Massachusetts became the first reformatory in the United States designed with small buildings known as cottages instead of dormitories or cell blocks. Boys' schools soon adopted the family plan as well, and increasingly groups such as the Massachusetts Board of Charities were recommending that "in providing for the poor, the dependent, and the vicious, especially for the young, we must take the ordinary family for our model." By the 1870s a number of institutions had adopted the domestic model, or cottage system, for their designs.[36]

Separate women's prisons were established just when the domestic model was gaining popularity. The Detroit House of Shelter, as Emma Hall made clear, approximated in design and routine the patterns of domestic life. A private room, "flowers, pictures, music and home industries" would "create a desire for a permanent home."[37] In New York, Josephine Lowell rejected the silence and hard labor of penitentiaries: "The reformatories must not be prisons, which would crush out the life from those unfortunate enough to be cast into them; they must be *homes*,—homes where a tender care shall surround the weak and fallen creatures who are placed under their shelter."[38]

According to Lowell the ideal reformatory would be set on a large tract of land (from 250 to 500 acres) in order to prevent communication with the outer world. Inmates would be classified and housed in several small buildings, with fifteen to twenty-five women in each, under the charge of female officers. Training would include traditional women's work: cooking, washing and ironing, gardening, and milking cows. Lowell stressed that due attention should be given to "mental and moral faculties" and to the physical health of the women. Like the Mount Joy prison and the Elmira reformatory for young men, a graded system of residences and progress to more privileged cottages would provide the incentives "necessary to a hopeful life."[39] Citing encouraging news from institutions that tried to implement familial routines, Lowell approached the New York State legislature to ask for a cottage plan institution for young adult female offenders.[40]

Largely due to her efforts, the Albany legislature passed a bill to establish New York's first "House of Refuge" for women in 1881. When appropriations were delayed, Lowell herself "bombarded" the lawmakers with letters and pamphlets and won her battle. The Hudson House of Refuge opened on 7 May 1887, the first cottage-system adult female reformatory. Staffed almost entirely by women, the institution embodied most of Lowell's plans, including an incentive grading system, cottages, and domestic routines. "The idea of a family and home life is carried out as far as possible in the cottages," the board of charities reported in 1888. "In the evening they are gathered together in a circle, of which the supervisor and assistant form the center. . . . The girls, while knitting or sewing, profit by some appropriate reading or oral instruction."[41] The Hudson House of Refuge was filled by 1889 and Lowell, along with Abby Hopper Gibbons and other WPA members, began to press for the establishment of two more New York women's reformatories.

Their WPA reports, testimony before the legislature, and support from the New York State Board of Charities helped establish the Western House of Refuge at Albion, New York, which opened in 1893. There, too, the management reported, "the regulations governing the household will follow as closely as circumstances permit those of any well regulated family of young people."[42] By 1892 the WPA had succeeded in securing legislation establishing a third reformatory, to serve the New York City area but secluded in Bedford Hills in Westchester County. Again insufficient appropriations delayed construction, but the institution finally opened in 1901.[43]

By 1900 methods to meet the distinctive needs of female prisoners—womanly sympathy, shelter, familial discipline, and domestic training—had been adopted by institutions in Indiana, Massachusetts, and New York. Although the separate women's institutions served only a small minority of all female prisoners, most of whom remained in sexually mixed local jails, they represented the new ideals of prison methods. Like the homes for released prisoners, the new institutions embodied the reformers' commitment to traditional definitions of womanhood. But while upholding these traditional definitions, reformers were also attacking barriers to women's entry into male domains, for the final goal of their movement was that women direct and control the reformatory process, an innovation which met initial resistance within the correctional profession.

Female Staff and Management

Elizabeth Fry insisted that prisons provide both separate women's quarters and female attendants within them. Fearing that male guards might abuse women prisoners, and reasoning that women would provide sympathetic counsel and good examples for female inmates, Fry advised: "It is absolutely essential to the proper order and regulation of every prison, that the female prisoners should be placed under the superintendence of officers of their own sex."[44]

American prisons adopted the practice of hiring matrons when women's departments were established in the first quarter of the nineteenth century. Rachel Perijo held the first matron position in 1822 at the Baltimore penitentiary, where she offered industrial, educational, and religious training to her female charges. In New York, first at the Auburn penitentiary women's department and later in the Sing Sing women's prison, matrons supervised female inmates. By 1845, when Dorothea Dix toured American jails, she found matrons in several Massachusetts houses of correction, at Sing Sing, in Maryland and Pennsylvania jails, and at the Eastern penitentiary.[45]

The early prison matrons, however, had neither the authority nor the assignment to reform fallen women, and they were invariably supervised by male officials. Most states still had too few female prisoners to warrant separate facilities and matrons, or they simply never considered them necessary. By 1870, though, the larger number of female inmates and women's criticism of male keepers raised new reasons to hire police and prison matrons. Moreover, during the late nineteenth century, American women were beginning to enter certain professions that were considered logical extensions of their domestic and nurturing roles. In addition to teaching, nursing, and social work, correctional jobs joined the list of acceptable women's careers after reformers successfully argued the necessity of female staff in women's prisons.

The major rationale for female staff was that men contributed to, rather than cured, women's delinquency. Just as they had focused on men's responsibility for female crime, so too did the prison reformers point out the victimization of women within the criminal justice system. The indiscriminate arrest of women who were alone on New York streets, for example, annoyed the Women's Prison Association. Their reports cited examples of police brutality en route to station houses, implying that potentially innocent women were commonly being assaulted under the guise of antiprostitution activity.[46]

Reformers claimed that arrested women faced further discrimination in trial and sentencing procedures. When Elizabeth Chace visited court during a case of assault on a woman, she was dismayed to find that not only the lawyers but even the judge treated the victim more harshly than they did her male assailant. Similarly, a female member of the Wisconsin charities board protested the unequal treatment of prostitutes and their customers after a police raid. "The male inmates are suffered to escape, or under an *alias*, fined and discharged," she bemoaned. But the arrested women, before their innocence or guilt had been determined, were "dragged through the streets, and into open courts for trial!" Unless women had "protectors" to pay their fines, the court sentenced them to jail, to be searched by men and possibly to be indoctrinated into the ways of crime.[47] In the opinion of these reformers, the system of justice appeared more criminal than the acts of prostitution for which women were arrested.

More disturbing than the accusation of unjust convictions was the sexual vulnerability of female prisoners. When women prison reformers declared that prison degraded rather than reformed women, they often spoke quite literally of sexual abuse. Hannah Chickering protested male officers' treatment of women, the WPA lamented that male doorkeepers physically searched the "poorer class" of female convicts, and the WCTU complained that male jailers had the keys to women's quarters. In station houses and prisons, Rhoda Coffin discovered, women were "huddled together like cattle in a pen," easily viewed and often assaulted by men. Josephine Shaw Lowell quoted a report about a jailer who "had wantonly assaulted and degraded numerous young women prisoners; and, when sheriff . . . had utterly brutalized three young girls."[48]

At least one woman prisoner confirmed reformers' fears that

sexual abuse in prison undermined all hope of reform. Addie Irving wrote to a woman prison visitor in 1866 that the warden of Blackwell's Island penitentiary in New York City had locked her in a room with a naval officer. The officer attempted to seduce her, explaining "that the authorities sent him there." "Now I ask you," Irving wrote, "after being in such a contaminating place is it any wonder i yealded [*sic*] to temptation again."[49]

Illegitimate births within charitable and penal institutions, noted in Connecticut, Michigan, New York, Indiana, Tennessee, New Jersey, and elsewhere, evidenced the extent of sexual activity in mixed prisons.[50] The paucity of convictions of male keepers suggests not so much that women were willing partners but, rather, that many were powerless to accuse or prosecute their attackers. One exposé of forced prostitution within a state prison did lead to convictions of male officers for assault on female prisoners, and it offers a rare insight into conditions within one of the worst mixed institutions.

The Indiana state prison at Jeffersonville represented a reformer's nightmare. In this "vast bawdy house," a young male prisoner revealed, younger female prisoners were "subjected to the worst of debasement at the hands of prison officials and guards," while the older ones were "obliged to do the work of all." When the warden "established the practice of concubinage," his deputy and other officers followed by making keys to the women's quarters and forcing the female inmates "to submit to their hellish outrages." The convict who authored this exposé may have been the same man who approached Charles and Rhoda Coffin when they visited Jeffersonville in 1868 and begged them "for God's sake, do something for those poor women, their condition is terrible." Sadistic beatings, rape, illegitimate births, "and more," the chaplain confirmed, had become part of the prison routine. A legislative investigation concluded that "the guards and other employees had free access to the female convicts, that the treatment of them has been disgusting, lecherous and brutal." These conditions moved Rhoda Coffin to declare to an APA convention that women confined in a men's prison "may be forced to minister to the lust of the officers, or if they refuse, submit to the infliction of the lash until they do. They are powerless, they are only convicts, and they do not have redress."[51]

Although not every prison was as corrupt as the one in Indiana, less-blatant abuses elsewhere angered women reformers. As in society at large, they concluded, so within the process of criminal justice—men contributed to women's delinquency. Their response evidenced a growing reliance on feminist rhetoric to attack men's authority. As one reformer reminisced, the call to aid her fallen sisters was in large part a response to what appeared to be male dominance gone rampant: "Arrested by men, given into the hands of men to be searched and cared for, tried by men, sentenced by men, and committed to our various institutions for months and even years, where only men officials had access to them, and where, in sickness or direst need, no womanly help or visitation was expected or allowed."[52] To remedy this situation the women offered an alternative: remove male influences by separating women from male prisoners, male officers, and male guards; and replace the demeaning influences of men with the uplifting force of women.

In the police matron movement, one of the testing grounds for this demand, reformers successfully argued that women's moral force qualified them as prison guards. The WCTU had succeeded in having matrons hired in several American cities between 1876 and 1888.[53] In New York City, however, the WPA encountered resistance to its campaign to require matrons wherever women were detained by police.[54] The men of the PANY opposed the WPA-supported legislation on the grounds that female prisoners did not suffer under men's authority and, even if they did, female matrons would be too weak to prevent abuse. PANY members especially disliked the provisions that police matrons would have the same salary as station-house keepers and the same right to trial before removal.[55] Women reformers avoided the questions of salary and status; they simply explained that women had special skills for protecting and reforming the female prisoner. No matter how depraved or unmanageable the prisoner might be, "a man has no right to go near her." Rather, she required "the shield of a pure woman's presence—, one who could bring to bear a force, often found more potent than muscular strength." The Police Matrons bill finally passed in 1888, though without mandatory status.[56]

Although some men agreed that women's moral force, sensitivity to their own sex, and domestic skills fit them for jobs in women's prisons, many remained reluctant to grant women authority over the new institutions.[57] When Rhoda Coffin first suggested to the APA in 1876 that a "woman's prison should be entirely under the control of women," her audience expressed discomfort. "I believe with the lady that every institution should be homelike," one man responded, "but the home for women without men is not the home for me."[58] The APA congress refused to accept Coffin's paper. Similarly, state officials remained wary of women's authority. In Indiana, a male board of managers controlled the finances of the women's prison during its first years and, according to Superintendent Sarah Smith, they encroached on the internal management of the institution. In 1877 Indiana reformers succeeded in installing an all-female board that was "watched by suspicious eyes" until members proved themselves competent. Massachusetts women's prison managers found it necessary to respond to critics by claiming that female staff subdued difficult prisoners "as successfully as if inmates had been under the control of men, and we believe, with better results to the character."[59]

Only a constant defense of the new women's prisons, argued at APA and NCCC meetings and in annual reports, convinced the profession that women had both the right and the ability to control their own institutions. The equality they won, however, rested firmly on the belief in a separate female sphere. Men who toured the Massachusetts women's prison in 1881 became convinced that "women can govern women."[60] As Pennsylvania prison chaplain J. J. Milligan confessed: "For ten years I have been doubting that the only persons to take charge of a female prison, were females. . . . But yesterday, I must say, that all my objections vanished into thin air."[61] The next year Milligan criticized his colleagues who remained skeptical of prisons "unreservedly in the hands of women." He exemplified the reasoning behind the gradual acceptance of women's prisons when he explained that they offered "the methods in nearest alliance with honest and pure home life. Girls and women should be trained to adorn homes with the virtues which make their lives noble and enobling. *It is only in this province, that they may most fittingly fill their mission.*"[62] The domestic basis of differential treatment proved to be the most convincing defense for women's prisons.

Both the NCCC and the APA followed Milligan's lead as members converted to the cause of female-controlled prisons. By the time Rhoda Coffin addressed the APA on the subject in 1885, delegates accepted a stronger statement of support.[63] By 1891 the NCCC acknowledged that female staff and management worked well in Massachusetts and Indiana. The organization listed as reasons for appointing women managers of state institutions that "woman's superior knowledge of domestic economy" would reduce state expenses, while in justice to female inmates, staff and management of the same sex offered sympathetic counsel and representation of women's own interests.[64]

By the 1890s the defense of women's prisons had been successfully accomplished. Separate penal institutions, run by and for women, and police matrons in major cities, supplemented the homes for discharged prisoners and the prison visiting of the antebellum period. The male prison reformers had gradually granted equal status to women and their institutions on the grounds that they constituted a separate female sphere within the correctional system. The legitimacy of women's prisons rested on women's uniquely feminine components—on their domesticity, their emotional sensitivity, and their greater moral force. Even as women encroached on men's professional world, they thus remained limited to the traditional feminine realm. As Milligan explained: "Home! a home is the place for the woman; there she belongs exclusively. Then make a reformatory like a home, educate her to that standard, and it is possible to train her *for a home*, in a home."[65]

The women's prisons established in the 1870s and 1880s set standards that survived almost intact for the next century. Differential treatment of women prisoners remained a central principle of American corrections until a new feminist approach emerged in the 1970s. Although the "separate but equal" argument long outlived its usefulness in justifying women's control of their own prisons, it cannot be totally dismissed as the anachronism it later became. In the end, the arguments based on difference furthered the breakdown of the separate spheres by enabling middle-class women to work and to assume authority in the public sphere. The principle of differential treatment of women provided an effective rationale to counter resistance to the reformers' entry into the public sphere while not conflicting with these nineteenth-century women's deeply held sexual ideology. In contrast to the few egalitarian feminists of their era, most prison reformers believed that they were different from men. Their faith in a common womanhood encouraged their concern for women prisoners; their discovery of sexual exploitation in prisons gave them good reason to believe that substituting keepers of their own sex would improve prison life for women.

The results of the "separate but equal" ideology, however, were as contradictory as were the reformers' plans for feminine prisons.

The two cultural models they hoped to combine—true woman-hood and the prison—were incompatible. How could the feminine principles they extolled—heart, home, sisterhood—thrive within an institution designed to facilitate the isolation and discipline of inmates? The histories of the first women's prisons reveal how "their sisters' keepers" responded to this contradiction.

Part 2

The Institutional Compromise

Women's Prisons in Indiana, Massachusetts, and New York, 1870–1910

Chapter 4

The Women's Prison Environment

In 1877, a new resident of the Massachusetts Reformatory Prison for Women wrote home to her sister: "I wish thee could see me! I cannot describe my surrounds. I might as well be in the desert of Sahara—for *human* companionship at this moment.—no, hark! in the distance I hear the rumble of a railway train, which means *life*. But I am separated from it by a high red fence—and from the other inmates of this building by wings—and corridors and doors."[1]

Although she came as a paid staff member, Dr. Eliza Mosher knew when she wrote these words that she was in prison. Her initial impressions offer a hint of how the buildings, their location, and their inhabitants must have affected the newcomers to women's prisons. Measured by Mosher's sentiments, the task of creating a homelike, reformatory environment posed a great challenge to prison reformers and administrators.

Both internal and external constraints contributed to this challenge. Within their own movement, reformers found themselves in a new relationship to prisons and prisoners once they had established their own institutions. Previously, they had criticized prisons from the outside, either as visitors, advocates for released inmates, or members of state correctional boards. Now, however, the reformers were inside, as keepers. Their very jobs constrained them as critics. Even as they remained sympathetic to the women under their care, they had to defend their institutions to the state officials who controlled their budgets and commitment policies. These external agencies—state legislatures, courts, and boards of control—imposed numerous constraints on prison funding, design, hiring, and inmate commitments.

As a result of both kinds of limitations, the histories of the first women's prisons, from approximately 1870 to 1910, reveal a narrowing of reformers' visions. The process of compromise first became evident in the creation of the women's prison environment—design, staff, and inmates—which is discussed in this chapter. The internal life of the institutions, the subject of chapter five, further illustrates the problems of implementing feminine prison reform.

Prison Design

Architectural design had been an important component of American prison reform since Jeremy Bentham's *Panopticon* of 1787 influenced the plans of the first state penitentiaries. Massive, imposing structures from the outside, the prisons built in the early nineteenth century reflected the goals of isolation, order, and discipline that were enforced within them. Central buildings housed administration and services, and from them emanated wings of long hallways with tiers of cell blocks easily viewed by guards. Miniscule cells, averaging fifty square feet, housed prisoners in isolation from each other. Like cogs in a machine, inmates moved according to strict schedules and, ideally, remained silent at all times. Even the late nineteenth-century reformatories, which rejected the punitive objectives of earlier institutions, retained their disciplinary goals. Reformatory design included greater specialization of interior space, with numerous workshops, classrooms, and usually a gymnasium, and with courtyards and a parade ground between buildings. But all these areas remained enclosed within an outer wall.[2]

In calling for unique, feminine prisons, reformers clearly stated that these institutions should not replicate the design of the penitentiary. Rather than a factory or military atmosphere, women required an environment suitable for their feminine temperaments. Josephine Shaw Lowell advocated the cottage system used in juvenile reformatories. Other reformers hoped to modify penitentiary or reformatory designs by making women's prisons less austere, less militaristic, and even less secure than men's. As a Massachusetts prison commissioner wrote, the "Proper Construction of Prisons for Women" did "not require the strength and solidity of a prison intended for the worst class of male convicts." Rather, he suggested, it should be relieved "as far as possible, from prison-like features" in order to be "homelike and cheerful."[3]

When women's prisons were constructed, their designs reflected a mixture of traditional and newer domestic styles. To a limited degree, the plans followed Lowell's recommendations. In 1877 the Massachusetts Reformatory Prison for Women (MRPW) opened on thirty acres of land in the village of Framingham (Sherborn). Its locale, thirty miles west of Boston, suggested a retreat from the city to a pastoral setting. Instead of cells, the reformatory had "private rooms" which ranged from fifty to ninety square feet, slightly larger than most men's prison quarters. Iron bedsteads and white linen, not the typical bare cot, adorned each room. Well-behaved inmates could decorate their quarters, enjoy unbarred windows, and have wood slats instead of grating on their doors. Room size and location was determined by a merit system, with six-by-ten-foot rooms for most and nine-by-ten-foot rooms for the honor class.[4]

The New York refuges at Hudson and Albion adopted the cottage plan. The numerous small structures there made it easier to classify inmates and to approximate domestic life. The Hudson House of Refuge, set on 40 acres in northeastern New York State, had four cottages at its opening in 1887 and added three more later. Each cottage housed twenty-six inmates and officers and included a kitchen and dining room. "The 'cottages' are fitted up as nearly as possible like an average family home," the *Charities Review* observed. In later years, the board of managers assigned the cottages names instead of the original numbers "in furtherance of its plans to free the institution from the appearance of a place of imprisonment." The institution also had a main building with office, work, and school rooms. Similarly, the Western House of Refuge opened in 1893 on a 100-acre campus adjacent to a park. It provided seven residential cottages, surrounded by ten other buildings.[5]

Indiana's prison, situated on 15.6 acres in Indianapolis, consisted of a superintendent's residence connected to a traditional congregate prison with a central administrative section and two wings. One housed forty to sixty adult felons in cells 8-by-11½ feet. The other had a capacity for 200 juvenile offenders. The two divisions had separate facilities, except for a common chapel located in the girls' school wing.[6]

In Massachusetts, New York, and Indiana, the women's prisons rejected the penitentiary plan of individual seclusion. Specialized interior rooms encouraged inmates to circulate throughout the prison to the chapels, workrooms, libraries, and infirmaries. Access to the outdoors also helped "naturalize" the settings. At each of the institutions, even the one in downtown Indianapolis, officials encouraged inmates to cultivate the prison gardens. In Massachusetts and New York the presence of children contributed to a domestic atmosphere. The former provided a nursery for infants born within the institution until they reached age two. The Western House of Refuge at Albion had a separate cottage for mothers and infants. Babies remained there until "suitably placed" in families, where mothers could reclaim them after their release.[7]

Unfortunately, these innovations could not compensate for the limitations of traditional prison design. Of the four women's prisons constructed during the nineteenth century, two—in Framingham and Indianapolis—were traditional congregate buildings: massive stone structures with wings containing rows of rooms. Only the New York Houses of Refuge used the cottage plan. Furthermore, all four of the institutions suffered from inadequacies in design resulting from shortsighted economic concerns and inexperience in structuring adult reformatories.[8]

The Indiana and Massachusetts prisons ignored the call for "family-style" designs. Stone walls and elevated fences enclosed their grounds, while double doors and iron gratings further insured prison security and discouraged efforts to provide a domestic atmosphere. Punishment cells, sometimes in the basement, revealed the expectation that intransigent prisoners would be beyond the reach of moral suasion. The Massachusetts edifice, despite the contention that it was a "beautiful, castle-like building, surrounded by ample grounds," more nearly resembled a "grim, dark, 'bastille'-like structure."[9] Even at the Hudson refuge a ninety-six cell prison building housed new arrivals and punishment cases.

Although the founders of women's prisons called for vocational, medical, and child-care services, it became painfully apparent in the first few years of institutional life that insufficient space hampered their provision. The New York Houses of Refuge lacked chapels, assembly rooms, and adequate school rooms. Indiana officials soon found the combined girls' school and women's prison inadequate and regretted their failure to provide a library and enough schoolrooms. The Massachusetts prison hospital was overcrowded within a year of its opening. In both of the congregate-system prisons it was nearly impossible to classify inmates satisfactorily within one building. Massachusetts employed different wings for the various grades of prisoners, but Indiana officials had no means of separating classes of inmates.[10]

Separate female prisons, then, were handicapped from the outset by inadequate buildings and poor planning. The congregate-prison design was more economical to construct and more conducive to the supervision of a large number of inmates, and so in spite of the commitment to reformatory design, it, rather than the campus-style cottage plan, prevailed in Massachusetts and Indiana.[11] Major concerns of classifying inmates and providing special services were impeded by the limitations of space in these prisons.

Even in the cottage-plan reformatories, medical and educational facilities were often too limited to meet institutional needs.

Management and Staff

The first women's prisons were somewhat more successful in realizing their goals of female control than in realizing those of design, but only after an initial period of struggle to oust male managers. At first men maintained ultimate authority over the Indiana and Massachusetts prisons, and male physicians served in New York and Indiana. Their presence contradicted the theory that women's problems, whether medical or emotional, could best be treated by members of the same sex. Other men worked at each institution, not only to calm fears that inmates would overrun their too-gentle female keepers, but also to perform engineering, firefighting, and carpentry tasks for which there were few women available.[12]

It was not easy to attract capable women who were willing to direct prisons. In Massachusetts, where the governor appointed prison superintendents, and in New York, which early relied on civil service to recruit officers, the first "professionals" chosen did not necessarily meet the standards of competency and kindness that reformers had set. The Massachusetts prison commissioners, for example, included the problem of finding suitable administrators among the "great disadvantages" at Framingham in 1879, suggesting their disappointment with Eudora Atkinson, the first superintendent.[13] Low salaries, too, created "great difficulty in securing officers," and resulted in frequent turnover of personnel. At one point the Hudson House of Refuge had to close its schoolrooms for lack of teachers and Massachusetts governors had to cajole women into accepting the apparently unpopular position of superintendent.[14]

Gradually, however, official constraints on female control eased and new personnel entered the institutions. Indiana rejected its male board of managers in 1877, and in 1883, along with Massachusetts, it dispensed with the male-held office of treasurer-steward. Women doctors joined the Indiana and New York prisons during the 1880s and 1890s and continued to serve at Framingham. In Indiana a "nightwatch-woman" joined the staff.[15]

By 1900 the managers of the women's reformatories could boast the attainment of female control. "Every officer, from the head down to the lowest matron, is a female," explained Warren Spalding, Massachusetts prison commission secretary, "and no man goes into the institution for any official business whatever." Not only could the women workers "hitch up a horse as readily as a man," superintendent Sarah Keely of Indiana told charity workers, but in spite of the presence of difficult inmates, "we have found that women are just as able to govern unruly women as men."[16]

The acceptance of female authority seemed to be based as much on women's ability to control prisoners as on their feminine skills in reforming them, and this attitude influenced the goals for women's prisons. Just as women's prison structures resembled traditional penal institutions', so, gradually, the goals of women's prison administrators came to approximate those of other penal reformers. At first, feminine solicitude seemed to prevail in Indiana, under superintendent Sarah Smith, and in Massachusetts. In the latter state, the different personal styles of the early administrators reveal the shift toward more orthodox methods that occurred during the last part of the century. They illustrate as well how individual superintendents could shape institutional life and how they were affected by it.

Eliza Mosher had never intended to enter prison work. Born in 1846 into a Quaker family in New York State, she studied medicine at the New England Women's Hospital in Boston and the University of Michigan. She later practiced in Poughkeepsie, New York, where she volunteered to work with boys at a local church. In 1877 Mosher entered the women's reformatory at Framingham as the prison physician. Her initial impressions, cited at the opening of this chapter, revealed how isolating and alienating her new home could be. Still, Mosher found comfort in her well-furnished quarters and looked forward to the chance to equip a small hospital and help steer the new institution. Soon she had decided to stay, insisting that "I have consecrated myself anew to my Master, for service here."[17]

Her first year as prison physician sorely tested that commitment. Venereal disease, insanity, drug addiction, and births of illegitimate or syphilitic infants overwhelmed her. Moreover, superintendent Atkinson, who had initially impressed Mosher with her "elegance," proved to be an obstacle. Atkinson interfered with medical procedures in the hospital and, in Mosher's view, inflicted "unduly severe punishment"—an average of ten cases of solitary confinement each day.[18] While Atkinson "hindered and oppressed" the doctor and other staff members, Mosher and her ally, chaplain

Sarah Pierce, met with the inmates to attempt reformatory treatment. "I had such a satisfactory time reading to some of the women this afternoon," the doctor wrote. "When I was done with the story they asked me to read in the Bible to them and pray, and I think they really were stirred for the time being. But alas that it is so evanescent."[19]

Such hopes and doubts recurred throughout Mosher's career. She shared earlier reformers' sympathies for the lot of the fallen woman, but she often felt helpless to relieve it. She had alternately been shocked and disappointed when inmates' "good intentions" were lost "the first time a temptation" came. But, Mosher added, "They are morally deformed, these women! How far are they responsible for their actions?" Like earlier reformers, she increasingly answered that they were not to blame. As the prison official most aware of their physical health she often cited disease and what she considered the "tainted" inheritance of alcoholism or venereal infection as the root of inmates' problems. Privately she wrote: "I feel so unspeakably thankful for the purity of all the parents who are pure. Oh you have no idea of the things which I come in contact with daily! The wretched lives, the hardened—and even lost image of the Maker. Tender spots, covered with rubbish tho' they may be, are often to be found, but the response is lost amid the influences which surround them even here."[20]

The pressures of work, the antagonism of superintendent Atkinson, and the deaths of both chaplain Pierce and a close relative caused Mosher to resign in September 1879. But, after visiting her family and traveling to Europe, she returned to Framingham within a year, when Governor John Davis Long threatened to appoint a male superintendent if Mosher would not accept the position. Although she only served from 1880 to 1882, Mosher had a significant impact on the institution. After her first year in office, the prison commissioners found that the institution was "now doing the work for which it was established in a much more satisfactory manner than heretofore."[21]

Now the highest ranking official at the reformatory, Mosher attempted to improve the conditions that had irritated her as prison doctor. Contrary to the common practice (then and now) of referring to inmates as girls, she indicated her respect by calling them "women," "the ladies," or "the prisoners." She instituted a merit grading-system, attracted new staff members, and attempted to provide "individual teaching and training." In her first year as superintendent, Mosher organized numerous "entertainments" for inmates, including speeches by feminists like Lucy Stone, talks by Governor Long, and readings, musical performances, and recitations. She began the practice of inviting students from nearby Wellesley College to visit prisoners and, along with their professors, to entertain inmates on Thanksgiving.[22]

As Mosher would have been the first to admit, it is difficult to evaluate her efforts. In a characteristic moment of doubt she wrote that "it is so hard to know how much is superficial and how much is heartfelt in the words and actions of those under our care." But if the strength of personal commitment provides any measure of the prison's development, enthusiasm for the institution grew under Mosher. "This is a work which tries women's souls (and men's, when they do it)," she once wrote to her niece. But in the end she persisted: "This *is* a wonderful field! As thee said Hannah last summer, it grows upon me. Am I doing the work day by day as it *ought* to be done. God knows I *want* to. And truly I am doing it for Him."[23]

In spite of frequent longings to return to medicine and to her family, Mosher continued her administrative work until 1882, when a serious knee injury forced her home to recuperate. Although she returned on crutches to supervise the institution, the election of Benjamin Butler as governor of the state, she claimed, took "a great deal of pleasure out of state work" for her. She resigned in April 1882.[24]

Butler had little sympathy for the women's prison and threatened to cut off its appropriations or appoint a male superintendent. The only woman he would accept for the position was Clara Barton, whose labors on the Civil War battlefields had won the former general's respect. Barton at first refused to relinquish her work for the International Red Cross, but with the encouragement of other women reformers, including Mary Livermore, Frances Willard, Marion Talbot, and Ellen Johnson, she agreed to serve and reluctantly remained at Framingham for nine months, until Butler had left office.[25]

Barton's reluctance to accept the superintendency did not seem to hinder her enthusiasm for the work. She made clear to inmates that her door was open to them and encouraged the women to write her whatever requests, problems, or experiences they wished to share and to make appointments to speak with her. Many did approach the superintendent, and whenever possible she tried to resolve their legal or personal difficulties. Inmates responded with lavish affection, and several formed friendships with her which continued through correspondence after their release. Barton meanwhile handled state officials as effectively as she did women prisoners. She kept Governor Butler and prison visitor Burnham Wardwell, both skeptics about the institution, at bay. She was partly responsible for the success of the legislation that abolished the male-held office of treasurer-steward.[26] She furthered the professionalization of women's prison reform both by assuming financial management of the prison and by disappointing observers who had expected her to serve without salary.[27] By the time Barton left, even Benjamin Butler concluded that "fit women are the fittest to take care of women."[28]

Although Barton was anxious to return to her work for the Red Cross at the end of the year, she wrote with extreme fondness of the women on her staff and in her care when she left Framingham. Both groups had enjoyed her presence and regretted her departure. "There was not one of whom I could ask forgiveness," Barton wrote in a letter shortly after leaving, "for I had offended none, and none have offended me." This evaluation continued, with overtones of the superiority of feminine prison reform:

> I knew then, as I know now, that I could conduct that prison from one years end to the other, holding it in good, and ever increasing order, without a punishment. [A]nd if *"Reformation"* ever comes to any, it must come under such elevating influences, and conditions of self-respect, self reliance, honor, love and trust:—penalties, degradation, distrust, disgrace never yet reformed any human being, and the more *Reformatory* people come to understand and regard that fact the better it will be for their work.[29]

It is unfortunate that the women's prisons could not attract and retain more administrators like Clara Barton and Eliza Mosher. Not only did they respect and comfort inmates, but they also maintained good working relationships with their staffs, making it more likely that qualified women would join them. However Mosher and Barton were exceptional, two of the outstanding women of their generation. Neither of them remained in the institutions, where they had felt as imprisoned as the women in their care. Each went on to accomplish broader humanitarian and women's reforms. Whether it was the low pay, the uncomfortable living conditions, or the questionable status of the work which repelled more qualified women is indeterminable. In any case, later staff members had difficulty living up to the early standards of feminine care.

More typical of the administrators who would dominate the

women's prisons until the early twentieth century was Ellen Cheney Johnson, who succeeded Barton at Framingham. From 1884 until her death in 1899, Ellen Johnson ruled at Framingham and made herself the spokesperson for women's prison reform throughout the country. As a newspaperman analyzing her portrait once wrote, Johnson had "a good combination of the feminine and the masculine . . . which qualifies her to comprehend all sides of human life and enables her to dominate her own sex and lead the other."[30] At Framingham she indeed combined the sympathy and domesticity of feminine reform with traditional penal concerns: discipline, control, and efficient management.

As a member of the prison commission that successfully argued for a separate institution in the 1870s, Ellen Johnson was a central figure in the establishment of the Massachusetts women's reformatory. She maintained close contact with the managers after it opened, occasionally taking charge when the superintendent was ill or away, and locating homes for released inmates and their children. Her frequent offers to aid Clara Barton were sometimes coupled with apologies for interfering in the superintendent's work, for Johnson was sensitive to her own need to find worthwhile activities to occupy her. She had been lonely and depressed since her husband's death in 1881 and turned to her work for solace. "There is no place so dear to me as that Prison now," she wrote to Barton. Even on vacation, Johnson confessed, "my mind often wanders back to the Prison," and to thoughts of uplifting an inmate, so that "at night I should not feel so absolutely *good for nothing.*"[31]

After Barton resigned in January 1884, Johnson became superintendent. Enthusiastically she proceeded to organize the institution around the theme of training for self-control. Johnson saw no contradiction in the tasks of reforming and disciplining prisoners. For her, rehabilitation came through control, first by the prison routine, and then by the inmates themselves. The prisoner "must learn to do right without compulsion or she will cease to do right when the compelling force is gone." Johnson's methods, nonetheless, were compelling. She combined a merit system with strict discipline and appeals to inmates' emotions. Her dual precepts were: "No lesson is more important than that which teaches respect for the law, and dread of its wrath. At the same time, it is a fundamental point in our theory that every criminal can be won by gentleness and patience."[32]

Of the two strains, Johnson emphasized the need for discipline, not only among inmates but with her staff as well. Some workers complained about their duties and resented Johnson's supervision. They breathed a sigh of relief when she was absent for a day and thought longingly of former superintendent Barton's "words of cheer and comfort."[33] The same methods which drove these women away, however, gave legitimacy to women's prisons in the opinion of others. The Massachusetts legislature, for instance, decided with Johnson's administration that the prison which many "regarded as an experiment, may now be said to have attained a degree of success far exceeding the most sanguine expectations of its projectors."[34] Their acceptance signaled that only with a heavy dose of traditional prison methods would women's work in the profession be considered legitimate.

The Massachusetts Reformatory Prison for Women may have been unique in the fame achieved by some of its administrators, but its history suggests several themes common to all of the institutions: first, women's prison reform became, in fact, a mixture of "masculine" and "feminine" concerns; second, the personality of a superintendent largely determined correctional treatment; and third, the new prisons were hard-pressed to find adequate staff. At least three women turned down the superintendency in Massachusetts, and only the threat of the appointment of a male head compelled the services of Mosher and Barton. Those who did remain, like Johnson, may have needed institutional work—for personal or financial reasons—too desperately to leave.

In Indiana and New York, as well, the search for competent staff repeatedly troubled the managers of the women's prisons. At the Western House of Refuge, not only were there difficulties finding teachers, but at one point the entire board resigned over criticisms of their mismanagement. The state prison commissioners admitted "serious embarrassment from [the] difficulty of procuring satisfactory officers from the Civil Service list for assistant matrons and assistant superintendent," and attributed the problem to both hard work and low pay.[35] In Indiana, after a decade during which Sarah Smith had continued the religious uplift of her former rescue work, the women's prison faced recurrent conflicts between managers and staff. Superintendent Sarah Keely failed to gain the respect of her subordinates, one of whom lamented in 1892 that "there is not the good done that use to be [sic]."[36] Members of the board of managers agreed, accusing Keely of unethical practices and harsh punishments. She responded with counteraccusations that board members misused state funds and interfered with prison discipline. The next superintendent, Emily

Rhodes, faced similar charges, including specific accusations of negligence leading to inmates' escapes; cruelty in tying women up in cold cells; refusal to parole those due to leave; and "working the women to death."[37]

The record of female correctional personnel during the late nineteenth century, then, was decidedly mixed. Women did achieve control over the penal institutions they had established and helped make prison administration a new female vocation. However they did so in part by identifying with traditional prison standards. Gradually the nurturing approach of Eliza Mosher and Clara Barton became heavily tempered by the disciplined control emphasized by Ellen Johnson. Moreover, there were perhaps too few qualified female correctional workers to run the institutions, and those hired were both poorly paid and overworked. Without the infusion of new ideas and experiences, the reformatories often succumbed to stagnation. Though women had gained the right to run their own prisons, they had yet to establish a pool of qualified persons to do the work in the manner reformers had envisioned.

Inmates

One of the prerequisites set by reformers for successful women's prisons were inmates who seemed open to reformatory treatment. Only a small minority of all women criminals could be accommodated by the new institutions (most would remain in jails, houses of correction, or state prisons).[38] Those who were young, who were relatively unhardened, who had committed misdemeanors, or who had been the victims of difficult circumstances were the most desirable prisoners.

Each state used different criteria for commitment to its women's prisons. At the Indiana institution, approximately fifty adult female felons entered annually to serve lengthy sentences—up to life—in the prison wing of the building. (Misdemeanant women remained in local jails.) The reformatory wing housed a girls' school for incorrigibles, petty offenders, and neglected children under the age of six.[39] In contrast, the New York houses of refuge for women at Hudson and Albion represented halfway measures between juvenile reformatories and adult prisons. They annually admitted several hundred misdemeanant women between the ages of fifteen and thirty, ages chosen to "include women likely to have children." Sentences ranged, with a high of five years.[40]

While the Indiana prison admitted only felons and the New York refuges concentrated on young misdemeanants, the Massachusetts Reformatory Prison for Women at Framingham accepted prisoners for crimes ranging from stubbornness to murder. For most crimes against public order or chastity, the courts were required to commit women to this institution. If the prison was not full, the court also could transfer women prisoners from jails and houses of correction. Framingham officials resented this provision, claiming that many women sent there were unfit for its treatment. Women officials preferred to take "those who have but recently begun lives of crime, than those who have spent years in prisons and alms-houses, until they have lost ambition for better lives."[41]

Who, in fact, did fill the women's prisons? Were they the "reformables," or habitual criminals, or both? Did they represent the female prison populations of their states or were they a select group? What characteristic types of inmates did the prisons serve?

The detailed statistics kept by several institutions provide a composite view of the inmates which can be broken down to account for individual variations. Table 3 presents an overview of the populations of the women's prisons from their openings until approximately 1910.[42] In general, the majority of inmates were under age twenty-five, white, and native-born, although often of immigrant parents. Nearly two-thirds had been married at some time in their lives, but half of these were widowed, divorced, or separated at the time of their incarceration. As prison officers pointed out, the family life of those who were married was erratic, or, as they put it, "fruitful of the worst possible evils."[43] Most of the women had no prior convictions, and those who did usually had only one, often for drunkenness. The crimes for which they were serving in New York and Massachusetts were minor—under 20 percent had committed dangerous offenses against person or property. Drunkenness and prostitution alone accounted for about half of the commitments (table 4).

In some respects, the prisoners in the all-female institutions of Massachusetts and New York differed from women in otl.er penal institutions in those states (table 5). For example, fewer foreign-born inmates appeared in the reformatories than appeared in the total state prison populations. The age groups represented at Framingham and at the New York refuges were predominantly younger than the total female convict group. The high percentage of single women, particularly in New York, reflected the lower age range. Massachusetts figures show a lower incidence of recidivism in the women's reformatory than in other state facilities for both men and women. The distribution of crimes, however, is less unique in the all-female institutions than might be expected. The

TABLE 3. Profiles of Inmates at Separate Women's Prisons: Massachusetts, Indiana, and New York

	Massachusetts	Indiana	New York (Albion)
	%	%	%
Age			
Under 25	50	50	95
Race			
White	95	72	95
Religion			
Protestant		51	
Catholic	not given	10	not given
None		39	
Nativity			
U.S. born,		90	
American parents	17	not given	42
Foreign parents	41		42
Foreign born	41	10	16
Marital Status			
Married (at some time)	57	65	28
Widowed, divorced, separated	36	24	22
Single	42	35	72
First Offenders	61 to 75	89	80
Intemperate	78	30	not given
Illiterate	20	25	15

Sources: Massachusetts: inmate sample, 1877–1913, from "History of Inmates," at Massachusetts Correctional Institution, Framingham, Mass., and mean of annual aggregate data, Massachusetts Reformatory Prison for Women, Annual Reports, 1878–1915; Indiana: mean of annual aggregate data, Indiana Woman's Prison, Annual Reports, 1873–1913; New York: mean of annual aggregate data, Western House of Refuge, Annual Reports, 1893–1900, and records of all admissions in Minutes of Board of Managers meetings, Executive Department, Board of Officers of State Institutions, New York State Library, Albany.

overall proportion of female offenders against person or property in Massachusetts and New York—between 15 and 20 percent—is similar to the proportion in the women's institutions. Indiana statistics are exceptional for in that state the women's prison took only the most serious offenders.[44]

TABLE 4. Types of Offenses Committed by Inmates of Separate Women's Prisons: Massachusetts, Indiana, and New York

Offense	Massachusetts %	Indiana %	New York (Albion) %
Public Order			
Vagrancy	4		33
Drunkenness	38		8
Idle and disorderly	10		3
Stubborn (child)	4		1
Other	1		1
Total	57		46
Chastity			
Prostitution	13		—
Lewd, wanton, and lascivious	7		—
Other	7		—
Total	27		36[a]
Person or Property			
Larceny	11	72	16
Assault	1	2	
Murder		9	
Arson		2	
Other	4	15[b]	1
Total	16	100	17

Sources: Massachusetts: inmate sample, 1877–1912, from "History of Inmates," at Massachusetts Correctional Institution, Framingham, Mass. (comparison with aggregate annual offenses shows discrepancy of less than 5 percent); Indiana: mean of annual aggregate data in Indiana Woman's Prison, *Annual Reports, 1873–1908;* New York: mean of annual aggregate data, Western House of Refuge, *Annual Reports, 1893–1900,* and records of all admissions, 1904–1909, in Minutes of Board of Managers meetings, Executive Department, Board of Officers of State Institutions, New York State Library, Albany.

a. Total only, not broken down by offense.
b. Includes some public order.

This overview demonstrates that the inmates of the new women's institutions differed only slightly from other imprisoned women, but the distinctions that did exist were important to the reformers: inmates at the new prisons were often young morals offenders who fit the reformers' definition of fallen women in need of aid. A sample of case records from Framingham confirms the profile: the women there were predominantly white, young, and American-born. The typical sentence was less than two years for a minor offense against public order. Most inmates had some formal education before the age of fourteen, when they began to work, 37 percent of them as domestic servants and 39 percent in factories and mills. Usually, but with notable exceptions, a first conviction

TABLE 5. Characteristics of Female Prisoners in All Penal Institutions, by Percentage of Institutional Population: United States, Massachusetts, New York, and Indiana, 1880, 1890

	U.S.		Mass.	N.Y.	Ind.
	1880	1890	1890	1890	1890
Age					
Under 20	11.45	13.74	7.89	9.84	23.21
Under 25			26.20	25.42	53.57
Race					
White	75.06	62.42	97.06	94.07	79.46
Nativity					
Foreign born	34.13	36.14	57.30	49.80	3.57
Offense[a]					
Person	9.46	12.02	3.97	5.61	16.96
Property	23.72	20.69	13.37	14.54	48.21
Public order			9.89	50.26	4.46
Chastity	55.68	59.83	70.99	26.01	25.89
Other	11.14	7.46	2.67	3.65	4.46

Sources: 1880: United States Department of the Interior, Census Office, Report on the Defective, Dependent, and Delinquent Classes of the Population of the United States, F. H. Wines, special agent (Washington, 1888), "Statistics of Crime," pp. 477–574; 1890: United States Department of the Interior, Census Office, Report on Crime, Pauperism and Benevolence in the United States at the Eleventh Census: 1890, Frederick H. Wines, special agent (Washington, D.C., 1895), pp. 3, 12–24, 45.

a. Offense categories have been rearranged from the United States Census listings to match as nearly as possible those used by the prisons studied; thus the crimes under public order and chastity may differ, and the two groups should be considered as one category. Rounding error accounts for totals ranging from 99 to 101 percent. Because the 1910 census combined juvenile and adult prisoners, the data are not presented here.

brought them to the reformatory, where they remained for an average stay of one year.[45]

The inmates by no means comprised a homogeneous group, however, for distinctions among types of offenders were significant. The Massachusetts records provide sufficient evidence to analyze the types of female criminals who entered that prison. Although they do not represent all women offenders, they do shed light on the problems faced by the women's prisons. An analysis of published annual aggregate statistics, a sample of 640 prisoner records, and a study of 2,000 inmates conducted by Dr. Eliza Mosher[46] reveal the characteristics of three classes of offenders.

The women in the first category, offenders against public order, were clearly not the intended beneficiaries of reformatory treatment, as the case of Mary M. suggests.[47] Committed for drunkenness at age sixty, she was Irish-born of "good parents." She had married forty years before, and six of her nine children were dead. Mary could not find work, and her "bad" husband lived with other women and beat her "terribly." For the past ten years she had been intemperate periodically. Her case was typical of offenders against public order, the majority of whom were committed for drunkenness. They were older than the other inmates, having a mean age of thirty, with the highest proportion over age twenty-one. Like Mary M., half were foreign-born, particularly Irish. About three-fourths had married. Dr. Mosher found among this group the highest incidence of syphilis, alcoholism, insanity, illiteracy, and recidivism in the prison, with a recommitment rate of over 70 percent.[48]

Prison officials seemed sympathetic to these women as victims, in spite of their pasts and their poor chances of reformation. A forty-eight-year-old Irish widow, for instance, had been intemperate all of her eleven years in the United States. Her previous sentences included fourteen trips to Deer Island, the city penitentiary, and one term at the House of Correction. She asked the judge to send her to Framingham, and officials there recorded that she was "anxious to reform." Another drunkard, age thirty-nine, had become intemperate some time after entering the mills at age thirteen. Yet her record claimed that "she never drank until after marriage." Apparently these older alcoholic women were given the benefit of the doubt by their keepers.

Different backgrounds characterized the second group of inmates, the chastity offenders—nightwalkers, adulteresses, or "lewd, wanton and lascivious" women. Younger, with a mean age of twenty-six, usually single, separated, or divorced, they were often American-born (50 to 66 percent), or from Britain or Canada. Margaret T., for instance, a common nightwalker, age twenty-four, was American-born of "good parents," both of whom had died. She had attended school (as had many of this group) and then married, but had not seen her husband for two years. Her sentence was a mere four months. A less-hopeful but not unusual case was Annie B. Though only nineteen, this was her fourth arrest for nightwalking. She was born in Lowell, Massachusetts, of intemperate parents, entered the mills at age ten, and was intemperate by age fifteen. She left home, became a prostitute, "married a known scoundrel," and "has led a life of blackest sin during the past year."

Thus the second type included the so-called fallen women, toward whom prison officials were sympathetic and for whom they took special pains. Many of these women were, in fact, the perpetrators of victimless crimes. The case of a twenty-five-year-old uneducated white woman illustrates both the actual nature of many offenses against chastity, and prison officials' response. Although committed for lewdness, she was described as "A quiet, well-behaved simple woman" whose crime was really an illegitimate pregnancy. Considered "reformable" and thus more likely to benefit from her incarceration, she received an eighteen-month sentence, six months longer than the mean for this group and a year longer than the sentences of most prostitutes. Another chastity offender, a thirty-five-year-old black woman, was sentenced to one year for adultery. Her crime consisted of living with a white man after her own husband had remarried. Reformatory treatment was apparently ineffective; like 16 percent of all chastity offenders, she later returned to the institution. In another case, common-law marriage proved a crime. Emma D., a native-born woman who was adopted after her own parents died, went to school until the age of fourteen. She lived with her husband for five years, but "not happily," so she left and "lived with a man unmarried." At first officials considered her a "Good, useful prisoner," but a doctor's report indicated that Emma "always had evil tendencies," and then officials discovered that her real parents had never been married! Now defined as an unhopeful case, it probably did not surprise the staff when she returned to prison the following year.

The chastity offenders included young women sentenced for "stubbornness" when their relatives could not control their behavior. Sixteen-year-old Eliza L., for example, committed for two years as a "stubborn child," had been "weak and licentious rather than deliberately bad." Another sixteen-year-old who had run away from home was sentenced at her grandmother's request. The length of these sentences reflected officials' belief that the young, promising cases deserved fuller treatment. As the court explained in the case of a seventeen-year-old girl sentenced for two years for idle and disorderly behavior, the sentence was made "not as a punishment, but to see what can be done for her in a reformatory way." But the younger inmates were not necessarily the most malleable. After three years in the girls' industrial school, for example, one inmate, an eighteen-year-old stubbornness case, became a "difficult prisoner" at Framingham who was at one point "sixty days in solitary and still continuing."

In some instances the prison served as a home or hospital, as in the case of Mary D. Her respectable family had moved from New Brunswick to Fall River, Massachusetts, where Mary attended school, worked in the mills, and then ran away to a house of ill fame. Her father found her there, pregnant, possibly the cause rather than the result of her new life. Sent to Framingham, she gave birth and was then discharged. She later married the child's father.

Chastity offenders, then, included a mix of young women committed for sexual or moral offenses; only a few, the professional prostitutes, were truly criminals. Most had committed victimless crimes and many needed medical and social services. Instead, however, they received inordinately large doses of reformatory treatment.

More dangerous criminals fell into the third category, offenders against property and persons. A representative subgroup, the larcenists, were young, though often married, with a high proportion from Canada and few from Ireland. The age range for this group varied widely (estimates of the mean ranged from fifteen to thirty-three). Occupation became relevant in this category only. Domestic workers tended to be convicted for property offenses, probably petty larceny from their employers, while factory workers seemed to commit crimes against the person. The latter group, however, was so small that the data may be misleading.

Members of this group received the longest sentences, with means of twenty-two and twenty-four months for property and person crimes, respectively.[49] One twenty-five-year-old woman, possibly insane (she spent part of her sentence in the Worcester Lunatic Asylum), received five years for trying to shoot a man. In a pathetic case, a sixty-two-year-old American woman professed her innocence in the charge of procuring an abortion for a woman who had died. A "very large, fleshy woman, almost helpless from size," and with an invalid husband, she pled ill-health but was nonetheless committed for five years. She died in prison. In each of these cases, the object of the long sentence was punishment or deterrence; for these women the institution was more nearly a prison than a reformatory.

In addition to these severely treated first offenders, the professional or habitual criminals often fell into this third category. They provided the most colorful as well as the most tragic cases at the prison. One woman operated a successful burglary team with her niece, winning people's sympathy by feigning invalidism. But when her husband discovered their cache of stolen goods, the women were brought to court. The older one received a three-year prison term while her niece got only eighteen months, a reversal of the usual pattern. In the courtroom the niece "cooly requested the judge to make her imprisonment equal" to that of her aunt, a request he denied. For these serious criminals, too, long sentences had the traditional goal of punishment, not reformation. Other professionals who appear in the prison records include the "notorious Dr. Emma Hudson," confidence woman from New York and Boston, perpetrator of fraud, theft, and blackmail. Another inmate, a forty-three-year-old Irish larcenist, remarried a professional thief, and the pair made their separate domiciles in various Massachusetts and New York penal institutions for years.

But the most dedicated, as well as colorful, character, a three-time resident at Framingham, was "Captain Jack"—alias Arthur Holmes, alias Fred Fiske, and actually a twenty-seven-year-old woman, arrested with her husband for horse stealing and sentenced on the charge of being "idle and disorderly." Her behavior, as described by the press, was anything but idle, though certainly disruptive. With "a hard, masculine face and a strong frame," the Captain wore men's clothes and worked as a teamster, sailor, bartender, and sea cook. She had repeatedly "made love to blue-eyed misses and been passionately loved by them" until her true identity was revealed, usually by herself when drunk. "Her mishaps are all owing, she says, to her passion for strong drink; if it were not for this she could wear pants with impunity and teach young men the superiority of woman."

Other inmates convicted of property and person offenses had more pitiful than flamboyant personal tales. They were the victimized women who had not committed willful acts of violence but had paid the price of drugs, drunkenness, and unwanted pregnancies. Eliza W., American-born of good parents, was committed for larceny at age twenty-four. She had once taken morphine on a doctor's advice and, addicted for three years, she stole "when under the influence of the drug." Another case, an alcoholic larcenist, committed for the seventh time, was considered a "poor miserable creature." A female doctor, convicted of abortion at age seventy-one, served five years, the minimum sentence, as "an exemplary prisoner." The charge of child abandonment brought a young woman to prison for a year; she had left her unwanted child on the almshouse steps, where it died. While adequate medical and social services might have prevented many of these so-called crimes, the reformatory at least provided a less-condemning atmosphere than did local jails or state prisons.

The population of the Massachusetts Reformatory Prison for Women consisted of a diverse group of inmates, many of whom did not meet reformers' definitions of hopeful cases. A large proportion—almost half of the inmates in the early decades of the prison, and between a fourth and a third thereafter—were alcoholics over the age of thirty. Chastity offenders, the original fallen women whom reformers wanted to rescue, made up only a fourth of the inmate populace. The dangerous criminals were either professionals and habitual offenders, or women whose crimes had been precipitated by dire circumstances.

Each of these groups brought to the institution different personal experiences which required a variety of responses. Few deserved punishment, as reformers were quick to acknowledge. Many needed social services and medical care, and others would have benefited from some form of personal rehabilitation, particularly the alcoholics. Once incarcerated, however, all inmates could expect a standard form of retraining, based on a traditional ideal of womanhood.

The design, personnel, and inmate populations of the original women's reformatories all fell short of reformers' ideals. The structure of the institutions usually resembled traditional prison buildings, although features of juvenile reformatories were incorporated, particularly in New York. Inadequate space and facilities plagued the institutions, as did the problem of attracting qualified staff, especially after the 1880s. To this setting were added inmate populations that rarely fit the mold of young, first offenders. The prisoners were of diverse backgrounds, both in age and criminal experience. Most inmates had only a grade school education and had entered low-paying jobs as domestic or mill workers before they were fifteen years old. Though many had married, their family lives were unstable. As the reformers had expected, their crimes were often victimless and due to external circumstances.

Despite their limitations, the new institutions opened their doors to women who would otherwise have served in state prisons or houses of corrections. Although they were, in several ways, poorly equipped for the task, the keepers of these institutions attempted to fulfill their charge of reforming women criminals. To do this they evolved a mixture of feminine reform and traditional penal discipline that was to retrain inmates to their model of womanhood.

Chapter 5

Domesticity, Discipline, and Prisoners' Response: Retraining Women in Prison

On 8 October 1873 Mrs. Sallie Hubbard—the "Wabash Murderess"—became the first inmate of an exclusively female prison in the United States. Along with her husband, she had murdered a pioneer family of seven which had sought refuge in their home. Mr. Hubbard was executed while his wife received a life sentence. The sheriff and two deputies who transported Sallie Hubbard to the new women's prison applied heavy manacles to contain her. But when superintendent Sarah Smith received the woman, she dramatically heralded the contrasts of men's and women's prison reform. Directing the men to "Take off her shackles; she is my prisoner, not yours," Smith embraced her fallen sister, prayed for her, and showed her to a room decorated with bedspread, clothed table, curtains, a pot of flowers, a Bible, and a hymn book. In time, Hubbard became a model prisoner.[1]

The Massachusetts women's prison opened with comparable ceremony. When inmates formerly confined in state houses of correction arrived at Framingham on 7 November 1877, they immediately received bright, blue plaid dresses. The superintendent explained that the institution "was not designed for imprisonment alone, but for reformation." It would be "a starting point in their existence for all eternity, a pause in this earthly life, a time for reflection, an opportunity for new principles to be formed, holy resolutions to be made, in the strength that God alone can give."[2] Similarly, managers explained that the New York House of Refuge at Hudson "is not a prison . . . but an educational institution." The Western House of Refuge promised to "give such moral and religious training as will induce [inmates] to form a good character and such training in domestic work as will eventually enable them to find employment, secure good homes and be self-supporting."[3]

Each women's institution thus rejected traditional penal goals of punishment and deterrence. The new prisons opened as alternatives to the penitentiary, with its silence and hard labor, and to the men's reformatory, with its military and industrial atmosphere. In contrast to both, women's prisons were intended to retrain women through sympathetic female staff, prayer, education, and domesticity.

Despite the founders' self-conscious differentiation of women's prisons from other nineteenth-century institutions, the feminine experiments eventually resembled traditional prisons in many respects. Like other efforts to humanize institutional care, such as the "soft-line" in juvenile reformatories or "moral therapy" in insane asylums,[4] women's prisons increasingly relied on traditional methods of discipline. In each of these experiments the underlying function of prisons and asylums—the control of inmates—repeatedly asserted itself. The women's institutions did remain unique in the domestic content of their retraining programs, but they too ultimately shared the disciplinary values of the prison system. In both skill training and character building the tension between domesticity and discipline pervaded the internal life of the women's prisons.

Retraining Skills

Women prison reformers insisted on the importance of teaching inmates some remunerative skills so that they would not be tempted to commit crimes after their release. They had suggested several types of training, including academic classes, industrial trades, and domestic skills. For several reasons, domesticity eventually prevailed at each institution. First, academic classes proved frustrating to teachers and inmates because of insufficient staff and resources and the difficulty of teaching so diverse a group. Only the New York houses of refuge, with their younger populations, maintained a commitment to remedial education.[5] Industrial training, favored at first by some administrators, faced the opposition to prison-made goods raised by the labor movement during the 1880s. Furthermore, the realities of women's employment opportunities discouraged industrial training, for only a small number of women could get jobs in skilled trades.[6] Because most women who worked for pay were domestics, and because domesticity was central to the reformatory scheme, administrators focused on training in domestic skills.

Some of the founders of the new prisons had hoped to expand training and job placement beyond the domestic work offered in the homes for discharged women prisoners. In advocating women's reformatories in 1870, Elizabeth Chace had questioned training for domestic service, noting that "men are more generally taught trades, both useful and profitable, . . . in shops, factories and on farms."[7] Rhoda Coffin suggested in 1876 that an inmate learn both the "duties of housewifery, and if possible, . . . some kind of trade— a trade which could be carried on without machinery."[8]

The Indiana Woman's Prison did try to identify some training that was "fit for women to do," offered possibilities for self-supporting employment after release, and did not undercut the incomes of the working women in the area. The managers, possibly seeking a profit-making industry, experimented with chair caning, paper-box making, and glove stitching, all of which proved financially disappointing. Finally, they settled on a prison laundry and brought experts from the Troy, New York, laundry workers to initiate Indiana inmates into "the secret of *starch*, ironing," and other skills.[9]

The Indiana industrial laundry employed about half the prisoners, but it was tiring, routine work and the superintendents disapproved of it.[10] Thus, by the 1890s Indiana's annual reports stressed domestic training: "A love for women's work should be carefully instilled into the minds of the girls." Cooking and cleaning, sewing and quilting occupied inmates. Superintendent Sarah Keely proudly told the 1898 prison congress that her institution had no steam laundry and no power sewing: "All work is done as it would be in a private family, thus fitting the women for work as they will find it in the outside world."[11]

As an "incentive to good behavior," indoor domestic work was later supplemented by outdoor activities. In addition to working in the chicken farm and in vegetable and flower gardens, Indiana inmates made institutional repairs. They painted most of the rooms, renovated the chapel, repaired walks, built steps, and cemented floors. They were not encouraged, however, to seek work using these skills.[12]

During its opening decade, the Massachusetts reformatory had contracts from private industries for machine knitting, chair caning, straw work, and the manufacture of corsets, brushes, and hammocks. When contract labor came under attack, a state-use system limited the amount of goods the prison could market. During her term, Ellen Cheney Johnson established outdoor labor, for, she believed, "To rouse an interest in country life and pursuits is likely to make the woman more contented when she is placed in a quiet home away from the city." Thus, those inmates not working in the prison laundry might be found whitewashing walls and ceilings, painting buildings, and taking care of prison grounds. Johnson also set up an experiment in silk culture that was briefly successful. As in Indiana, these outdoor activities were less a form of training than of moral treatment. As superintendent Frances Morton wrote, "while it is health-giving, it also suggests new thoughts which must be uplifting to many minds, if not at the time, we hope for the future."[13]

Massachusetts prison managers claimed that it was difficult to find "mechanical work" for inmates after release and, as in Indiana, the managers' ideals of the country home required training for domestic tasks rather than for trades and industry. Thus, in spite of an initial interest in training for less-traditional skills, the major emphasis at Framingham was domesticity; Framingham's unique contribution to prison reform was the indenture program, or conditional early release, when prisoners served as domestic servants in neighboring homes.

The indenture system provided an incentive for inmates to acquire domestic skills. Only those who displayed "fitness for service" while in prison qualified for placement. As Ellen Johnson explained, the program fulfilled several of the goals of training. It was intended to bring the inmate "under the influence of family life and to keep her from old temptations; at the same time she is trained to domestic duties, and her earnings are entirely under her own control."[14]

The indenture law passed the Massachusetts legislature in 1879, a year after the women's reformatory opened. In the twenty-five years during which the Massachusetts institution found placements for inmates, approximately 1,500 women went "to service," about one-fourth of all those sentenced there. Fewer than 9 percent of the servants returned to the prison from their positions, and the state considered the program highly successful.[15]

To be eligible for indenture, an inmate had to be in the highest grade in the prison, which usually meant that she had served about three-fourths of her sentence. The superintendent had the authority to recommend prospective servants. (Ellen Johnson once stated that a woman was never recommended "until we feel she can make bread," a comment which won a round of applause at the National Prison Congress.) A housewife usually asked the Massachusetts prison commissioners to assign a domestic to her, and when an inmate had been approved, the prisoner had the choice of consenting to the contract or remaining in prison. The employer could reject the candidate, too. In one case a Jamaica Plain housewife declined an inmate who was known for her drunkenness, claiming, "We are too near the city, and the neighborhood abounds in temptations." In another instance, one inmate refused a position which was then accepted by another.[16]

"As a rule," the superintendent explained, "the homes selected have been in the country, away from evil influences." Most of them were in the semirural towns surrounding Boston, especially in South Framingham, near the prison, and Weston, West Newton, Ipswich, or, for a few, western Massachusetts. The wages ranged from $1.25 a week during the first months of service to $2.50 a week in the more generous households; these wages were slightly lower than most domestics earned. The money earned belonged entirely to the inmate, who sometimes received a bonus when her term expired and she left her place of indenture.[17]

The housewives who accepted servants took their responsibilities as seriously as did the prison officers. They claimed to welcome inmates "right into the family," and treated them like daughters, with the hope that the former criminals would marry and establish their own domiciles. Not only the domestic duties, but also the personal lives of servants came under their employers' surveillance. As one woman wrote to the prison when accepting a released inmate: "What are the woman's weak points of history and character? I will protect and guide her to the best of my ability." To ensure proper conduct, employers supervised private hours, required permission for visitors or for trips away from the house, and set standards of acceptable behavior.[18]

Most servants completed their contracts of indenture without incident. Their incentive was to remain outside of the prison; to run away from service became a criminal offense in 1880. The employers profited by acquiring a sometimes grateful servant and the possibility of future indentures if the current one was successful. Occasionally, however, household conflicts became too serious and the indenture was terminated. In one case an inmate indentured to a couple on a small farm left after four days, explaining that "the man was not a good man to his wife and he didn't act proper to me; he was always flirting and it made me feel sorry for his wife." When employers sent servants back to the prison they often did so with apologies for failing to uplift their charges. One woman claimed that she had borne the drinking, temper, and late hours of her worker, but regretted that her husband couldn't overlook the language used toward him. Another employer, who paid her servant's fine when arrested, wrote: "I thought I could reform her but have come to the conclusion there is no such thing . . . If it had not been for her appetite for drink she would have remained here." In another case, police followed a servant home and nearly arrested her for soliciting. The housewife lamented that "I could not keep her with my family of boys . . . I lost in other ways one of the best workers I ever had."[19]

But for each unsuccessful indenture there were nine in which women served their terms completely, often winning the praise of employers. One servant who had been unsatisfactory at first "turned over a new leaf," her employer wrote to the superintendent. Other participating housewives sent back periodic reports on former servants who were happily married or successfully employed, such as the "colored girl released three years before who is now a housekeeper in Connecticut making $3.23 a week, very respected, responsible." Inmates, too, wrote to the prison from their placements. One claimed to be "very happy in my new home," while another asked the superintendent to "tell all the girls for me to get a place . . . on a farm."[20]

The Massachusetts indenture plan succeeded because it fulfilled several functions for the prison. First, it provided suitable feminine training that did not compete with men's labor (although it did undercut the wages of other women servants). Second, sending inmates out to neighboring housewives gave added incentive for good behavior in prison and opened spaces for new commitments when necessary. Finally, indenture served as a form of parole, with individual homes serving as halfway points to release. Although it did reflect the narrowing of training in the prison, the indenture plan was one of the most progressive plans of its time. It offered better training than women received in the houses of corrections and may have been more welcome to prisoners than the industrial work done by inmates in penitentiaries.

The reliance on domestic training made more sense, however, in the early to mid-nineteenth century, when most women viewed household management as their primary occupation. By 1900, when the women's prisons had reverted to domesticity, more American women were leaving the home for public activities ranging from higher education, the professions, and social reform for middle- and upper-class women, to factory work for immigrant and working-class women.[21] Some women did continue Catharine Beecher's tradition of trying to elevate housework to a profession, particularly through the domestic science movement. But the women's prisons did not view indenture as professional or scientific training. The domesticity they cultivated looked backward, rather than forward, suggesting how firmly the prisons were rooted in the traditional female sphere.

The indenture program also suggested an attitude on the part of reformers that might be called, for lack of a neutral term, maternalistic. Although the keepers themselves had entered the public sphere as paid workers and social reformers, they discouraged prisoners from leaving the home. Women who had committed crimes, they implied, could not be trusted on their own, especially in the cities. Therefore, to protect them from either their own "bad inclinations" or from men, the reformers sent prisoners to small towns and rural families. Unable to teach inmates how to support themselves in an urban industrial economy, they chose to return them to an older, increasingly anachronistic, women's world.

Character Retraining

A dual ideal of womanhood guided the staff who worked in the new reformatory prisons. It drew upon the values of the female sphere, especially piety, domesticity, and purity. At the same time, though, it called for self-sufficiency, echoing reformers' concerns that sexual or economic dependence led to women's crimes. Prison officers believed that women were more emotional than men and thus cultivated their sentiments; they also argued that women needed self-control and attempted to encourage it.

Staff members themselves provided a model of this dual ideal. They assumed the roles of loving but demanding mothers who forgave past errors but insisted on obedience. For Indiana superintendent Sarah Smith, the first principle of corrections was love; the second, the strength to resist temptation and care for oneself. Her methods, she explained, consisted on the one hand of constant personal oversight, special care in sickness, little acts of kindness, and, on the other hand, prompt punishment and firm training. Like Ellen Johnson in Massachusetts, Smith and her chief matron, Elmina Johnson, won praise for uniting "womanly kindness and sympathy with great firmness and skill in governing."[22]

The superintendents and chaplains appealed to traditional feminine ideals of piety and domesticity to aid inmates' retraining. The chaplains mainly provided spiritual and nurturing services. They visited new prisoners in solitary, made sick calls at the hospitals, and wrote letters for the illiterate. Daily religious services,

Sunday schools, and prayer meetings, as well as sermons by visiting ministers, exposed all inmates to Protestant teaching, with an emphasis on "a full and free salvation." Ellen Cheney Johnson donated a painting of "Christ and the Erring Woman" to remind prisoners they were "a downcast, but not forsaken sisterhood."[23]

Officers also used nature to cultivate piety. One night Johnson awakened prisoners and sent them outside to view a night-blooming flower. During the day Massachusetts inmates sometimes sat in the mulberry grove to hear visiting speakers. The superintendent of the Western House of Refuge led inmates on a hike one day. The managers exclaimed that it was "one of the great events of the season. Although the girls were tired from the walk, . . . still they were delighted to get outside the fence. After the walk, dancing was indulged in until supper time."[24]

Prisoners' maternal feelings could be aroused by the children of inmates who resided, up to the age of two, in most institutions. By allowing prisoners to visit and care for the infants, the staff both feminized the prison routine and provided an outlet for otherwise-disruptive inmates, as the story of Margaret B. illustrates. A "poor old creature," for years "drunk and knocked about," Margaret complained, "I've been in every institution in the country and I'm tired of institutions. Won't you let me go home?" Prison physician Lucy Hall recalled her response: "'I can't let you go home,' I said, 'but how would you like to help take care of the babies?' I took her to the nursery, and in twenty-four hours that insane look of misery had left her face . . . I fully believe I saved her from insanity."[25]

The emphasis on piety, nature, and maternity may indeed have comforted many inmates. In contrast to mixed institutions where women prisoners were objectified as sexually fallen outcasts, the new feminine methods stressed the other parts of inmates' female identities: their nonsexual, maternal, sentimental sides. The women's world in the prison offered a potentially supportive atmosphere for those inmates who wanted to affirm these values in themselves. The Massachusetts reformatory was said to have provided such an environment at first, at least according to one observer. In 1879 Louisa May Alcott spent a "very remarkable day and night" at the prison, where she read to the 400 inmates and listened to their stories. She judged the institution "a much better place than Concord Prison, with its armed wardens, and 'knock down and drag out' methods. Only women here, and they work wonders by patience, love, common-sense, and the belief in salvation for all."[26]

Although these efforts to strengthen the feminine elements of the prison environments continued, they coexisted from the outset with more authoritarian means of enforcing feminine behavior. In Indiana superintendent Smith prohibited "the unwomanly vice of tobacco-smoking" at the institution's opening, even though the practice had been permitted for women in the state prison. Furthermore, she immediately banned the popular *Police Gazette* and allowed only religious newspapers. The board of visitors welcomed these dictates as "the forerunner[s] of other voluntary [*sic*] reforms that will . . . lead to a restoration of an effaced or lost womanhood." When inmates protested these deprivations, prison officers relied on their maternal skills. Even prisoners who were wild and unmanageable, they explained, could be "hushed for a while, at least, into quiet submission by the power of song and prayer."[27]

The Massachusetts superintendents who followed Mosher and Barton epitomized the harder line of women's prison reform. Ellen Cheney Johnson disapproved of unsupervised conversation among inmates. When she took charge in 1884, she suspended recreation periods and scheduled special events instead. The Silver T Club (Temperance, Truth, and Trust) occupied the evening hours which had originally been a time for informal meetings. Johnson claimed that she encouraged self-sufficiency among inmates by allowing prisoners to manage the clubs themselves. Similarly, the badges worn by those privileged to belong were supposed to instill self-respect. But, as Johnson herself revealed, her methods manipulated inmates and imposed her will on them: "Of course the prisoners themselves are not aware of our wish to interfere with their recreation time. They are very jealous for what they consider their rights, and whatever we do must be managed with tact, not to antagonize them and so destroy the good effect of our efforts."[28]

Johnson's successor in 1900, Frances Morton, openly rejected kindness for authority. She cut out recreational hours entirely because they were "great sources of evil and detrimental to discipline." Morton told the women they would do better to use the time learning to sew. The message she repeated to her professional colleagues was "Obedience is the first lesson taught each woman."[29] Morton may have been idiosyncratic in her authoritarianism, or her approach may have marked a break with the past tradition of hiring sympathetic reformers as administrators. In either case, she spoke more freely about control, relying less on the principles of sisterhood than had her predecessors.

These personal methods employed by prison officials were combined from the outset with formal structures for overseeing the daily behavior of inmates. The merit grading-system—an integral part of British and American reformatory penology—placed upon the prisoner herself the burden of maintaining order. The elaborate rules governing daily life illustrate both what prison routine was like and how the emphasis on self-control resembled the traditional goals of prison discipline.

Ellen Cheney Johnson's merit system, instituted to encourage "self-conquest," consisted of four stages, each of which granted wider privileges of dress, mail, and recreation. A woman could advance from the blue denims of Division I to the gingham dress of Division III. Then, if she had a perfect record, she earned a red ribbon with the silver letter T (for the Temperance Club), to be worn over her left breast. These trusted women had the best rooms and took responsibility for prison chores. In Indiana a three-tiered system operated after 1896, regulating inmates' food, dress, and letter-writing privileges. The "honor system" at the Hudson House of Refuge asked inmates to report their own misbehavior (which one critic found "absurd"). The superintendent of the Albion House of Refuge prided herself on the absence of such a system, since she found it inimical to "well regulated family methods." However, the institution did eventually accept a plan by which inmates received 10,000 marks on entry that had to be worked off through good behavior in order to earn parole.[30]

With the introduction of the indeterminate sentence at the end of the century, the merit systems assumed new significance. These sentences, long advocated by prison reformers as incentives to good behavior, gave a minimum-to-maximum range (e.g., two to five years), with the inmate's record determining her date of release. In 1903 the Framingham officials reorganized the merit system with a complicated plan of credits and demerits which required "perfect conduct and industry" for months at a time to reach the highest grade, from which parole was possible. Backsliding meant serving extra time. The system confused many prisoners about the length of their stay and no doubt created enormous tensions.[31]

The self-discipline imposed by such positive incentives did not suffice to produce model prisoners, as the use of punishments indicated. According to the early statements of prison reformers, women would be hindered rather than reformed if punished by confinement in the typical nineteenth-century dark cell. Yet solitary confinement and a diet of bread and water awaited a woman who was disrespectful, talked at meals, or attempted to escape. As Clara Barton pointed out when requesting several punishment rooms at Framingham, solitary provided a more humane method of dealing with noisy and unruly women than did handcuffs, strait jackets, or lashes, which were still in use in state prisons. Perhaps with this thought in mind, but also because the reformatories admitted some inmates whom the staff found "perverse, obstinate, and wicked," each one soon provided punishment rooms, and some resorted to corporal punishment.[32]

The use of disciplinary measures varied by state, by superintendent, and by institution. Ellen Johnson punished misbehavior at the dinner table by solitary meals; "further insolence" resulted in confinement in a solitary work room (ten by twelve feet) for up to three weeks, plus the loss of ten credits and one day of commuted time. Extreme insubordination earned confinement on bread and water, with no company or books allowed, until the offender declared her penitence. The "dungeon" (basement cells and a diet of bread and water) was reserved for those who attacked officers, destroyed property, or threatened the safety of other inmates. Johnson claimed that she seldom used this last resort.[33]

In Indiana, where more felons were incarcerated at the women's prison, administrators seemed less averse to discipline. Superintendents' official reports often described punishments of solitary confinement, a bread and water diet, the loss of good time, and corporal punishment. In addition, periodic charges of extensive physical discipline reveal that handcuffs and beatings were also used.[34]

Severe treatment characterized New York's Hudson House of Refuge, even though its inmates were young, minor offenders. For "pouting, loud talking, and failure to comply with the spirit of the rules and unwritten laws of the institution," inmates lost points in the merit system. For more serious problems, solitary in a dark cell with disciplinary diet and handcuffs was reportedly "in vogue" at first, while long confinement in uncomfortable positions and corporal punishment frequently occurred in later years. Excessive physical punishment provoked a riot in 1899, one of the rare incidents of active resistance that officials recorded. An investigation disclosed not only harsh punishment but also complete mismanagement. A new administration closed the dungeon and revised the merit plan, but within a year their reports mention punishment cells again.[35]

Reformers had argued that women's institutions must be places of reformation and not of punishment, yet some punishments did appear throughout the records. Compared to mixed penal institutions the level of physical discomfort in the women's reformatories was mild. Women who remained at Sing Sing, for instance, endured gags, strait jackets, short rations, hair croppings, as well as solitary in the dark cell.[36] The women's reformatories relied more heavily on systems of merits and demerits, imposing less corporal punishment and employing alternate means of discipline. Combined with emotional and spiritual appeals, their methods of inculcating "self-control" seemed to succeed in creating orderly, well-disciplined penal environments.

The Effect on Prisoners

The most difficult problem in prison history is reconstructing the inmate experience. Although quantitative data tell something about who went to prison and why, they do not record feelings. Most statements about inmates come from reformers and officials, and thus must be read with care. No doubt the women who were retrained in the reformatories reacted as have other subjects of "total institutions": rebellion by some and submission by others. Unfortunately for historians, the institutional records mainly report grateful responses from former inmates and glowing accounts from visitors. Only two outbreaks appear in the sources. Of the one at Framingham in 1888, a legislative investigation insisted it was merely "born of a spirit of bravado and of a desire to have some fun." New York officials took the riot of 1899 at Hudson more seriously; they blamed management for the mistreatment of inmates and instituted some reforms. And, of course, the use of disciplinary measures which had not been anticipated by reformers suggests that on an individual level, prisoners resisted the retraining process.[37]

The bulk of the evidence indicates, however, that most inmates complied with the official routines. Whether inspired by the examples of the staff, encouraged by the incentive systems, or discouraged by punishments, they seem to have become the dutiful daughters required by the institutional regimens. Like the group of life-term prisoners observed in Indiana, many inmates of women's prisons seemed "docile, industrious, even pleasant, and . . . apparently resigned to their fate."[38] An observation by national prison reformer Frederick H. Wines shows the extent to which order prevailed, in this case under Ellen Johnson:

> I applied to the discipline at Sherborn every known test. I saw no conversation in the shops, certainly less than in a well-governed school. . . . I stood in the halls at night and listened for a sound, but could hear none. I noted the generally respectful manner of the prisoners to their officers. I sat upon the platform in the chapel, and again in the rear, without detecting a symptom of disorder.[39]

A similar scene at the Indiana Woman's Prison impressed reformer Isabel Barrows:

> The bell signals for dinner. The inmates file in but there is always a pause of perhaps five minutes before the last one is in her seat and they are ready to sing grace. Out from every pocket, as soon as she sits down, comes the bit of fancy work and they may sew till the signal for grace before meat [*sic*]. . . . after certain meals they are allowed to turn and face the officer, who sits on a platform at the side, and while the tables are noiselessly cleared by those on duty for that work, the rest may sit for fifteen minutes or half an hour at their needlework while the officer reads aloud to them some interesting book.[40]

The authors of these observations, sympathetic to the women's prisons, wanted to emphasize that female staff could maintain order. They revealed that the women's reformatories did not differ greatly from men's prisons. Each required a degree of regimentation which could not have been achieved without "constant pressure and vigilance," according to Wines.

Officials succeeded in maintaining this level of control by carefully inculcating prisoners with the values of reformatory treatment. The prisons, like other "total institutions," facilitated this process.[41] Isolation stripped inmates of their normal identities, while keepers had absolute power to impose their ideals on them.

The type of inmate, discipline, and design in the women's prisons may have made this task easier. First, many women were already humiliated when they arrived at the institutions. Some had not realized they had risked imprisonment when they drank, left home, or had sexual relations. Others had actually been the victims of sexual mistreatment. As one woman who had been seduced and abandoned wrote: "Ever since I came here it has seemed as if I should die of ashame [*sic*]."[42] Next, solitary confinement during the first stage of classification isolated inmates. Later, complicated merit systems regulated the minute details of prisoners' behaviors, including their food, clothing, rooms, and correspondence. The threat of punishment may have been responsible for the absence of rebellion, but equally important was the reformatory design itself. The semblance of domesticity masked the fact that women were indeed prisoners; without consciousness of their position, prisoners were less likely to strike out at their keepers. The rhetoric of sisterhood, moreover, may have convinced some inmates that institutional controls were indeed for their own good.

The reminiscence of one prisoner at the Massachusetts reformatory suggests how individual resistance gave way gradually to identification with reformatory values. A woman "of culture and education," the prisoner resented the deprivation imposed on her during her solitary probation period—"so little water, so few towels . . . tin plate." Then, "As the days went on through probation," she wrote, "a feeling that being shut up indoors was far worse than having to eat from a tin plate; that I would give anything in all the world for some of my own books." When she entered Division II and met the other inmates, her first reaction was that the women were "hardly human," but she then became interested in their reformation. "It began to be a pleasure to feel that I could keep one group of women from more harmful talk by telling them stories or picking out library books." This behavior earned her reclassification. She recalled leaving Division II "with a feeling that I could trust the matrons," and, granted the privileges of dress and movement of Division III, she reached the point of complete identification with the staff and the values of order and discipline. She wrote:

> In Division III the world began to change. I began to know the place better. I began to find more of bad and more of good in women. Many, many—indeed most of them—were hopeless. They are coarse, vulgar, but not all bad. They are generous among one another; many of them are truly fond of their matrons; they do appreciate kindness. They value the flowers in chapel on Sunday. One not very well behaved woman said, and she meant it: "I'd like to be good just to let Mrs. Johnson know it." To sum it all up, the place is to me a reformatory, not a prison; clean, orderly, systematic, managed and governed with a judgment that is beyond criticism.[43]

In this case and others, isolation and the grading system helped convert new inmates. As an educated woman who considered herself better than the others, the above case was atypical; the inmate became an active partner in the reformatory process. Other women gradually stopped resisting and accepted the fate assigned them by the staff because they had no explanations for their predicament. For example, a woman who had been at the Massachusetts prison for only one month, on a vagrancy charge, revealed both discontent and resignation when she testified during a legislative hearing:[44]

Q. This is the first time you have been sent to Sherborn?
A. Yes. . . .
Q. How do you like it here?
A. Don't like it at all.
Q. Like that uniform you have to wear?
A. No, I don't.
Q. How long you got to stay?
A. I don't know . . .

In another case, a woman who claimed to have miscarried and disposed of the fetus was convicted of murdering her illegitimate child. She had served only two months when interrogated and was already learning to accept a penitent role.

Q. How long have you got to stay here?
A. I don't know. . . .
Q. Did the court say anything as to how long you were to stay?
A. I don't know; I was so hysterical all I could hear was Sherborn. . . .
Q. Got any curiosity [about length of sentence]?
A. It would not shorten my stay if I had.
Q. Are you pretty well satisfied here?
A. In a way I am. I have no reason for being dissatisfied, except that I am away from the few relatives that I have.
Q. There is nothing in the institution that you can complain about, is there?
A. No, sir.
Q. You have to be up day and night? [She worked in the infirmary.]
A. Up and down.
Q. That is voluntary on your part.
A. I was put in there and it is my duty to do whatever is expected of me.

This woman, because of the shock of finding herself sentenced to prison, had no idea how long she would have to remain. She resigned herself to doing whatever was necessary to avoid further trouble.

An older Irish woman who had served five years, apparently for adultery, was about to be released. Her attitude is precisely that which legislators hoped the prison would mold:

Q. You won't have that fellow around the house again?
A. No; nor any other fellow.
Q. Have you made a good many acquaintances among the women?
A. I saw a couple of women I know from Charlestown.
Q. When you go out are you going to keep up any of the acquaintances you have made here?
A. I am going to keep my business to myself.
Q. There is no one here you care to continue acquaintance with?
A. I am going to keep to myself.

For inmates like her, prison had become a way of life. When one woman's sentence expired, for example, she asked to remain at the Massachusetts reformatory until she could arrange a place to live rather than return to her husband. "I never want to see the face of that man again," she wrote, echoing officials' views: "as to live with him I never shall for he is not my Equals he is a drunkard and I am better without him."[45] No doubt she was. Yet while the prison had fostered this insight, the woman still did not have the skills to become self-supporting and so be able to act on it.

Those inmates who accepted the values of temperance and obedience became success stories for the official record. Annual reports to state legislatures recounted grateful tales of former criminals who thanked the reformatory for their new lives as wives, mothers, or domestic servants. "I have got a good man, don't drink or no bad habits," one wrote. "Your place was a making of a good woman of me. I go to meeting every Sunday and do just as my husband want to do and we live happy together." An employer complimented the reformatory for a released inmate who was "the best girl with children that we ever had. She has behaved herself in every particular and has not given us the least bit of trouble." Another case, representative of several, reported on a released inmate: "You will be glad to know that she is thoroughly reformed, is married, and living in X [another city]." Such was the power of this system that one dismayed husband wrote to the prison that his reformed wife might "go bad" unless he received word from them which would "tone her down." And according to the superintendents, former inmates sometimes returned to the reformatory for their own reencouragement and to provide models for other prisoners.[46]

The programs to retrain women in the Indiana, Massachusetts, and New York reformatory prisons between 1870 and 1910 had a mixed record of success and failure. On one level, prison reformers won legitimacy by proving that women could manage institutions and adequately control female prisoners. As Frances Morton wrote in 1902: "Twenty-five years ago the eyes of the world were looking with incredulity on the experiment of a women's prison, governed by women; to-day the experiment stands pre-eminently a grand success,—a monument of woman's work whose foundations are very strong, for in the very beginning they builded stronger than they knew."[47] Reformers from the nation and the world visited the women's institutions and found them "far more enlightened" than most penal facilities and an inspiration for future reformatories.[48] Compared to most prisons' treatment of women, the female institutions were exemplary. They enabled thousands of women who would otherwise have served in men's institutions to avoid the neglect and abuse that continued here.

However, only half the goals of retraining were met. While inmates were taught to value traditional feminine ideals of purity and submissiveness, this training often defeated the concurrent goal of teaching women to be self-sufficient. Although reformers recognized that women's dependencies were a source of their crimes, they cultivated new dependencies on the prison and taught domestic skills which ill-equipped inmates for economic self-support.

The ideas reformers had used to justify the establishment of separate women's prisons rested on important assumptions about sex, class, and power. Because they perceived women as a sexual class, separate from men, nineteenth-century reformers crossed the boundary between themselves and fallen women. Once they took charge of prisons, however, sex was no longer the determinant of power. A new hierarchy placed the keepers above the inmates, in part because of the privileges they had enjoyed as middle-class women, but also because of the nature of institutional relationships.

Reformers had tried to bridge the divisions based on purity and class in order to reach out "the helping hand" to fallen women. As keepers, however, they fully exercised their authority in the unique, single-sex, power hierarchy of the institution. Power triumphed over sisterhood not because these were single-sex institutions, but because they were prisons; female-directed colleges, settlement houses, and political organizations did not necessarily recreate this pattern.[49] The women's reformatories recapitulated the histories of other nineteenth-century institutions for deviants and dependents; the contradictory notion of "feminine prisons" remained unresolved.

Part 3

The Progressive Approach,
1900–1920

Chapter 6

The New Criminology of Women, 1900–1920

By the close of the nineteenth century, women's prison reform had reached a point of stagnation. As the first spate of institution building ended, reformers increasingly defended rather than improved upon their past accomplishments. Between 1890 and 1910, the original activists who had lived long enough to influence the separate prisons—Abby Hopper Gibbons, Rhoda Coffin, Elizabeth Buffum Chace, and Josephine Shaw Lowell—all died.[1] Women entering prison reform as paid administrators during the 1880s and 1890s did not share the missionary spirit that had motivated these founders.

Within a decade, however, new life reinvigorated the movement. A generation of reformers came of age in a time of educational and occupational expansion for middle-class women. They did not have to argue for the right to work in prisons for they had inherited these institutions from the previous generation. These "new women," however, did not necessarily accept their predecessors' sexual ideology or penal methods. A small vanguard of educated, middle-class criminologists and reformers questioned the biological basis of the separate spheres and elaborated an environmental analysis of women's crime.

The different personal experiences of nineteenth- and twentieth-century reformers help to explain the new direction of women's criminology (see table 2, chap. 2). The earlier generation had shared backgrounds of religious training, education at a female academy, benevolent reform, marriage, and child rearing. Even as they entered the public sphere as volunteers and later as professional reformers, they continued to value domesticity and female moral superiority. Politically they fell into the category of social feminists; a few eventually supported women's rights.

In contrast, a majority of the Progressive-era reformers were single, divorced, or separated.[2] Like their generation as a whole, those who did marry had fewer children than their predecessors.

109

Unlike most American women they were highly educated. Several attended the eastern women's colleges that had opened in the late nineteenth century. When research universities, such as the University of Chicago, admitted women graduate students in the 1890s, several of these women earned advanced degrees. Almost all members of the latter generation of prison reformers worked for pay. Some lived for a time in settlement houses in New York, Philadelphia, and Chicago. Half of them actively supported the suffrage movement and none publicly opposed it. A few engaged in partisan politics during their lives.

Twentieth-century women had both different reasons for entering prison reform and a different approach to women prisoners than had the earlier generation. Although still concerned about attitudes toward prostitutes, fewer of the Progressives had a religious impulse to convert fallen women. Those trained in social work, law, medicine, and the social sciences approached female prisoners as professional clients or subjects of research. Reflecting their own personal experiences, the Progressives found problematic the arguments that woman's nature confined her to maternal and domestic tasks. Increasingly they dropped the principle of female moral superiority and questioned the implications of "biology is destiny."

The criminology developed by Progressive-era women was in part a response to a movement known as the "new penology." From 1900 to 1920 male and female prison reformers sought innovative methods to replace those used in the discredited nineteenth-century prisons. They instituted preventive social services, probation, and specialized courts for juveniles and women. To inform their work, many Progressives called for scientific investigations of the causes of crime.

In the recently established social sciences, which provided much of this research, the debate over hereditary and environmental determinants of crime moved into the laboratory. Criminal anthropologists carefully measured prisoners' bodies, psychologists tested mental skills, and sociologists studied criminals' backgrounds. Until World War I, most investigators stressed physical traits and mental ability as determining an individual's propensity for crime.[3] They based their conclusions on new discoveries in biology and, after 1906, on intelligence tests, which provided a tool for correlating mentality and crime.[4]

Hereditarian explanations of crime appealed to a conservative strain of American social thought. Nativism and racism flourished at the beginning of the century in reaction to the new immigration from southern and eastern Europe and the black northern migration, and in support of American overseas imperialism. These themes influenced the eugenics movement, which used scientific theories of Anglo-Saxon superiority to justify immigration restriction and population control. Hereditarian criminology used similar theories to support the view that criminals formed a separate biological class that had to be controlled.[5]

Despite the popularity of biological determinism in both pure science and crude propaganda, influential social scientists criticized hereditarian theories.[6] A growing number of criminologists questioned the validity of correlating crime with physiological and mental traits. After 1915 a new "multi-factor" approach, pioneered by the staff of the Juvenile Psychopathic Institute in Chicago, forced American criminologists to study criminals' family lives, educations, and economic conditions.[7] Nevertheless, the concept of the defective delinquent remained powerful, and hardcore biological determinism waned only after the 1920s.

Women prison reformers joined in this Progressive-era debate over the causes of crime. Many of the first women social scientists worked within separate women's prisons, where they found, literally, captive populations to use as subjects for testing criminological theories. Although women were as susceptible as other Progressives to nativist fears, they often remained more suspicious of biological determinism. Three types of studies by women researchers questioned prevailing theories and contributed to an environmental, or social, explanation of crime. First, at the opening of the century, Frances Kellor, a young sociologist, attacked Cesare Lombroso's concept of the physiological criminal type. Then, between 1910 and 1920, researchers at the New York women's reformatory grappled with the relationship of mental ability to crime. During the same period women social scientists' quantitative studies of female crime, along with Progressive social reformers' writings on prostitution, argued for an economic interpretation of women's crime.

Biology and Crime

Frances Kellor was representative of the unique group of women who combined academic inquiry with social action during the Progressive era. Kellor received a law degree from Cornell University in 1897 and then began graduate school in sociology at the recently established University of Chicago. There she studied "criminal sociology," a topic on which she elaborated in her 1901 textbook, *Experimental Sociology*. She later wrote on unemployment, prostitution, and immigration. In 1910 Kellor became chief investigator for the New York State Bureau of Industries and Immigration and two years later she directed the Progressive Service, the social welfare branch of the national Progressive party. Her feminist concerns included suffrage, women's athletics, the rights of Negro women, and the prevention of prostitution. During the 1920s and 1930s she specialized in labor arbitration.[8] Kellor began this notable career by being the first woman and one of the earliest Americans to attack Cesare Lombroso's biological interpretation of crime.

Lombroso, the Italian physician who popularized the idea of a physiological criminal type, had for many years commanded the respect of criminologists.[9] In *The Female Criminal*, published in English in 1895, Lombroso applied his theory of biological atavism, which held that primitive physical traits indicated criminal tendencies, to women prisoners. He concluded that female offenders differed from normal women by the greater frequency of pathological anomalies of their skulls. They physically resembled more closely either normal or criminal males than they did normal women. Moreover, his anthropometric measurements showed that women who committed different types of crimes varied by weight; that all female offenders were shorter than the norm; that they had an abundance of hair, often gray or (with the exception of prostitutes) dark. Sensory tests indicated these women had notable dullness of vision, hearing, smell, and taste, but normal perception of touch. The female criminal type was akin to the savage woman, he explained. She had an excess of male characteristics— eroticism, dominance and violence—and a paucity of female attributes, such as maternal feeling and morality.[10]

The criminal type was rarer among women than among men, Lombroso held, because of women's congenital disinclination to crime. But that small percentage who were "born criminal" had propensities "more intense and more perverse than those of their male prototypes." They were more greedy, more vengeful, more cruel, and more deficient in moral senses: "Women are big children; their evil tendencies are more numerous and more varied than men's but generally remain latent. When they are awakened and excited they produce results proportionately greater."[11] Thus, like earlier American moralists who believed in woman's greater fall, Lombroso reasoned that when a woman committed a crime in the face of countervailing social forces, "we may conclude that her wickedness must have been enormous before it could triumph over so many obstacles."[12]

Lombroso's tone was somewhat anomalous itself in the 1890s, when scientific terms were replacing moral ones in the language of criminologists. That the concept of women's greater fall persisted, even though cloaked in biological theories, endangered whatever progress women reformers had made toward removing the greater stigma of female crime. Few critics appreciated this implication of Lombroso's conclusions. At least one, however, Frances Kellor, saw clearly both the flaws in Lombroso's methods and the dangers for women in his conclusions.

Several scholars had questioned Lombroso's studies during the 1890s,[13] but Frances Kellor first replicated his experiments and used sociological evidence to refute them. The results of her research, reported in 1900 in both the *American Journal of Sociology* and the *Arena*, showed that the physiology of female criminals did not differ significantly from noncriminal women and that biology was less important than environment in encouraging deviant behavior. She insisted as well that women criminals were no more depraved than male criminals.

Kellor began her articles with a general critique of anatomical studies which ignored the social, mental, and emotional determinants of crime. "Workers in criminal sociology have become too accustomed to accuse heredity of all the results for which no other cause can be found," she wrote in the *Arena*. Kellor made a point of denying any "socialistic or anarchistic tendencies" on her part, although she emphasized class and culture rather than heredity as the root of crime.[14] First she faulted Lombroso, in particular, both for ignoring the "tremendous forces of social and economic environment" and for using inadequate methods to test his narrow theories. His sampling technique included too few noncriminals for valid comparison and his generalizations were based on "doubtful documentation." She also pointed out that Lombroso's methods could easily confuse ethnic and national traits with criminal ones. Only tests of normal and criminal women of comparable nationality would avoid this pitfall, a particularly significant one for the diverse American criminal population.[15]

In an effort to overcome these methodological flaws, Kellor compared sixty-one female prisoners and fifty-five female students. At the end of a lengthy series of anthropometric tests she was "unable to verify" Lombroso's results. The bone structure, weight, strength, facial characteristics, handwriting, and other traits of the criminals did not differ significantly from those of the students. The imprisoned women were no heavier, nor more frequently left-handed, no longer-lived, nor more masculine in appearance. In fact, when "the classes from which these people come, who are not criminal, but who have the same cultural and educational acquirements, are observed, it is difficult to determine any marked difference."[16] Kellor attributed the differences in tests of touch, taste, vision, and smell to the poor health and frequent injuries of prisoners.[17]

To further her goal of "a closer union of psychology and sociology," Kellor investigated prisoners' social backgrounds. She studied institutional records and prison matrons' reports, interviewed prisoners and visited their homes. Her report emphasized that women from large, lower-class families, whether married or single, committed crimes mainly through a combination of economic need and lack of economic opportunity.[18]

Married women's entry into prostitution, for instance, resulted from the influence of men or economic want. Kellor echoed nineteenth-century prison reformers when she suggested that immoral women "often marry men who continue or induce their depravity." For others, frequently "the dissipated habits are traceable to domestic troubles and to the struggle for existence," especially if the wife was supporting the family. Married women had fewer economic opportunities than did single women or men. The only skill which many of them could market was domestic service, a poorly paid job and one which, she believed, was an "easy route to seduction in the home or through phony employment bureaus who procure prostitutes."[19]

Kellor detected social origins of female crime in other evidence from her case studies. The parental homes from which the prisoners had come were usually poor, and had family sizes averaging over five children. Many women had run away from these homes to support themselves, but they found few remunerative positions open to them. One-half of the prisoners had been unemployed when convicted. Furthermore, after visiting their homes, Kellor concluded that many came from "crime-breeding" districts, those with poor sanitation and overcrowded housing.[20]

Unlike earlier women reformers, Kellor did not single out

women as the victims of social conditions. She recognized that male prisoners came from similar backgrounds and reasoned that the so-called criminal traits which had been attributed to offenders of both sexes were in fact the products of environment. Kellor perceived a danger in regarding women criminals as separate and more degraded, and she blamed the double standard for this phenomenon. "We say that a woman is worse, but we judge her so by comparison with the ideal of woman, not with a common ideal." Under a similar standard and given equal opportunities, she believed, members of both sexes would commit the same crimes.[21] Kellor seemed to believe that class was more important than sex in the making of a criminal. She found, for example, that in workhouses, women and men "come from similar environments, possess the same moral standards, and the life of both sexes within the group is upon the same plane."[22] Although she minimized sex differences, Kellor did add that women were tempted to prostitution because of their more limited economic resources and their physical incapacity to commit crimes of force.[23]

In these pioneering studies of female criminality, Frances Kellor laid the groundwork for the environmental analysis which would eventually replace Lombroso's biological categories. Her work encompassed both the strengths and weaknesses of environmentalism. She did expand the parameters of criminology by emphasizing careful methodology and well-researched case histories. Her discussions of women's marital, sexual, and work experiences usually avoided the moralism of earlier reformers' writings. Kellor's ideas, however, were limited by individualistic environmentalism.[24] She opposed biological categories, yet like Lombroso she focused on individual behavior. Although she constantly pointed out both flaws in the social structure and economic causes of crime, she failed to acknowledge any systematic injustice based on economic class or on sex. Like other Progressives at the time and other liberals since, Kellor believed in reducing crime by ameliorating the symptoms of class or sex exploitation, rather than by attacking the source of the problem.

Despite these limitations, Frances Kellor deserves credit for waging one of the first scientific battles in the ongoing struggle against biological determinism. If theorists can now develop alternatives to both biology-as-destiny and to Kellor's individualistic reforms, it is because innovators like her made their work possible.

Mentality and Crime

Despite recurrent fascination with the idea of a physiological criminal type, most social scientists did reject Lombroso's crude biological determinism by 1920. In the meantime, however, a new argument for a distinctive, hereditary criminal type—the defective delinquent—became extremely influential in America. Eugenicists popularized the idea that mental deficiency, or feeblemindedness, caused crime, prostitution, and vagrancy.[25] Even respectable social scientists presented data to support this relationship.[26] As Frank Tannenbaum later observed, "A new species of Lombrosianism came to plague criminological theory just about the time that the older and simpler 'criminal anthropology' was being repudiated. . . . We had returned once more to the Lombrosian theory of the 'born criminal' except that now our evidence was derived from the measuring of intellectual capacity."[27] Until the results of the mental tests of World War I draftees discredited some of the uses made of IQ tests, low intelligence scores became associated with potential deviancy. The defective delinquent joined the insane and the epileptic as the object of stigmatization, institutional segregation, and sterilization.

During the heyday of the mental testing of criminals, the women's prisons were becoming centers for research on female criminality. Administrators called for mental tests of inmates and presented the results along with other research findings, sometimes accepting the dominant opinion about defective delinquents and sometimes raising serious questions about it. In general, environmentalism, so well represented in Frances Kellor's earlier work, characterized women's approach to the subject. The studies produced at the New York Reformatory for Women at Bedford Hills, under the direction of Katharine Bement Davis, illustrate how the environmental theme persisted.

While Kellor had provided a direction for female criminology, the career of another woman trained at the University of Chicago fostered it within the women's prisons. Katharine Bement Davis had taught high school for ten years before she entered Vassar College in 1890. After receiving her bachelor's degree two years later, she studied nutrition at Columbia University; directed a model workingman's tenement at the World's Columbian Exposition in Chicago; and worked at a settlement house in Philadelphia. In 1897 she began her doctoral work at Chicago, where she studied with Thorstein Veblen. When she received her Ph.D. in 1900, the third New York State reformatory for women was about to open. Marion Talbot, a dean at Chicago, recommended Davis as superintendent, and with the support of Josephine Shaw Lowell, she got the job. Davis would eventually hire a number of women trained at her alma mater to aid her effort to make the women's reformatory a model of Progressive penology. Later, in 1914, she would leave Bedford Hills to become commissioner of corrections for the City of New York, its first woman cabinet member, and would go on to chair the city's parole board. An active suffrage leader, Davis is perhaps best known today for her 1929 study of female sexual behavior, *Factors in the Sex Life of Twenty-Two Hundred Women*.[28]

When Davis had been at Bedford Hills for several years, she began a social survey of inmates in order to determine a basis for treatment. She studied the records of the first 1,000 commitments (between 1901 and 1909) and subsequently investigated over 600 prostitutes at the reformatory to identify their common problems. The results showed, among other things, that 15 percent appeared to be feebleminded and that "degenerate strains" appeared in the heredity of 20 percent of the cases. At the same time Davis pointed out that one-half of the women were not fully literate and that most came from large, urban families.[29]

Although her preliminary impression was that "environment and heredity are so closely related that it is difficult to draw a line," Davis did initially classify on these grounds. On one hand, she wrote, were "congenital defectives," those women who were susceptible to delinquency because they were feebleminded or mentally imbalanced. The other group she singled out were criminals created by the environment, "through lack of moral, mental or physical training." "For this class," Davis wrote, "society is directly responsible." Urban crowding, unsanitary housing, insufficient public education, unjust economic conditions, and "the low moral standard among men which prevails in our cities" were at fault.[30]

Davis encouraged outside experts to investigate the Bedford Hills inmates. In 1910, Reed College psychologist Dr. Eleanor Rowland conducted psychological tests on inmates. A third of her subjects had subnormal scores, but Rowland hesitated to draw conclusions because of complications presented by both immigrant and illiterate prisoners. Meanwhile, Katharine Davis, possibly alarmed by these findings, sought a more systematic evaluation of incoming prisoners. She successfully applied to the New York Foundation for funds to hire a psychologist and in July 1911, Jean Weidensall filled the position.[31]

In addition to hiring women social scientists, Davis was responsible for establishing a psychological clinic at Bedford Hills, thanks to a chance association with John D. Rockefeller, Jr. In 1910, during the "white slave scare" that had been created partly by New York City politicians, Rockefeller chaired a grand jury investigating prostitution. The millionaire moralist wanted to eliminate the social evil and decided to create an Institute, the Bureau of Social Hygiene, to study the problem. Impressed by a pamphlet Davis wrote in 1911, Rockefeller invited her to join the board of his bureau.[32]

At Davis's suggestion Rockefeller chose Bedford Hills as the home of the Bureau's Laboratory of Social Hygiene. He purchased eighty-one acres of farmland adjacent to the reformatory at a cost of $75,000 and leased the land and its buildings to the reformatory managers at a nominal rent for five years, hoping that at the end of the lease the state would take over the facility. During those years the laboratory employed a staff of up to twenty women social scientists. They observed incoming prisoners at the Elizabeth Fry Reception House, conducted mental and clinical tests, and reported their findings in numerous bureau publications. The official purposes of the laboratory were to determine a proper sentence for each woman; to furnish a diagnosis for treatment; to collect data "which shall throw light on the causes of prostitution and crime"; and to suggest "a basis of remedial measure to prevent crime."[33]

Jean Weidensall became the chief psychologist at the laboratory. Like Davis, Weidensall had attended Vassar and the University of Chicago, where she had completed her doctorate under James Angell in 1910. She had taught at Bryn Mawr for a year and had worked at the Juvenile Psychopathic Institute in Chicago.[34]

Weidensall first undertook an investigation of feeblemindedness. Both she and Davis were skeptical of prisoners' low IQ scores because the normal distribution for standard scores was based on college students' performances. After comparing inmates, students, and a group of working women, Weidensall concluded that the tests may have measured mental training, but they did not measure mental capacity. She carefully avoided linking a prisoner's mentality with her delinquency and called for "a more

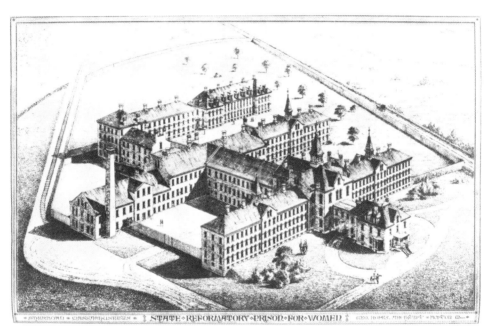

Massachusetts Reformatory Prison for Women, Framingham (Sherborn), Massachusetts.

Elizabeth Buffum Chace, 1806–99. Prison reformer, abolitionist, pacifist, and suffragist.

Rhoda Johnson Coffin, 1826–1909. Prison visitor and member of the board of managers, Indiana Woman's Prison. *(Courtesy of the Indiana Yearly Meeting of Friends.)*

Dr. Eliza Maria Mosher, 1846–1928. Physician, educator, and superintendent of the Massachusetts Reformatory Prison for Women, 1881–83. *(Courtesy of the Bentley Historical Collections, Bentley Historical Library.)*

Ellen Cheney Johnson, 1829–99. Superintendent, Massachusetts Reformatory Prison for Women, 1883–99. *(Courtesy of Basic Books.)*

Room for inmate, Massachusetts Reformatory for Women, ca. 1920. The ideal of domesticity in women's prisons encouraged inmates to decorate their rooms; at the same time it helped mask the reality of their imprisonment. *(Courtesy of Massachusetts Correctional Institution, Framingham.)*

Room for inmate and infant, Massachusetts Reformatory Prison for Women. *(Courtesy of Massachusetts Correctional Institution, Framingham.)*

"Our Babies," Massachusetts Reformatory for Women, 1916. The early women's prisons allowed infants under the age of two years to remain with their mothers in prison. Both mothers and other inmates visited the nurseries, which, reformers hoped, would encourage maternal feelings in prisoners. *(Courtesy of Massachusetts Correctional Institution, Framingham.)*

Recreation, Massachusetts Reformatory for Women, 1920. *(Courtesy of Massachusetts Correctional Institution, Framingham.)*

Keystone Kops, inmate performance, Massachusetts Reformatory for Women, ca. 1920. For an evening's entertainment, prisoners dressed as male police, offering comic relief from the usual gender and social roles. *(Courtesy of Massachusetts Correctional Institution, Framingham.)*

Recreation, Massachusetts Reformatory for Women, 1920. *(Courtesy of Massachusetts Correctional Institution, Framingham.)*

Farm labor, Massachusetts Reformatory for Women, 1911. *(Courtesy of Massachusetts Correctional Institution, Framingham.)*

Harvesting berries, Massachusetts Reformatory for Women, ca. 1911. Outdoor labor was characteristic at both the Massachusetts and New York reformatories for women after 1910. *(Courtesy of Massachusetts Correctional Institution, Framingham.)*

Farm labor, Massachusetts Reformatory for Women, 1911. As part of the "Fresh Air Treatment" advocated by Progressive era prison reformers, inmates worked on the farm land surrounding the Massachusetts reformatory. (*Courtesy of Massachusetts Correctional Institution, Framingham.*)

exacting understanding of her family conditions, her social and industrial history, her physical conditions, and her mentality."[35]

Over the next few years, the Laboratory of Social Hygiene attempted to fulfill Weidensall's call for more social data. In *The Mentality of the Criminal Woman*, inmate histories were compared to groups of working women and students. Prisoners at Bedford Hills had less formal education, more conflicts while in school, and fewer motivations to work than the other groups tested. No "unusual gift or impelling sex impulse" had made those who engaged in prostitution enter their trade. The most interesting result of intelligence tests, Weidensall found, was the bimodal, rather than bell-shaped, distributions of prisoners' IQ scores. Weidensall suggested that "inmates constitute two pretty distinct groups." The significant minority who were mentally impaired might require separate treatment from the majority, who had average or above average intelligence.[36]

The idea that defective or disturbed prisoners might benefit from special treatment recurred in the reformatory literature. One study at the Laboratory of Social Hygiene, for instance, showed that two-thirds of the disciplinary cases at Bedford Hills involved psychopathic or psychotic women.[37] Reports by institutional superintendents had long noted such problems, but few prisons could afford to provide separate care for those cases. Bedford Hills, however, had the resources to do so through the Bureau of Social Hygiene. In September 1916 a hospital for psychopathic delinquent women opened at the reformatory.[38]

Dr. Edith Spaulding directed the Psychopathic Hospital. Another former staff member of the Chicago Psychopathic Institute, she had served as resident physician at the Framingham, Massachusetts, women's reformatory since 1913. In an article co-authored with psychologist William Healy, Spaulding rejected the principle of direct inheritance of criminality; Spaulding and Healy also wrote that "indirect" inheritance, including mental ability, could have an influence on deviant behavior.[39] Although her own studies of Framingham inmates showed a high proportion (two-thirds) to be of subnormal mentality, Spaulding agreed with Weidensall that low intelligence alone did not cause crime.[40]

Spaulding's book on the psychopathic hospital included a chapter on etiologic factors in crime. In it she emphasized that antisocial behavior resulted from a "network of causes and effects, mental, physical and social, interwoven and interactive." Rather than investigate the inheritance of criminal traits, she explained, her study viewed "unfavorable inheritance" such as disease and insanity in the family history as "handicaps with which our patients may have begun life." More than half of the case studies did show significant hereditary handicaps. Environmental factors, including poverty, parental death, incest, and either prostitution or alcoholism at home appeared in 45 percent of the cases. Lack of parental supervision was noted frequently.[41]

The intellectual status of the psychopathic group was not uniformly low. In fact, mental tests tended "to substantiate the belief that the 'defective delinquents' as a class include individuals with superior as well as inferior intellectual capacity." When compared to the test scores of United States Army draftees, the scores suggested that a mental defect "is not necessarily of primary importance as an etiologic factor."[42]

A follow-up study conducted four to five years after the inmate's release indicated that one-third of Spaulding's former patients were doing well outside of prison. But her prognosis for psychopathic criminals in general was not encouraging. In evaluating the hospital experiment, she noted that disciplinary action had taken more time and energy than the staff had anticipated, cutting into their therapeutic work. Furthermore, the New York experiment was isolated and unique; it could do little to relieve the reformatory there or prisons elsewhere of difficult cases. Spaulding called for more wide-ranging responses to the psychopathic delinquent, including early detection of troubled children, special schools for the feebleminded, and more separate institutions like the hospital she directed.[43]

Davis, Weidensall, Spaulding, and their colleagues at Bedford Hills asked many of the same questions that other Progressive Era criminologists asked. Sometimes they accepted the standard solutions, such as segregation of seriously disturbed inmates. However their research on female criminality differed significantly from the mainstream of writing on the issue of mental deficiency. At a time when eugenicists claimed that segregation or sterilization of mental defectives would eliminate most deviancy, and at least one psychologist explained that female criminals, even more than male, were the products of feeblemindedness,[44] the Laboratory of Social Hygiene publications seem impressive for their moderation. They adopted neither biological nor psychological nor economic determinism. They followed the lead of Katharine Bement Davis in concentrating on the individual case and its complexities. Like Frances Kellor, however, the New York researchers made no systematic analysis of crime, despite the existence by 1910 of a radical critique of prostitution.[45]

The training of the women social scientists who questioned mental testing certainly influenced their conclusions. Experience at the University of Chicago and the Juvenile Psychopathic Institute may have inclined them toward an environmental or "multifactor" criminology. In addition, these women shared the experience of working at Bedford Hills. Brought together as a group by Katharine Bement Davis, they worked in a separate female institution, with access not only to women inmates but also to women colleagues who supported their critique of the established literature. Indeed, the fact that they were outsiders in the profession and were themselves breaking with tradition simply by becoming criminologists may help account for their willingness to question the prevailing theories about the nature of women's crime.

Economics and Crime

The studies published by the Laboratory of Social Hygiene and those of Frances Kellor shared the common themes that there was no female criminal type and that social forces had a large part in shaping female crime. In new theoretical works published after 1912, both European and American criminologists who supported this view began to focus on the relationship of economics and crime.[46] At the same time, feminist theorists like Charlotte Perkins Gilman and Emma Goldman were arguing that the economic system channeled women into prostitution.[47] Both women criminologists and social reformers echoed these concerns as they investigated the relationship between women's work and women's crime.

Occupation commanded the attention of a number of Progressives. Some claimed that women's entry into traditional male jobs led to more female crime.[48] To this charge the women social scientists, themselves participants in the trend toward new careers for women, responded in character. Not only did they refute the claim, but they did so with finesse, piling statistical proofs upon their own argument that traditional "women's work" was in fact an incentive to crime. Of a slightly different character were the writings of charities and corrections workers that cited women's poor wages and working conditions as the causes of prostitution. Both sources shared the environmentalism of earlier women's writings.

While other social scientists, including Weidensall and Spaulding, had pointed out the high percentage of domestic workers who became prison inmates, it was Mary Conyngton who provided the major critique of the view that entry into the paid work force led women to crime. In a study prepared for the United States Department of Commerce and Labor's *Report on the Conditions of Women and Child Wage Earners in the United States,* Conyngton studied 3,229 adult female offenders in six manufacturing states. Her results appeared in a 1911 volume, *Relationship between Occupation and Criminality of Women.*

Conyngton found that in 78 percent of the cases studied women had been employed in domestic or personal service—four times the frequency with which all women held such positions. After analyzing the occupational histories by region, Conyngton concluded that women's entry into new, industrial, clerical, and professional jobs did not result in more female crime. Rather, traditional "women's work" more often led to delinquency.

Like Kellor, Davis, and Weidensall, Mary Conyngton found no one "criminal type." She suggested instead that a combination of hereditary handicaps, lack of early training, and poor environment produced three categories of women's delinquency. A small group of antisocial women of normal intelligence committed crimes against chastity; some women criminals had subnormal intelligence and required custodial care; but the "great masses of female offenders" were "victims of poor birth, poor environment, poor training, and bad association."[49]

Conyngton's main purpose, though, clearly was to defend women's entry into nontraditional occupations. Her study suggested, both in its tone and in specific conclusions, that women committed crimes when they could not fit into the new industrial order. Thus, to prevent crime or to rehabilitate female offenders, women should be trained not for domestic tasks but for skilled labor and trades. She wrote that the "newer occupations" offered a woman "interest in her work and the hope of advancement" which could help produce "right living."[50]

Occupation was just one of the concerns of the authors of *A Study of Women Delinquents in New York State,* but they, too, offered new insight into the relationship between work and women's crime. Their ambitious project, undertaken between 1915 and 1917, produced a lengthy, statistics-packed testament to the Progressive criminologists' penchant for quantification. It classified, averaged, correlated, and analyzed variables ranging from age, religion, marital status, nativity, and criminal offense to degree of sexual irregularity, IQ score, wages at first and subsequent jobs, and the use of tobacco, alcohol, and drugs.

Mabel Ruth Fernald, a Chicago-trained psychologist who became director of the Laboratory of Social Hygiene, conducted the New York study, along with psychologist Mary Hayes and sociologist Almena Dawley. Their staff gathered data on 580 women, including inmates from a state penitentiary, the women's reformatory, a county penitentiary, the New York City workhouse, a Magdalen home, and a group of women on probation from the courts. The study compared women of various ages, offenses, and criminal records as well as male inmates in Sing Sing prison and the Elmira reformatory.

The Fernald study dismissed Lombroso at the outset and rejected the concept of a predetermined female criminal type. Their data, the authors wrote, "fail absolutely to justify the view expressed recently by certain propagandists that delinquency and defective intelligence are practically synonymous."[51] Of greater interest to the researchers were the quality of offenders' homes, educations, and "the economic stress to which they have been subjected."[52] They found that "less than ten percent came from homes considered better than mediocre in respect to economic status, moral standards and parental supervision."[53] Although unskilled, with less than a fifth grade education, 97 percent of the women studied had had to earn a living. Most had worked in domestic service or factories, and half were unemployed when convicted. The Fernald study suggested that "the greater probable lucrativeness of prostitution, shoplifting, or other forms of delinquency" explained women's crimes "in at least a fair proportion of the cases."[54]

Like Conyngton's study, *Women Delinquents in New York State* implied that women's crime could be prevented by expanding occupational opportunities for women. In contrast to nineteenth-century reformers who stressed the need for differential, feminine care in reformatories, the new studies suggested that women, and particularly women prisoners, could benefit from training which prepared them for the formerly male world of paid labor.

A similar critique of women's economic plight can be found in the writings about prostitution that proliferated during the Progressive era. Reformers and radicals, ranging from Jane Addams to Emma Goldman, pointed to societal responsibility for the "social evil." Even more than their predecessors of the nineteenth century, Progressive-era charity and corrections workers pointed to low wages and menial jobs as sources of vice.

A sampling of comments on the roots of prostitution suggests that reformers had an economic analysis of crime. For instance, one 1911 survey of prostitution noted that "the barometer of crime rises as that of prosperity falls, and this is particularly true as regards the crimes of women."[55] Mary Boyle O'Reilly, a prison commissioner in Massachusetts, claimed that women criminals there were "almost entirely the victims of the parasitic season-trades that by piece work and starvation wages drain the workers of life, liberty and happiness." Kate Richards O'Hare, who spent over a year in prison herself, stressed the "vicious results of women's economic dependency."[56]

Other reformers blamed female crime not on simple economic exploitation, but on the dreariness of life for working girls, particularly the immigrants. Louise de Koven Bowen, active in the Chicago Women's Club and the Juvenile Protection Association, wrote pamphlets like the *Temptations of the Shop Girl* which blamed long working hours and lack of vacations and sick leave for young women's discontent. As one pamphlet, *A Girl Starving for Pleasure is an Easy Prey*, concluded, "Is it any wonder that she sometimes chooses 'the easiest way'?"[57] New York reformer Alice Davis Menken also wrote that young girls desired "unhealthy excitement" to release them from the daily grind of shop and factory, making them easy prey for procurers.[58] Maude Miner, Secretary of the New York Probation Association, claimed that the lack of healthy recreation was one cause of prostitution. Working girls in search of entertainment frequented dance halls where they might meet prostitutes, or even worse, male procurers.[59]

The reports of vice-commission investigations in dozens of cities repeated these explanations of prostitution and recommended higher wages and better working conditions, as well as supervised recreation, to destroy the flesh trade.[60] In their writings, women like Miner, O'Hare, and Menken made similar suggestions. To help "Our Unfortunate Sister," Menken advised the study of housing and working conditions. Improve home life, the factory, and recreation, Miner recommended, while giving wise sex instruction and waging a "constant war against the procurers."[61]

Although they often concentrated on wages and the workplace, these reformers actually explained prostitution by a generalized environmentalism akin to that of the women criminologists. Both groups, for instance, wanted to expand opportunities for working women and to improve family life, especially in the cities. But like others of their generation, they failed to appreciate the difficulties women faced in trying to gain some measure of economic security without the restructuring of both work and family roles. If women were to enter the labor force as anything but low-paid menials with the added burden of household responsibilities, inequalities based on sex, class, and race would have to be eliminated. That task, however, was not the goal of the Progressives. Rather, reformers and social scientists alike hoped to improve working conditions, wages, education, and recreation until women would no longer be tempted to the more profitable and exciting life of crime.

A criminology of women had emerged by 1920 that consistently rejected the physiological or mental criminal type and looked instead to home environment and economic causality to explain women's delinquency. Although an environmental analysis of crime was not unique to women social scientists, the writers discussed above were in the vanguard of their profession; American criminologists did not generally adopt the multifactor or environmental approach until the 1920s.[62] Most historians have explained the shift to environmentalism as due to either the general intellectual climate of pragmatism or the self-interest of professionals who needed to believe in the possibility of curing deviancy.[63] For women criminologists, however, other factors may have influenced their ideas. In particular, their personal experiences as educated career women who had themselves rejected the separate female sphere may have made them more critical of biological determinism. Collaboration with women like themselves may have encouraged them to undertake the investigations that questioned dominant theories of hereditary and mental defect.

The women criminologists of the Progressive era drew upon and refined the environmentalism of earlier prison reformers. They continued to focus on the effects of social conditions on the individual but still did not question the sexual definition of women's crime. However, the Progressives applied new scientific methods to support environmental theories. In addition, they began to reject sexual difference in favor of sexual equality, both in their lives and in their work. They not only contributed to the transition from biological to sociological criminology, but at the same time they helped redirect the goals of women's prison reform.

Chapter 7

The Limits of Progressive Penology, 1900–1920

The Progressive reformers who revised theories of female criminality also called into question the methods employed by women's prisons in the previous century. Separate, feminine institutions had appealed to an older generation who viewed women as a separate sexual class in need of protection from male influence. The Progressives, however, identified environmental sources of women's crime, including poverty, lack of education, and low-paying, tedious work. Prisons alone could not resolve these problems. Moreover, both the personal lives and the published writings of the new reformers rejected the traditional boundaries of the domestic sphere. Thus they did not share the traditional reformatory goals of building feminine characters and training for domesticity.

As a result of these new ideas, women's prison reform both expanded beyond its institutional focus and modified older penal methods. On the one hand, Progressive reformers who favored extrainstitutional, preventive services over incarceration concentrated on changing criminal justice practices before the stage of imprisonment. On the other hand, superintendents Katharine Bement Davis and Jessie Donaldson Hodder tried to improve the women's prisons through better classification and education, and diversified training. Ironically, the very successes of extrainstitutional reforms often undermined efforts to improve the prisons, for they helped create institutions of last resort.

Extrainstitutional Reforms

A widespread concern over prostitution, which peaked around 1910, facilitated the expansion of women's prison reform during the Progressive era. Exposés about the sexual exploitation of young women, popularized in newspapers, magazines and through dozens of vice-commission reports in American cities, provided both social-purity and prison reformers with new reasons to criticize the treatment of fallen women. In contrast to the nineteenth-century reformers, who had concentrated on the possibility of uplifting the prostitute, the Progressives sought new ways to prevent her fall.[1]

The Progressive responses to prostitution revealed a deep ambivalence toward the fallen woman.[2] Many journalists and civic reformers pointed to commercialized vice as proof that working women, along with urban political machines and immigrants, were destroying American society. But at the same time, social justice reformers, more interested in the female victims of the trade, aided young urban women as a way to prevent the spread of prostitution.

Social services for immigrants and new migrants to the cities contributed to the wider scope of preventive work. Immigrant Protective Leagues helped women traveling alone to avoid exploitation by employers and landlords, as did the Young Women's Christian Association, the National Council of Jewish Women, and the Clara deHirsch Homes for Immigrant Girls. Investigations by Frances Kellor and other women reformers identified fraudulent employment agencies and rooming houses that allegedly procured girls for brothels.[3]

Other preventive services reached out to the young woman on the verge of a criminal career. The Big Sisters, organized in several cities after 1910, offered social hygiene instruction, recreation, and home placement for delinquent girls and monitored the girls' court proceedings.[4] Rescue homes aided other women who had taken the first step. Under the leadership of Kate Waller Barrett, the Florence Crittenton Homes rejected their earlier mission of converting prostitutes and became refuges for unwed mothers, to prevent them from falling into prostitution.[5] Other homes served as quasi-public reformatories to which the courts sent convicted first offenders.

Closely related to these private, preventive agencies was the movement to hire policewomen in American cities. Although police matrons had been introduced in American jails in the 1870s and 1880s, they had performed largely custodial duties. In 1905 the city of Portland, Oregon, first delegated police power to women volunteers at the Lewis and Clark Exposition, setting the precedent for the creation of women's divisions in police forces throughout the country. Between 1910 and 1925 over 150 cities appointed policewomen to duties which centered around protecting women and children. Experience in social case work was often a prerequisite for the policewoman, who supervised dance halls and movie houses and enforced youth curfews. In addition, they handled detective work on cases involving women and accompanied these women to court.[6]

Policewomen, reformers agreed, would improve conditions in city jails and station houses, where the majority of all women prisoners served during short sentences and while awaiting trial. Separate women's prisons had alleviated the abuses of mixed institutions for only a few prisoners. Police stations and jails, with scenes reminiscent of those Elizabeth Fry confronted in 1815, still mixed first offenders and hardened criminals in close, unsanitary quarters. Juvenile reformer Martha Falconer called the jail a "perverter of womanhood" and criticized prison reformers who "devoted all of their time to the improvement of convict prisons and the reformation of convicted criminals." She explained, "The time to reform a criminal is at the beginning of her career and not at the end. . . . caring for prisoners awaiting trial [should] be emphasized in the highest possible degree. The treatment of men in jails and police stations is bad enough, but the treatment of women is generally worse."[7]

Women in several states attempted not only to have female staff hired for mixed institutions but also to have separate women's quarters established. In Massachusetts special women probation officers interviewed female offenders at the jails, accompanied them to court, protected them from false accusations, and tried to keep them out of prison by recommending probation. In Chicago the deplorable conditions in the women's quarters of the Cook County jail prompted an experiment in 1915 in which local women's groups oversaw the renovation of three station houses as "Detention Homes for Women." This project was abandoned, however, after the police rejected the recommendations of the Women's Advisory Committee.[8]

The women's courts established in several cities during the Progressive era had greater success. The main functions of these courts were to centralize preventive services and to provide a more dignified atmosphere for trying morals cases. In New York an additional purpose was to try prostitutes as soon as they were arrested, usually at night, and thus avoid detaining them in police stations. Women's courts would help separate prostitutes from their pimps, who often attended trials, paid the fine or bail, and returned their workers to the streets directly from the courthouse. In addition, medical and social workers would, ideally, be attached to women's courts to diagnose physical, mental, and social problems and to recommend the best form of treatment for each offender.[9]

The separate women's court originated in New York City in 1908, when the night court was divided into male and female branches. After 1910, all women from Manhattan and the Bronx charged with prostitution (either soliciting or loitering), and all girls charged with incorrigibility, went to the women's night court (which became a day court in 1918). There they were finger-printed, tested for venereal disease, and investigated by case workers.[10]

For those convicted, reformers from the Women's Prison Asso-ciation urged probation instead of fines or imprisonment.[11] New York did abolish fines for prostitution as part of the effort to un-dermine the control of pimps, and the number of probation cases doubled between 1907 and 1913. Female probation officers began their supervision of a convicted woman by investigating her home environment. If it seemed inadequate the officer might recom-mend a suspended "sentence" in an approved home, such as Wav-erly House, affiliated with the New York Probation Association, or a private agency like the Magdalen Homes. In addition to the court officer, social service volunteers often stepped in to help first offenders. Alice Menken and her coworkers in the Jewish Big Sis-ters would appear at the New York women's court and invite the Jewish defendants to attend Sunday morning meetings at Shear-ith Israel, the Sephardic congregation. They sometimes became official or quasi-official probation officers for Jewish prostitutes.[12]

Other cities established variations on the separate women's court. The Chicago morals court, for example, was founded at the request of that city's vice commission, both to heighten public awareness of the extent of prostitution, and to coordinate special-ized law enforcement and social services for its defendants. In Chi-cago and in the Philadelphia women's misdemeanant division, the courts handled morals charges for both sexes, but female clientele predominated. These courts provided special facilities for prosti-tutes, including detention quarters for women, medical examina-tion rooms, and probation departments which hired female offi-cers.[13]

Although the women's courts intended to improve the quality of criminal justice for moral offenders, in practice they discrimi-nated against their clients in a number of ways. Like juvenile courts, they often dispensed with jury trials, giving the judge extraordinary powers to convict and sentence. Although they tried to protect women from the exploitation of men, the courts did little to prosecute either pimps or customers. Even though compulsory hospitalization of venereally infected women was ruled unconstitutional in New York,[14] physical examinations of all accused women continued there and elsewhere. The courts dismissed male customers without tests or treatment for venereal disease. Furthermore, due process was effectively abrogated in the women's courts because complaints were not filed until after arrest and bail (as in the Chicago court) and cases were postponed pending results of physical examinations.

The extrainstitutional methods which Progressive reformers introduced had many shortcomings, yet they did evidence a willingness to experiment outside of the prison.[15] Preventive social services, homes for female delinquents, and probation officers all were attempts to eliminate the environmental causes of crime. Perhaps they kept some women from becoming prostitutes. More importantly they kept many from becoming inmates of penal institutions. At the same time, these extrainstitutional reforms integrated women professionals—lawyers, probation officers, and policewomen—throughout the criminal justice system, not simply in separate women's prisons. In expanding women's prison reform beyond its institutional base, however, the Progressives also forced a reconsideration of the prison itself.

Institutional Adjustment

Even as prevention became the watchword of the Progressives, both male and female reformers experimented with a "new penology" that attempted the rehabilitation of prison inmates. Advocates of the new penology criticized the traditional mechanisms of prison discipline that trained good prisoners but did not prepare inmates for lives outside institutional walls. Reformers like William George and Thomas Mott Osborne tried to transform juvenile reformatories and penitentiaries into what one historian has termed "anti-institutional institutions."[16] George's "Junior Republics" were coeducational, self-governing communities for young delinquents. Under Osborne's superintendence, a "Mutual Welfare League" at the Auburn, New York, penitentiary and a "Golden Rule Brotherhood" at Sing Sing prison granted self-government to inmates on the principle that "it is liberty alone that fits men for liberty."[17]

Of the women prison reformers who shared the "anti-institutional" outlook, the most influential were Katharine Bement Davis and Jessie Donaldson Hodder. In New York and Massachusetts, respectively, they pursued two lines of innovations. First, they attempted to transcend the physical limitations of women's prisons by emphasizing the cottage system, parole, outdoor work, and recreation. Secondly, they pressed against the less-tangible boundaries of domesticity by expanding training to include academic and industrial classes and nontraditional women's work.

Modifications in women's reformatories occurred within several types of settings. In New York the opening of a new institution provided an opportunity to incorporate the lessons of both earlier women's prison reform and of the new penology. In Massachusetts new personnel tried to adapt an older institution, despite limitations of design and tradition. Both of these experiments influenced the founding of other women's reformatories, especially in Connecticut and New Jersey.

The New York reformatory enjoyed the advantages of a longer period of planning and the lessons of older reformers. Although the legislation establishing Bedford Hills had been passed in 1892, appropriation and building delays kept it from opening for nearly ten years. During that time reformers who had witnessed the problems of the first prisons insisted that Bedford's planners secure adequate land, facilities, and staff. Abby Hopper Gibbons, then in her nineties, reminded the managers that "criminals are made what they are by association and treatment. Let us turn over a new leaf and remember they are human." Josephine Shaw Lowell, who joined the Bedford board of managers in 1899, asked the advice of women educators in hiring staff. As a result, Katharine Bement Davis became the first superintendent.[18]

When Bedford Hills finally opened in May 1901, it represented an improvement on earlier designs. Located on over 200 acres in a rural area of suburban Westchester County, with no fences surrounding it, the reformatory was modeled on the cottage plan. In addition to a reception hall for new commitments, four cottages were ready at the outset in which inmates could be classified by age and behavior. Sanford Cottage housed married women, mothers, and inmates over age twenty-one. With good behavior they could be promoted to Huntington Cottage. Those under age twenty-one resided in Gibbons, and the best behaved under age eighteen lived in Lowell. Cottages were an attempt to mask the fact that this was a prison; thus they were named after founders and provided the comforts of home. Each cottage had a flower garden, a kitchen equipped with "good linen and china," and twenty-eight pleasantly furnished single rooms that inmates could decorate.[19]

Lessons in democratic self-government, along with the cottage system, modified the older reformatories' intensive supervision of inmates' lives. Davis explained that she wanted inmates to learn that the law was not merely an abstract authority, but a method of conducting relationships between people. Therefore, she started a series of talks on the law, beginning with its origins and development, working up to American democracy, citizenship, and the "importance of women in such a democracy [even] though they take no part in actual government." All of this was a means of preparation for residence in the Honor Cottage, where inmates elected their officers and tried their own cases of infringements of rules.[20]

The parole system at Bedford Hills also differed from nineteenth-century penology. Although early release had been a feature of the Massachusetts women's prison, it was used there largely as an incentive to promote good behavior within the institution. In Davis' view, however, the essential goal of the prison was getting women out through early parole. "No person should be sentenced to an institution who can be cared for outside with hope for herself and safety for the public," she once wrote. The Bedford managers agreed on a policy "to parole inmates as rapidly as they are found to be fitted to go out, and to do this without regard to the period of time spent in the institution."[21]

Preparing inmates for life outside required new training methods. The original women's prisons had abandoned formal classroom work for all but illiterate inmates and had taught mainly domestic skills. Now, however, both the new penology and the new woman demanded more diversified training than cooking, cleaning, and laundry. Katharine Bement Davis came closest to effecting this goal. In addition to academic subjects, inmates at Bedford Hills took industrial and recreational classes. Though her efforts fell short of the goal of training for self-sufficiency, they nonetheless varied the institutional routine and made it much less stifling than the older system.

Davis hired a full-time instructor who held academic classes throughout the week. In addition to basic skills, inmates could take geography, history, current events, or mechanical drawing. To supplement this curriculum Davis gave singing lessons, the assistant superintendent offered daily gymnastics, and the reformatory physician gave a weekly lesson in physiology and sex hygiene.[22] Recreational programs provided numerous breaks from the classroom. With the financial support of women reformers, Davis hired a summer recreation director from the College Settlement and a special matron for "outdoor work." One staff member produced amateur plays, Gilbert and Sullivan musicals, and other entertainments. Volunteers from almost every one of the Seven Sister women's colleges, plus students on vacation from the University of California, Cornell, and the University of Chicago, assisted the paid staff.[23]

To make classes more palatable, the Bedford Hills' staff adopted Progressive educational methods. All tasks, both in the classroom and outside it, were to be shared by inmates and teachers. The staff was expected to do as much menial work as their charges, and instructors tried to make subject matter relevant to the lives of the women. Daily institutional experiences became the subjects of the lessons. If students learned less history, it mattered little. "Our efforts," Davis wrote, "are to fit girls for life and not to pass examinations."[24]

Vocational training occupied the half of the day not spent in school, for, Davis explained, "our success will depend on our ability to train girls so as to enable them to earn a[n] honest livelihood." At one time, this would have meant only domestic training, but Davis departed from earlier policies saying, ". . . it is not every woman in our mixed throng who is adapted by nature or taste to domestic service, sewing or laundry work. In the reformatories for men, no one for a moment seriously considers limiting the trades taught to cooking and tailoring, though these occupations are highly respectable, and the remuneration of the chef or custom tailor is excellent."[25]

Although part of inmates' training consisted of cooking, laundry, and food service within the cottages, Davis supplemented this with nondomestic tasks as much as possible. Classes in hat making and machine knitting began in 1903. In 1904 several inmates took stenography and typing classes, and a few became aides in the institution's hospital and supply room. Over the next years, chair caning, cobbling, bookbinding, painting, and some carpentry filled out the industrial course offered by the reformatory.[26]

Unfortunately, women could not count on finding jobs which employed these new skills, and domestic service remained the easiest job placement for released inmates. Davis noted with some annoyance that while employers claimed that they refused to hire her inmates in industry because they feared "contaminating other employees," they didn't hesitate to take these same ex-prisoners into their own homes where they would be intimates of their children. By 1909 Davis acknowledged that "A large proportion of our girls go to domestic service and others go to their homes to do or assist in domestic service and homemaking." Like her contemporaries who wanted to elevate traditional women's work to a profession, Davis placed training for these tasks in the category of "domestic science" and offered them in a new "Industrial Building."[27]

Another of Davis's innovations, "Fresh Air Treatment," applied the Progressive era "back to nature" impulse to women prisoners.[28] Female criminals, Davis argued, even more than male, suffered from physical and mental deterioration. Fresh air, sunshine, and outdoor occupations would rebuild their bodies and their nervous systems.[29] Thus, on summer evenings Bedford inmates could remain outdoors until dark. During the day they could be found not only gardening, weeding, and planting, but also raising poultry, breeding stock, and slaughtering pigs. At first, Davis admitted, it seemed to the prisoners like "man's work," but once the female officers took part, the inmates followed suit. Besides gardening and farming, they learned masonry, built a road, painted the institution, built a conduit for a new steam laundry, and harvested ice in the winter.[30] Journalists, judges, and other visitors often marvelled at the sight of women grading an embankment or draining a swamp.[31]

Like Katharine Davis in New York, the new superintendent of the Massachusetts women's prison, Jessie Donaldson Hodder, brought innovative ideas to women's prison reform. An unconventional past had brought Jessie Hodder to this career. During the 1890s she studied music in Germany and lived with a young American philosopher, Alfred Hodder. The couple had two children. When her common-law husband abandoned his family to marry one of his Bryn Mawr colleagues, Jessie Hodder, left stranded in Europe, had to fend for herself and her children. Her friends in Boston, Elizabeth Glendower Evans and Alice James, helped her return to America and find work. After serving as a matron at the Lancaster State Industrial School for Girls, Hodder began counseling unwed mothers at the Social Service Department of the Massachusetts General Hospital. In 1910 she became the superintendent at the Framingham, Massachusetts, reformatory, where she "brought a new education and scientific spirit to bear."[32]

Hodder thought of herself as the first of a new generation of administrators at Framingham. The founders of the women's prisons, she once wrote, had limited their sights to religious conversion and the maintenance of order. Even her immediate predecessor "came into the institution in its experimental years, when it was believed women could not handle 'women criminals.'" But Hodder had different goals. Like Katharine Davis, she wanted to modify institutional controls and individualize treatment.

Hodder's first annual report urged that the word "prison" be struck from the institution's name and that in the future the term "prisoners" should be replaced by "women." She succeeded in having the name changed to the Massachusetts Reformatory for Women in 1911 and described "joyous hand-clapping" and "sobs" by the women following the ceremony.[33]

But it was not merely the term "prison" that bothered Hodder. She raised severe criticisms about the building, the atmosphere, and the treatment at Framingham. For years, superintendents' annual reports had dutifully repeated the same platitudes about uplift and harmony; rarely did they question the function of the reformatory prison. Hodder's reports, in contrast, blasted her new home and claimed that the reformatory "is disintegrating." She called the Framingham facility a "big shut-in house" and requested a special state appropriation to transform the structure and change its routine. Either the institution should be remodeled, she argued, or, having outlived its usefulness, it should be abandoned. For a superintendent to suggest the closing of her own institution was an unusual recommendation, particularly since reformers had once been so defensive about their prisons. But in Hodder's opinion the Massachusetts reformatory was not fulfilling its potential as a superior home for women prisoners. Rather, it had "standards of care, education, industrial training, individual comfort and development . . . far below those for men in men's prisons and reformatories."[34]

To improve the physical plant, Hodder called for enlargement of the campus, transformation of the old cell block into a gymnasium, and the establishment of several outer cottages (including one for the feebleminded), with no walls enclosing them. Treatment should be adapted, she suggested, by separating old and young inmates, diversifying occupational training, replacing moral reform with academic training, and providing more outdoor recreation. Eventually she wanted to develop the reformatory into an "Industrial Training Institute for Women."[35]

Hodder also hoped to establish a "scientifically equipped clearing house" like that at Bedford Hills and a separate division for women who required psychological treatment. Unfortunately, she did not chance upon a Rockefeller to support her plan "to study prisoners and criminal motivation." She did try to segregate the most unstable women within the institution and hired women trained in criminology to help her. In 1913 she appointed Edith R. Spaulding as resident physician, and she invited Harvard students to use the reformatory as a summer clinic for their course on the psychology of delinquency. But Hodder's larger dream of making the reformatory "a laboratory of criminalistics" was frustrated; her requests for state funds were repeatedly ignored or denied.[36]

Hodder had limited success in implementing her plans for diversified training. By 1915 she had expanded the reformatory school beyond mere literacy classes. She had organized physical fitness programs, although her request for a gymnasium was not filled until 1925.[37] Inmates could also train in "scientific farming." But for the most part the old school of domesticity survived. Hodder repeatedly called for the institution to reject traditional domestic training and "to develop vocational training for the women,"[38] but her requests for an integrated program of classes and shops for industrial education went unheeded.

Transforming an existing institution like Framingham with any but minor, inexpensive changes proved far more difficult than starting a program from scratch. Hodder had more success influencing the new women's reformatories authorized in several states. Both Hodder and Davis advised the selection of land for the Connecticut state reformatory in 1917, and Hodder served temporarily as an "advisory superintendent" for the institution.[39] The impact of her ideas can be seen as well in the thirteen women's correctional facilities established between 1900 and 1920. All adopted the titles of reformatory, state farm, or industrial school, and over half of them required the cottage plan by law (see chap. 8, table 6).

The New Jersey women's prison offers a good example of the influence of Hodder and Davis on new institutions, as well as of the limitations of the Progressive-era experiments. After a decade of agitation led by state women's clubs, in 1910 the New Jersey legislature established a female correctional institution. It opened in 1913 to house women formerly held in the state penitentiary who were considered suitable for reformatory treatment and women sentenced directly from the courts. Although its official title was the New Jersey State Reformatory for Women, it was known as neither a prison nor a reformatory, but as "Clinton Farms."[40]

An "anti-institutional" structure was adopted at the outset. Built on over 300 acres in a rural setting, Clinton Farms used the cottage plan, at first with the original farm houses on the site. Eventually ten specialized cottages were opened, including those for honor inmates, black women and their infants, white mothers and infants, and problem cases. Inmate self-government began in 1914, partly because there were so few staff members that prisoners themselves supervised groups at farm work. Several years later, superintendent Mary Belle Harris recalled, inmates continued to work on their own. An elected inmate government took over when the cottages opened, and annual reports stressed its importance for morale and inmate self-respect. Training consisted of outdoor farm work and domestic science, with institutional sewing and a beauty school added after 1930.[41]

In New Jersey, as in New York, Massachusetts, and Connecticut, reformers attempted to transform women's prisons into more "anti-institutional" institutions. The choice of names, cottage systems, inmate self-government, and outdoor work did offer more freedom of movement to inmates than nineteenth-century prisons had allowed. They did not, however, meet the goal of the new penology that prisoners learn how to live outside of the institution. As in the first women's prisons, the training programs indicated the deep resistance to preparing women for roles in a modern economic system. Although increasing numbers of working women engaged in clerical and service jobs during this period, the new state reformatories adopted the farming model set by New Jersey and continued to rely on domestic science as a mainstay of training.[42] Outdoor work and recreation served to improve the prison environment, but did little for prisoners' lives after their release. In addition, serious problems at each institution made even the new penology unworkable before long.

Obstacles to Reform

Despite the achievement of structural modifications in women's prisons during the Progressive era, the institutional histories for this period resemble the earlier pattern of unfulfilled visions. Some states simply failed to adopt Progressives' recommendations, as in Massachusetts. But even in new institutions, persistent obstacles undermined the "anti-institutional" reforms. Bedford Hills provides a disheartening example of how even the best laid innovative plans were thwarted by judicial sentencing policies and legislative appropriations that were incompatible with reformers' methods.

From its opening, Bedford Hills suffered from its own good reputation. It became a popular place to send "incorrigible" women. Early administrative reports complained that habitual drunkards sentenced there by the courts would harm the institution more than it could help them. At the request of the Women's Prison Association and other reformers, New York established a separate state farm for women alcoholics in 1908.[43] Meanwhile, however, Bedford Hills's jurisdiction was expanded. By 1906 Katharine Davis began to notice a marked change in the kind of inmates committed by the courts. More New York City women, whom she considered the most difficult cases, entered the reformatory. Over the next few years she noted the burden of women who were mentally defective, venereally infected, or addicted to drugs. Other officials also pointed out an increase in the number of foreign-born, illiterate prisoners, especially the large percentage of Jewish immigrants. Davis feared that the "tendency of committing difficult women if continued will make our problems harder as it takes longer to get them in condition to profit by mental and industrial training."[44]

Both cutbacks in appropriations and increases in the number of women committed annually aggravated these problems. After 1909 "the most rigid economy" prevented the expansion of buildings and services. Serious overcrowding resulted, including the doubling up of inmates in rooms and the use of hallways for dormitories. These arrangements in turn added to the existing tensions within the institution over sexual relationships between inmates. Officials blamed the overcrowding for what they called "abnormal attachments" which were "not an uncommon manifestation" by 1911.[45]

Although overpopulation and underappropriation contributed to Bedford's problems, the Progressives' own policy of extrainstitutional reform created a dilemma for the prisons. Both probation (suspended sentence with supervision) and parole (early release) meant that the most hopeful cases either never went to an institution at all, or left as soon as possible. Any available rooms went to women without enough promise to merit probation. Those who were sentenced to the reformatory, Davis found, often needed a longer time "to adjust" to the institution. Many had to overcome their dependencies on liquor or drugs; others had to improve debilitating physical conditions before they began classes or vocational training. At the same time, overcrowding of the reformatory hampered the operation of the parole system. Whenever the inmate population became too large, the managers felt pressured to reach the "limits of propriety in granting parole." This policy undoubtedly increased the number of parole violators who returned to the institution.[46]

The problems of underappropriation, overcrowding, and the sentencing of difficult inmates were peaking around 1910, when Davis got Rockefeller to locate his Bureau of Social Hygiene at Bedford Hills. With the opening of the laboratory, some of the reformatory's difficulties seemed to subside. Now inmates were screened before entry, to isolate problem cases. The hospital for psychopathic delinquent women later segregated potentially disruptive cases. The presence of qualified psychologists and nurses supplemented the institution's own staff. During this period inmates and staff adjusted in spite of difficulties, but once Davis resigned in 1914 to become New York City commissioner of corrections, the institution deteriorated rapidly.[47]

A 1915 investigation revealed the serious tensions in the institution. Overcrowding, all agreed, presented the major problem. The facility housed over 100 more inmates than it could comfortably accommodate. Beds appeared in halls, the gymnasium, and wherever else possible. Overcrowding was complicated by the number of women who required some custodial care. The original system of classification had practically broken down. Furthermore, insufficient appropriations necessitated a monotonous diet and a poorly kept physical plant.[48]

Racial and sexual tensions at the reformatory first came to public attention through the 1915 investigation. Black and white women had lived in the same cottages at Bedford Hills because Katharine Davis had refused on principle to segregate the races. By 1915, with a larger number of black women sentenced from New York City, and a host of totally unrelated problems confronting Bedford Hills, investigators cited Davis' policy of integration as a source of the reformatory's ills.[49] The problem, however, was not one of racial antagonism, of which no evidence appeared. On the contrary, it was the revelation of homosexual attachments between black and white inmates that proved a source of embarrassment for the administration. Assistant superintendent Jessie Taft testified that sexual immorality was "the foundation of most of the trouble along disciplinary lines." She further explained that "there is no denying that the colored girls are extremely attractive to certain white girls."[50]

According to James Wood, president of the board of managers, lesbian relationships were nothing new at Bedford Hills. "The practices referred to have obtained to a greater or less extent during the whole existence of our institution," he said. Although the opportunities for sexual contact "have been much more frequent and general in the past year or two, because of our overcrowded condition," he felt that little could be done besides the usual attempt to separate inmates "in every case where these abuses have been discovered." Others, however, seized on the revelation to demand that the black inmates be segregated in separate cottages. Jessie Taft claimed that "Two institutions, I think, is the only thing that could really take care of it; two separate institutions in separate places." Wood later agreed that only complete segregation would prevent interracial sex.[51]

To what extent this episode reflected the increasing stigmatization of homosexuality in the society at large and to what extent it simply masked racial discrimination, is impossible to judge.[52] As Wood indicated, lesbian relationships between inmates had been common, even if not commonly acknowledged, while Davis ran the institution.[53] Now, however, either the taboo against interracial sex surfaced as a stronger one than that against homosexuality (for surely intraracial sex would continue), or the entire incident served as an excuse to segregate black women. The investigator's final report concluded that "While the committee makes no objection to this [integrated cottages] because of the color line, it is undoubtedly true that the most undesirable sex relations grow out of this mingling of the two races." In 1916 the annual report announced that two new cottages for black women had opened, allegedly at the written request of the Negro inmates.[54]

Besides channeling the blame for institutional problems onto blacks and lesbians, the 1915 investigation provided recommendations to improve Bedford Hills. It called on judges to exercise more care in screening commitments and asked the state to establish custodial asylums for female mental defectives. The report also recommended better management, an improved dietary plan, and the extension of self-government and recreation. Managers' best hopes rested on a new farm they had secured to offer more outdoor work, and on the nearby Laboratory of Social Hygiene, with its unit for psychopathic women.[55]

Whatever improvements these recommendations brought proved insufficient to restore the reformatory. By 1919 a new investigation reported a "failure to solve the real difficult problems of the institution." The trial of a former inmate had exposed "cruel and unusual punishment," such as "stringing up" inmates with handcuffs and a form of water treatment. New charges of mismanagement were leveled, and the familiar issues of overcrowding and mentally defective inmates surfaced. The administration placed some of the blame on the closing of the Laboratory of Social Hygiene, which neither Rockefeller nor the state would fund after 1918.[56] After its closure Bedford Hills had to contend with a new set of problems, the classification and treatment of women formerly handled by the laboratory.

By 1920 all efforts had largely failed. A combination of the closing of the laboratory, changes in inmate population, and revised probation and parole policies had undermined Bedford's innovations. The institution, the investigation concluded, "while serving in a very limited degree its original purpose, is in the main not a reformatory at all." Instead of the population of first offenders originally expected, their verdict continued, "the beneficent operation of the suspended sentence, probation laws and various social and religious movements have picked up from the courts a very large population of the accidental and even intentional first offenders. Young women are only sent to Bedford when . . . [they] could not be helped by probation. . . ."[57]

By 1919, the reformatory population at Bedford Hills consisted largely of recidivists (100 out of 167 inmates). About 75 percent of the prisoners were prostitutes, 70 percent had venereal disease, a majority were of low mentality, a significant minority needed custodial care, and 10 percent were psychopathic. With a "heterogeneous population largely drawn from the lowest strata of New York City life," Bedford Hills could no longer be the showcase that Katharine Davis had envisioned and struggled to achieve.[58] The final blow to the ideals of women's prison reform came in 1921 when, for the first time in the history of the movement, the state appointed a man, psychiatrist Amos Baker, as superintendent at Bedford Hills.[59] If the Progressive response could have succeeded anywhere, Bedford Hills was the likely site. The failure of this most promising experiment in structural change and diversified training highlighted the irony of the new penology. The logic of environmentalism called for societal change, not institutionalization, to reduce crime. Instead, new, extrainstitutional criminal justice procedures were founded to prevent delinquency, and institutions were expected to rehabilitate those who slipped through its network. The two methods, however, did not work well together. Probation and parole left the reformatory with the most difficult inmates. Reformers like Katharine Davis struggled to reinvigorate reformatory treatment, but they waged a losing campaign. In the case of Bedford Hills, and in later years at the newer state farms and reformatories, no amount of internal reform could resolve the dilemmas presented by institutions of last resort.

Chapter 8

The Legacy of Women's Prison Reform: An Epilogue and Evaluation

> If the reformatory could speak for itself . . . It would tell you of how inadequately it had handled the purely reformatory problems without the necessary classification, of humiliating punishments meted out because of inadequate quarters and tools, of the nervous and physical strain on officers . . . of their lack of restful or encouraging living quarters, and their wretched pay,—it would bare its heart to you and ask you to put an end to such a farce as "Sherborn" has long been and not force upon her a further destructive step without giving her assistance.
>
> Jessie Hodder, 1918[1]

Women prison reformers of the Progressive era had been prepared to reject the separate sexual spheres, both in their own lives and in their approach to women inmates. Their theories of crime questioned female uniqueness and their ideal of diversified training implied that the workplace should be sexually integrated. The failures of the women's reformatories to implement these visions testifies to the resistance to changes in sexual ideology in the early twentieth century. Although women were in fact entering a formerly male world, as students, workers, and, after 1920, as voting citizens as well, they were at the same time bounded by new versions of old ideas. So too in the prisons, domestic science replaced domesticity and outdoor work supplemented the nursery, but these institutions could not transcend their legacy of "separate but equal." Despite the new life brought by Progressive reformers, women's prisons, like other American institutions, would continue to reinforce sexual difference and sexual inequality.

The Triumph of Differential Treatment, 1915–30

By the end of the Progressive era, women's prisons were becoming a standard feature of the American criminal justice system. De-

143

spite the problems of the nineteenth-century institutions and the failures acknowledged by Progressives like Jessie Hodder, most reformers still believed that the separation of women prisoners would improve correctional treatment. After 1915 a host of organizations called for more women's prisons. The National Committee on Prisons and Prison Labor, the New York Prison Survey, and the Chicago Crime Commission all advocated women's prisons, as did individuals ranging from radical Kate Richards O'Hare to prison reformer Thomas Mott Osborne.[2] A dozen state reformatories for women opened over the next decades. By 1940 a total of twenty-three states had established separate women's prisons, and by 1975 only sixteen states lacked them (table 6). In the meantime, the first federal women's prison opened in 1927.

TABLE 6. State and Federal Correctional Institutions for Women, 1873–1975

State	Title at Opening	Date of Opening
Indiana	Woman's Prison	1873
Massachusetts	Reformatory Prison for Women	1877
New York	House of Refuge for Women, Hudson	1887
New York	House of Refuge for Women, Albion	1893
New York	Reformatory Prison for Women, Bedford Hills	1902
New Jersey	State Reformatory for Women	1913
Maine	Reformatory for Women	1916
Ohio	Reformatory for Women	1916
Kansas	State Industrial Farm for Women	1917
Michigan	State Training School for Women	1917
Connecticut	State Farm for Women	1918
Iowa	Women's Reformatory	1918
Arkansas	State Farm for Women	1920
California	Industrial Farm for Women	1920
Minnesota	State Reformatory for Women	1920
Nebraska	State Reformatory for Women	1920
Pennsylvania	State Industrial Home for Women	1920
Wisconsin	Industrial Home for Women	1921
United States	Industrial Institution for Women (now Federal Reformatory for Women)	1927
Delaware	Correctional Institution for Women	1929

TABLE 6 —*Continued*

State	Title at Opening	Date of Opening
Connecticut	Correctional Institution for Women	1930
Illinois	State Reformatory for Women	1930
Virginia	State Industrial Farm for Women	1932
North Carolina	Correctional Center for Women	1934
California	California Institution for Women	1936
Kentucky	Correctional Institution for Women	1938
South Carolina	Harbison Correctional Institution for Women	1938
Maryland	Correctional Institution for Women	1940
Alabama	Julia Tutwiler Prison for Women	1942
West Virginia	State Prison for Women	1948
Puerto Rico	Industrial School for Women	1954
Georgia	Rehabilitation Center for Women	1957
Missouri	State Correctional Center for Women	1960
Louisiana	Correctional Institute for Women	1961
Ohio	Women's Correctional Institution	1963
Nevada	Women's Correctional Center	1964
Oregon	Women's Correctional Center	1965
Tennessee	Prison for Women	1966
Colorado	Women's Correctional Institute	1968
Washington	Purdy Treatment Center for Women	1970
Oklahoma	Women's Treatment Facility	1973
South Carolina	Women's Correctional Center	1973

Sources: Helen W. Rogers, "A Digest of Laws Establishing Reformatories for Women in the United States," *Journal of Criminal Law and Criminology*, 13 (November 1922): 382–437; and American Correctional Association, *Directory 1977: Juvenile and Adult Correctional Institutions and Agencies* (Washington, D.C.: American Correctional Association, 1977).

Note: Women's divisions of mixed prisons are not included.

The initial impetus for a federal institution came in the years immediately after World War I, when the number of women imprisoned for federal offenses more than doubled as a result of the Harrison Act (1914), which outlawed narcotics; the Volstead Act (1919), which implemented prohibition; and the Jones-Miller Act (1922), which made automobile theft a federal offense. The state prisons that had previously housed these women began to refuse them or to raise their boarding rates. With the support of Assistant

U.S. Attorney General Mabel Walker Willebrandt, Congress began hearings on the establishment of a women's reformatory. In 1923 representatives from almost every major national women's organization convened in Washington and issued a set of recommendations for the new institution. Congress approved legislation based on their plan in 1924. In 1927 the cottage-style reformatory opened on a 500-acre campus in rural Alderson, West Virginia. Women managers and staff supervised domestic, industrial, and outdoor work. In a fitting tribute to a half-century of women's prison reform, buildings were named for Elizabeth Fry, Katharine Davis, Jane Addams, and other prison and social reformers.[3]

Women's prisons continued to appeal to reformers, despite the inability of the first institutions to live up to their founders' ideals, in large part because there were so few alternatives. Those who opposed women's prisons entirely favored more punitive measures in traditional penal institutions.[4] Other critics, such as Jessie Hodder, asked for assistance to improve the reformatory, but not to abolish it.[5] Even former prisoner and socialist organizer Kate Richards O'Hare, who concluded in 1920 that "Every existing prison should be abandoned as soon as possible," merely proposed that they be "replaced with hospitals and prison farms and small industries." Every women's prison department, she wrote, "should be separated from the men" and placed on farms according to the cottage system.[6] O'Hare and others believed that, when compared to sexually mixed jails or men's penitentiaries, the women's institutions were relatively successful. Their rural settings, cottages, and private rooms seemed much more palatable than the stone walls, iron gates, gun towers, and cell blocks typical of men's prisons.

Besides having continued support from reformers, women's prisons gained acceptance because they began to perform a new function, one very different from the individual regeneration intended by the earliest reformers. If Progressivism had two spirits, one of uplift and one of social control, it was the latter that lived on in the years after the Armistice in new efforts to repress vice by isolating and punishing its victims. During and after World War I, for instance, women's prisons incarcerated prostitutes rounded up under the auspices of the Committee on Training Camp Activities. In the 1920s and 1930s the reformatories received women convicted for alcohol and narcotics offenses under the Volstead and Harrison Acts.[7] The purpose of imprisoning these women, one reformer noted in 1922, "emphasized the old conception of the self-preservation of society" rather than the reformation of the individual.[8]

The treatment of prostitutes during the war illustrates this shift. In the late nineteenth and early twentieth centuries, the concept of woman as victim had inspired sympathetic treatment of prostitutes. After 1917, however, a resurgence of antiprostitution activity unleashed deeply held fears of the harlot as a threat to society. The wartime program did not seek to regenerate the fallen woman as had women prison reformers; its goal was rather the protection of American men from venereal disease. Patriotism motivated this national campaign, as an officer of the Sanitary Corps explained: "The struggle for the principles of democracy demands . . . manpower, and woman-power. The greatest destroyer of man-power . . . is venereal disease. The greatest source of venereal disease has been prostitution. . . . For military efficiency,—and for social welfare,—prostitution must go."[9]

Strict enforcement of antiprostitution laws during the war included closing red-light districts and hiring vice agents to arrest potential carriers of venereal disease. As a result, courts sent thousands of women to local jails and state reformatories. This new inmate population necessitated a program to build and expand women's prisons. Between 1918 and 1920, the United States government appropriated over $400,000 for "construction, enlargement, repair, or equipment of reformatories . . . for . . . delinquent women and girls." Of the forty-three institutions thus aided, at least sixteen remained in operation after 1920.[10]

Although usually operated by women, these new institutions abandoned most of the benevolent features of earlier women's reform. Sympathy for the fallen woman as victim declined as even some women reformers, such as program director Martha Falconer, justified their work as a way to "protect our men against prostitutes."[11] The government's official report calculated the cost benefits in terms of soldiers' health, not women's: detention cost only eleven cents per prevented sexual encounter (and potential venereal exposure), compared to an estimated seven dollars to treat an infected soldier.[12] Unlike Progressive-era reformers, the government administrators also found it necessary to "erect barbed-wire fences around the premises, to employ guards or watchmen, or resort to both expedients."[13]

The incarceration of prostitutes during the war, and of both alcoholics and narcotics addicts in the next decade, continued to transform the reformatory populations, a process which had begun well before the Progressive era. Instead of young and first offenders, women with serious medical and social problems now filled the institutions. In addition, the racial balance of the once predominantly white reformatories shifted due to the postwar acceleration of the black migration north. Black female prisoners usually lived in segregated cottages under the control of white staff. For this group, too, incarceration was used to control rather than restore. Thus the reformatories increasingly housed those women perceived by the society as the most dangerous, not the most hopeful, cases.

To some extent, then, the women's institutions became a standard feature of American penology by adopting the same practices that characterized the rest of the system in the twentieth century: incarcerating "hard-core" criminals and blacks as a means of isolating deviants and deterring crime. But at the same time the reformatories tried to maintain the distinctive feminine treatment which had justified their establishment in the nineteenth century. The women's prisons built after World War I incorporated the concept of feminine reform in their designs and the training they offered, creating what has been called a "dual system"[14] of corrections, one male and one female.

The legal sanction for the two systems emerged by 1920, notably in a 1919 Kansas decision, *State* v. *Heitman*, which permitted separate sentencing policies for each sex. Women, the judges argued, were the more reformable sex and could legally receive maximum indeterminate sentences at a state industrial farm, while comparable male offenders served shorter terms in local jails. The justification that male and female criminality presented two different problems was reminiscent of the United States Supreme Court's 1908 decision in *Muller* v. *Oregon*, which permitted state protective legislation for women workers. In 1920 the Kansas court declared, for instance, that: "Woman enters spheres of sensation, perception, emotion, desire, knowledge and experience, of an intensity and of a kind which men cannot know . . . the result is a feminine type radically different from the masculine type, which demands special consideration in the study and treatment of non-conformity to law."[15] Longer sentences that allowed more time for rehabilitation fell into the category of "special consideration," as did separate, less austere, institutions, like state farms, industrial schools, or reformatories.

The states that established women's prisons in the twentieth century perpetuated the ideal of a feminine institutional environment. Cottage systems and large, rural campuses predominated. The Federal Industrial Institution for Women adopted this plan in order to meet the special needs of female inmates, as its first superintendent, Mary Belle Harris, explained: "In women's institutions this breaking up of the large group into smaller housekeeping units we believe is the ideal, affording as it does greater opportunity for training in homemaking."[16] Other unique features that differentiated the women's prisons included less-stringent security provisions; private rooms rather than cell blocks; the right of prisoners to decorate their surroundings; less rigid clothing rules; and higher staff-inmate ratios.[17]

The most important remnants of differential treatment were the training programs offered to women inmates. Periodically, official reports called for the rejection of domestic chores and the adoption of industrial programs. The 1920 New York Prison Survey, for instance, termed the domestic training in women's prisons mere "busy work" and recommended "dual training" for homemaking and vocations. "We are likely to ignore the fact that women have vocational careers," the report admitted. "The State has no more right to exploit the time, energy, and latent ability of women prisoners than it has of male inmates."[18] Therefore they suggested that "Bedford and Albion be made strong industrial training centers and expand beyond the present conception of training women for duties related to the household."[19]

As in the past, such pleas had little effect. Training for employable skills in women's prisons remained "wholly inadequate," according to a 1927 survey made by the National Committee on Prisons and Prison Labor. It, too, recommended that the reformatories adopt new programs "to provide a woman with the skill which will find her a job when she leaves the institution." But the authors of this report revealed deep-seated sexual stereotyping of vocations when they rejected skill after skill for inclusion in women's prison workshops. Of industries in which women already constituted over half of the work force, they rejected 85 percent for "the most obvious" reasons. For example: ammunition was "psychologically wrong"; "printing is a man's industry"; dental goods require "too much skill and application"; pottery required too many men; tobacco was "inadvisable for women's institutions." Instead they relied on the traditional standbys of household work, power sewing, laundering, and farming because, they explained, "before the industrial revolution, women carried [these activities] on in the home and on the home farm."[20]

Official reports and reformers' private writings repeatedly called for more useful training and repeatedly met resistance.[21] When in 1923 a congressional committee suggested industrial training for the new federal women's reformatory, the United States superintendent of prisons responded by defending differential treatment:

> I have never known of the building of factories for women offenders, and the care you give to women prisoners is vastly different from the care you give the men and the kind of training you give them is different. You have to train them as individuals in a sense that you do not deal with men prisoners. We will never have factories for women offenders. You would object to them and all of the women of the country would object to them.[22]

Not surprisingly, the Federal Industrial Institution for Women, despite its name, concentrated on traditional women's work. Home-hygiene classes offered by the Red Cross, office work, and farming predominated. ("The care of helpless animals is work that appeals particularly to women," prison superintendent Harris once wrote.) Alderson originally offered only one factory skill, power sewing.[23]

This retreat from Progressives' efforts to reinvigorate women's prisons with diversified training occurred during a period of reaction to reform in general and to feminism in particular. Progressivism diminished in the face of postwar "normalcy" and the repression of radicalism. Furthermore, the women's movement, weakened by external pressures and internal conflicts over political strategies, could not provide a supportive climate for women's reform activities. Like the young women coming of age in the postsuffrage period, the inmates of women's prisons suffered from the societal pressure for conformity to a new stereotype of femininity.[24]

The prison reformers, too, faced opposition to their roles as new women. After several decades of expanding public authority for women, the 1920s witnessed a leveling off of professional opportunities.[25] Although women continued to work in separate prisons and to study female criminals, their influence on the prison system, outside of the field of juvenile justice, was minimal.[26] Jessie Hodder, who remained at Framingham until her death in 1931, could not implement her Progressive reforms. In New York and Indiana no outstanding reformers or administrators even attempted to revitalize women's prisons.

The fate of Ann Vickers, a fictional prison reformer created by Sinclair Lewis in 1933, suggests the cultural forces at work during the 1920s. A suffragist, social worker, superintendent of a model women's prison, and author of a book on vocational training in women's reformatories, Vickers is the prototype of the Progressive female penologist. Her first marriage disintegrates as a result of her conflicts between career and womanhood. But Lewis resolves this dilemma by having Vickers sacrifice her work in order to marry a judge, move to a suburban cottage, and bear a child. Glowing with maternal and conjugal pride, Ann tells her husband in the concluding passage that "You, you and Mat," their son, "have brought me out of the prison, . . . the prison of ambition, the prison of desire for praise, the prison of myself. We're out of prison!"[27]

By the 1930s separate women's prisons had become acceptable to American penology by conforming to the values of both traditional prisons and contemporary sexual stereotypes. Although Progressive criminologists had attempted to drop sexual distinctions and diversify training, the backlash of the postwar era, along with the inherent contradictions of feminine prisons, combined to defeat their efforts. Like the suffrage victory of 1920, the success of the women's prison movement testified to the ability of American institutions to accommodate reform for conservative ends much more than it signaled a triumph for women's progress.

The Impact on Women Prisoners

For a century, small groups of middle-class American women sought to improve the treatment of female prisoners. Their major contribution, the separate women's prisons, has influenced inmates' lives from the 1870s to the present. In many ways, prisoners benefited from reformers' efforts to change attitudes toward fallen women and to provide more humane penal environments. At the same time, however, the differential treatment that originally justified the establishment of women's prisons perpetuated sexual inequalities. An evaluation of contemporary women's prisons illustrates this dual legacy.

The most widely adopted theory of women's prison reform was that female inmates should be housed separately from men, both to prevent sexual abuse and to alleviate overcrowding in inadequate women's quarters. This stipulation was met not only by the separate women's prisons but also by new departments for women at older state institutions and in city and county jails.

Sexual segregation has made incarceration less oppressive in many ways. With few exceptions, separate prisons prevent men's abuse of female prisoners, while in mixed institutions, rape and harassment continue to the present, as the case of Joann Little brought to public attention.[28] Separating women under female guards has not only eliminated the fear of attack; it has also lifted many of the constraints imposed on women to deter heterosexual contact between prisoners. Formerly in mixed prisons women could not circulate where men might view them. When Kate Richards O'Hare served time at the Missouri state penitentiary during World War I, the windows had been covered over with gray paint, excluding all natural light, "to prevent the women flirting with the men on the other side of the wall."[29] Women's prisons require no such barriers and allow more freedom of movement within and between buildings.

Sexually segregated prisons have freed women from some exploitation of their labor. In mixed prisons, Jessie Hodder once wrote, "It is not humanly possible to avoid making women subservient to men so it results that women prisoners treated on this principle major in mending, washing, ironing and sewing for men prisoners."[30] The domestic work women prisoners continue to engage in is at least for themselves, not for male inmates. Furthermore, the absence of men requires that women perform a variety of tasks, including farming, carpentry, and painting.

Finally, the centralization of several hundred women from throughout a state into one institution has created some social and economic benefits. Inmates can enjoy the companionship of other women to a degree impossible when only a handful of women served at each predominantly male prison. Equally important for the large number of prisoners who are mothers has been the availability of nurseries, or of cottages for women with infants, at some women's prisons. In mixed institutions, female inmates continue to suffer the additional punishment of being separated from their young children. Centralization also has allowed a greater range of vocational training, for at men's prisons all women must do whatever single task is assigned to their small group.

Women's prisons, then, can potentially improve the treatment of female inmates. The reforms which grew from sexual segregation, particularly the elimination of constant sexual vulnerability, were impossible within male-dominated institutions. That many of the shortcomings of the separate prisons were due to lack of cooperation or funding from state officials suggests that these prisons could have come closer to fulfilling reformers' goals. Moreover, many of the worst features in the historical record can be attributed to the contradiction inherent in "prison reform"—a term that implies that an institution designed to deny individual liberty can be made more palatable.

Nevertheless, sexually segregated prisons have left unresolved many of the problems reformers identified in the past and have never addressed many others. Sexual segregation has not necessarily alleviated the sexual tensions of prison life. Until very recently, neither male nor female inmates had access to heterosexual partners and officials diligently suppressed homosexual relationships between women inmates. The original women prison reformers, Victorians who were eager to uplift the fallen from sexual degradation, could not conceive of women prisoners having legitimate sexual needs. In the twentieth century a few reformers recognized the problem. Katharine Bement Davis seems to have tolerated lesbian relations at Bedford Hills, although subsequent officials reversed her policy. Kate Richards O'Hare recommended in 1923 that inmates be permitted to meet with their spouses, but her unique suggestion rested upon a condemnation of all homosexual activity.[31]

Women's prisons haven't eliminated the problem of overcrowding that has plagued mixed institutions as well. At some time in the history of each prison, overcommitment from the courts or underappropriation from the legislatures has created population pressures that have undermined prison functioning. Judges have tended to sentence female offenders to the few "good places" available, without considering which women were the best subjects for reformatory treatment. Thus the women's prisons often became "dumping grounds" for the courts, which forced them to provide custodial care from which few inmates could benefit.[32]

The difficulties of classifying inmates have also plagued women's prisons. Because sex is the primary criterion for commitment, it has been difficult to provide specialized treatment on other grounds. Almost every state maintains a variety of institutions for men, depending on age, offense, and previous record. A young male misdemeanant could serve in an institution with similar offenders. A young woman, though, must enter a reformatory which houses all types of women offenders. She is treated there as a woman, not as a misdemeanant, youth, or recidivist.

The legacy of differential, feminine care has placed other limitations on female prisoners. On the one hand, the rural settings, less-stringent security provisions, and the private rooms and cottages of women's reformatories have allowed female inmates to enjoy more comfortable surroundings than male prisoners. But at the same time, differential treatment has narrowed the opportunities for women prisoners by channeling all inmates into sexually stereotyped programs for character development or job training. The training programs available to women prisoners from the founding of the institutions to the present have reinforced the economic disadvantages that some reformers blamed for causing female criminality. In spite of Progressives' effort to deemphasize domesticity, it has remained the core of reformatory training during most of the twentieth century. Eventually some new skills were introduced, and by 1970 women inmates could learn clerical work, beauty care, and key punching—all sexually segregated, low-status, poorly paid women's jobs. While men's prisons offer training for the higher-paying, male-stereotyped skills—auto mechanics, electronics, welding, and machine repair—two industrial jobs have predominated at the women's prisons—garment making and laundry.[33]

Differential treatment has also resulted in other, less-tangible forms of discrimination, including the imposition of demeaning stereotypes of feminine behavior. From the founding of the first homes for discharged prisoners, through the family-style reformatory systems, to present-day correctional institutions, women prisoners have been forced to play the parts of children. Just as some superintendents in the past called their charges "the girls," so later prison personnel have continued to view inmates "as being weak, like children," and have treated them accordingly. In all of the early institutions staff used first names in addressing prisoners, who had to use the officers' appropriate titles. The Progressives tried to modify these and other older practices, for example by introducing inmate self-government and allowing prisoners more responsibility and freedom of movement. But the older attitudes have persisted. As one inmate told an interviewer in the 1970s, "They think we're four years old. They think we can't think for ourselves."[34]

The historical link between juvenile reformatories and women's prisons no doubt has encouraged similar attitudes. Women's institutions were modeled on the same domestic structures as became popular for juvenile offenders in the mid-nineteenth century. The similarity in names (house of refuge, industrial school, state farm) has further cemented the parallel. But beneath all of these circumstances has lain the paternalistic view that women and children are inherently dependent, while men, even when incarcerated, retain a degree of adult status.[35]

When nineteenth-century women first crossed the boundary between the pure and the fallen, they revealed their strong identification as a sexual class. In the separate prisons they established, however, the boundary between keepers and prisoners, one based on both class and power relations, revealed the tensions in the ideology of sisterhood. After the 1920s, the women who administered prisons had neither the belief in a common womanhood nor the critical approach to men's prisons that characterized earlier reformers. The separate prisons, though run by women, no longer existed to serve women. Rather, they supported the male-dominated prison system and adopted its values.

This history of accommodation to the larger penal system may help to explain why the nineteenth-century separate-but-equal ideology has proved to be so resilient. Granting women authority over institutions that housed their sex gave only limited power to a few women. Separate but equal thus helped maintain both the sexual status quo and the legitimacy of the prison system as a whole. The risk that women would transform the institutions was slight, for prisons had as much influence over reformers as reformers had over institutions. Thus, despite feminine training programs and rural environments, women's reformatories always reverted to traditional methods of prison discipline. Even during the Progressive experiments with less-feminine or authoritarian treatment, the underlying purposes of the prison—the isolation and control of criminals—reasserted themselves. Separate women's institutions that did not question the nature of the prison system proved to be equal to men's institutions primarily in their usefulness in maintaining that system.

The feminist movement of the 1960s and 1970s launched an ideological and political attack on the principle of separate but equal. As a result, for the first time in almost a century, the legitimacy of separate women's prisons has been called into question. Feminists have exposed the inequalities of feminine training and of longer sentences for women prisoners. New advocates of equality, however, do not seek to extend the hardships of men's prisons to women. Rather, radical feminists of the late twentieth century prefer to end the imprisonment of women.[36]

As in the past, women's ideas about female crime influence their models of treatment. Earlier reformers had either an individualist or environmental approach to criminality. Thus, they wanted to uplift the individual fallen woman and make the prison environment more conducive to her rehabilitation. Progressive reformers favored social services to prevent women from entering a life of crime. Contemporary feminists have extended the Progressives' social analysis to its logical, political conclusion: eliminate societal racism and sexism, allow economic and sexual autonomy for all women, and women's prisons will no longer be necessary.[37]

Short of these long-range goals, contemporary reformers seek to minimize the incarceration of women and to expose abuses in women's as well as men's institutions. Both women and men have called for the decriminalization of victimless crimes, such as prostitution and drug use, for which many women serve in prison. Feminists have rediscovered the traditional problems faced by women prisoners and added new concerns to those of the nineteenth-century reformers. As one group explains its focus on women in prison:

> there are problems special to women in prison, as distinguished from the oppression faced by all those in prison: the presence and physical threat of male guards, the overall sexism of the prison system, the lack of specialized training which leads to fewer available jobs, the tragedy of mothers separated from their children, the assault on the women's reproductive organs, and much more.[38]

In response to these problems, feminists have attempted to open new lines of communication with "sisters inside." Through the feminist media and innovative legal projects, women outside the prison system serve as advocates for inmates in their legal appeals, child custody conflicts, parole hearings, and disciplinary complaints.[39]

At the same time that feminists have initiated these new, noninstitutional reforms, the prison system has offered its own reform measures. In response to criticisms of both women's and men's institutions, several states have begun to reverse the century-long trend of separate women's prisons. In 1973, the Framingham, Massachusetts, women's reformatory admitted its first male inmates, and other institutions have since joined in the reintegration of the dual prison system. Moreover, gender is ceasing to be a qualification for prison staff. Despite resistance from male guards, women have become guards and wardens at men's prisons. By the same process, men have become superintendents of the Framingham and Alderson women's reformatories and male guards have been working at Bedford Hills.[40]

Sexual reintegration has yet to prove of great benefit to women inmates. At Bedford Hills, for instance, prisoners brought suit to protest the invasion of their privacy by male guards.[41] Their complaints echo those of nineteenth-century reformers, but significantly, it is now inmates themselves who are demanding an end to male surveillance. Reintegration has not necessarily ended discriminatory training programs, although some traditionally male skills, such as auto mechanics, have been introduced for a small number of women. Thus far, "coed prisons" seem most useful in maintaining discipline in men's institutions, for the promise of transfer to a women's prison offers an incentive to good behavior. Furthermore, coeducation as a reform may only divert attention away from the serious problems that were exposed by prisoner rebellions during the 1970s, rebellions that occurred not only at Attica, but at Alderson as well.[42]

Whatever the shortcomings of the institutions they created, earlier women's prison reformers had clear insight into the dangers of male-dominated institutions. Many of the hostile attitudes toward female criminals that they identified a hundred years ago persist today throughout the society. The stigma of woman's fall may be less critical, but the fact that most women prisoners are now not only poor but also non-white compounds their powerlessness. The old reformist concern for women's victimization has new foundations that necessitate continued scrutiny of the criminal justice system.

As long as police harass prostitutes and ignore their customers; as long as courts administer sexist justice to third-world women and women who defend themselves from sexual violence; and as long as mixed prisons continue to foster the sexual exploitation of women, then so long should women's prison reform continue. Feminist monitoring of police and court practices, and even the maintenance of single-sex prisons, may continue to serve the best interests of women inmates. Only when women have achieved full equality under the law will the movement begun by Elizabeth Fry become obsolete. At that time, "their sisters' keepers" can cease their watch.

Appendices

Appendix A. New York Criminal Conviction Rates, 1830–1900

Five Year Period	Courts of Record		Courts of Special Sessions				Sum of All Courts		Percentage Change	
			County		City					
	Male	Female	Male	Female	Male	Female	Male	Female	Male	Female
1828–32	166.72	13.97								
1833–37	150.35	10.28								
1838–42	165.06	13.83	297.74	49.34	131.83	35.60	594.63	98.77		
1843–47	164.52	9.21	324.45	55.63	189.09	41.17	678.06	106.01	+14.03	+7.33
1848–52	145.33	8.89	332.66	52.20	267.74	65.10	745.73	126.19	+9.98	+19.04
1853–57	142.57	9.50	477.78	97.10	544.74	230.60	1165.09	337.20	+56.23	+167.22
1858–62	137.23	12.75	678.76	174.41	1376.17	905.20	2192.16	1092.36	+88.15	+223.95
1863–67	143.80	16.09	663.18	211.97	1819.65	1126.93	2626.63	1354.99	+19.82	+24.04
1868–72	153.57	10.38	1176.49	238.68	2228.72	1281.98	3558.78	1531.04	+35.49	+12.99
1873–77	208.64	12.86	1717.63	356.23	2492.57	1157.87	4418.84	1526.96	+24.17	–.27
1878–82	176.79	9.32	1464.19	309.90	2857.92	1187.55	4498.90	1506.77	+1.81	–1.32
1883–87	134.63	7.29	2846.71	655.70	2944.64	1151.24	5925.98	1814.23	+31.72	+20.41
1888–92	150.09	7.08	2729.30	449.82	2594.58	965.75	5473.97	1422.65	–7.63	–21.58
1893–97	155.43	8.06	2599.69	292.00	2785.17	1015.83	5540.29	1315.89	+1.21	–7.50
1898–1902	137.07	8.13								

Source: New York Secretary of State, *Convictions for Criminal Offenses, 1830–1899.*

Note: Figures represent five year average conviction rates per 100,000 adults.

Appendix B.   Personal Backgrounds of Nineteenth and Twentieth Century Prison Reformers

Nineteenth Century Reformer	Lifespan; Birthplace; Religion	Highest Educational Level[a]	Paid Work or Occupation
Barney, Susan Hammond	1830–? Mass. Methodist	?	
Barton, Clara Harlowe	1821–1912 North Oxford, Mass. Universalist	A	Teacher; nurse; government clerk
Chace, Elizabeth Buffum	1806–1909 Providence, R.I. Quaker	A	
Chickering, Hannah B.	1817–1877 Dedham, Mass. Unitarian/ Episcopalian	?	
Coffin, Rhoda M. Johnson	1826–1909 Xenia, Ohio Orthodox Quaker	A	Teacher
Collins, Rebecca	? ? Quaker	?	
Comstock, Elizabeth Leslie Rous (Wright)	1815–1891 England Quaker	A	Teacher; minister
Daniel, Annie Sturges	1858–1914 Buffalo, N.Y. Episcopalian	G*	Physician
Dix, Dorothea Lynde	1802–1887 Hampden, Maine Unitarian	A	Teacher; supervisor, Civil War nurses
Doremus, Sarah Platt Haines	1802–1877 New York City Presbyterian	(at home)	

a. A = Academy, public school, Friends school; C = College, normal school; G = graduate degrees: *M.D., †Ph.D., ‡Ll.B.

Prison Reform Activities	Other Reform or Political Activities	Family[b]
Prisoners' Aid Soc., R.I.	Missionary Soc.; officer, WCTU, R.I.	M (1854)
Superintendent, MRPW	Antislavery; nurse, Civil War; founder, Red Cross	S
Board of Lady Visitors, R.I.; police matrons movement	Antislavery; women's rights; woman suffrage; pacifism	M (1828) W (1870) 10/5
Prison visitor; founder, Dedham Asylum; MPC	Teacher, Sunday school	M W ?
Prison visitor; founder, Home for the Friendless, Richmond, Ind.; board of managers, IWP	Chicago Women's Club; kindergarten movement	M (1847) 6/5
Penn. Prison Assoc.; Friends Visiting Committee, Phila.		M (?) ? ?
Prison visitor and minister	Antislavery; temperance; pacifism; women's rights	M (1847) W (1850) 1/1 M (1858)
Physician, WPA; police matrons movement	Woman suffrage; working women's societies; N.Y. Tenement House Commission	S
Survey of jail and prison conditions, 1844	Reform for insane, founder, asylums	S
Prison visitor; director, WPA	N.Y. Tract and Mission Soc.; founder, Presbyterian Home for Aged Women and Woman's Hospital; Woman's Union Missionary Soc.; volunteer, Civil War	M (1821) 9/4

b. M = Married (date); S = Single; W = Widowed; D = Divorced or separated (date);
No. children born/No. children survived

Nineteenth Century Reformer	Lifespan; Birthplace; Religion	Highest Educational Level[a]	Paid Work or Occupation
Durant, Pauline Adeline Fowle	1832–1917 Alexandria, Va. Protestant	A	
Farnham, Eliza Woodson Burhams (Fitzpatrick)	1815–1864 Rensselaerville, N.Y. Quaker/atheist	A	Matron; writer; nurse
Felton, Rebecca Ann Latimer	1835–1930 DeKalb County, Ga. Methodist	C	Educator; writer
Fuller, Margaret Sarah (Ossoli)	1810–1850 Mass. (Transcendentalist)	A	Teacher; writer; journalist
Gibbons, Abigail Hopper	1810–1893 Philadelphia, Pa. Quaker	A	Teacher
Gilbert, Linda	1847–1895 Rochester, N.Y. Protestant(?)	A	Inventor
Hall, Emma Amelia	1837–1884 Lenawee County,Mich. Congregationalist	C	Teacher; matron
Hall-Brown, Lucy	1845–1907 Vt. ?	G*	Physician
Homans, Eliza Lee	?–1914 Boston, Mass. Protestant	?	
Johnson, Ellen Cheney	1829–1899 Athol, Mass. Protestant	A	Teacher; administrator

a. A = Academy, public school, Friends school; C = College, normal school; G = graduate degrees: *M.D., †Ph.D., ‡Ll.B.

Prison Reform Activities	Other Reform or Political Activities	Family[b]
Prison visitor; volunteer, Dedham Asylum; MPC	Cofounder, Wellesley College; pres., board of managers, YWCA	M (1853) W (1881) 2/0
Head matron, Sing Sing; phrenology advocate	Perkins Institute; nurse, Civil War	M (1836) W (1848) 3/1 M (1852) D (1852) 1/1
Founder, Ga. State Training School for Girls; WCTU prison reform committee; opponent of convict lease system	Temperance; Women's Board, Chicago Exposition and International Exposition; delegate, Progressive Party; delegate, Democratic Party; U.S. Senator (one day)	M (1853) W (1909) 5/1
WPA supporter	Antislavery; feminism	M (1848) 1/0
Prison visitor; WPA	Antislavery; pacifism; nurse, Civil War; pres., Committee for the Prevention of State Regulated Vice (social purity)	M (1833) 6/4
Prison visitor; Gilbert Library and Prisoners' Aid Fund; Home for Fallen Women (Chicago)	?	S
Matron, Detroit House of Shelter; director, Adrian Reform School for Girls	Presbyterian Home Mission; worker, Sunday school; missionary teacher, Indian school	S
Physician, MRPW	?	M (1891)
Mass. Prison Commission	Antisuffrage	M(?)
Dedham Asylum; MPC; superintendent, MRPW	Temperance; urban missionary; founder, New England Women's Auxiliary Assoc.	M (1849) W (1881) 0

b. M = Married (date);   S = Single;   W = Widowed;   D = Divorced or separated (date); No. children born/No. children survived

Nineteenth Century Reformer	Lifespan; Birthplace; Religion	Highest Educational Level[a]	Paid Work or Occupation
Kirkland, Caroline Matilda Stansbury	1801–1864 New York City Protestant	A	Teacher; writer; editor
Leeds, Deborah	? Philadelphia, Pa. Quaker	?	
Leonard, Clara	? Mass. ?	?	
Lowell, Josephine Shaw	1843–1905 West Roxbury, Mass. Unitarian	A	
Mosher, Eliza Maria	1846–1928 Cayuga County, N.Y. Orthodox Quaker	G*	Physician; professor; college dean
Palmer, Phoebe Worrall	1807–1884 New York City Methodist	?	Evangelist minister; religious author
Poor, Mary Pierce	1821–1912 New York City Unitarian	?	
Sedgewick, Catherine Maria	1789–1867 Stockbridge, Mass. Unitarian	A	Novelist; educator
Smith, Sarah	1814–1885 England Quaker	?	Minister

a. A = Academy, public school, Friends school; C = College, normal school; G = graduate degrees: *M.D., †Ph.D., †Ll.B,

Prison Reform Activities	Other Reform or Political Activities	Family[b]
Sec. and director, WPA	U.S. Sanitary Commission	M (1828) W (1846) 7/4
Prison visitor, Pa.; WCTU prison reform committee	Temperance; social purity	M (?) ?
Mass. Prison Commission; director, Home for the Friendless, Springfield, Mass.	Antisuffrage	M (?) ?
Police matrons movement; advocate, separate women's reformatories; member, board of managers, BH	Antislavery; U.S. Sanitary Commission; N.Y. Charity Organization Soc.; N.Y. Board of Charities; N.Y. State Aid Assoc.; Women's Municipal League, N.Y.C.; N.Y. Freedman's Relief Assoc.; Consumers' League	M (1863) W (1864) 1/1
Resident physician and superintendent, MRPW	Pres., Women's Medical Assoc. of N.Y. State; pres., Medical Women's National Assoc.; Amer. Social Hygiene League	S
Prison visitor and minister	Founder, Five Points Mission; sec., N.Y. Female Assistance Soc.	M (1827) 6/3
Prison visitor; volunteer, House of Industry; WPA; board of directors, Dedham Asylum; sec., League to Establish a Separate Reformatory for Women	Antislavery; temperance; antisuffrage	M (?) 4
Director, WPA		S
Prison visitor; founder, Home for the Friendless, Richmond, Ind.; superintendent, IWP	Nurse, Civil War	M (?) 3/3

b.   M = Married (date);   S = Single;   W = Widowed;   D = Divorced or separated (date); No. children born/No. children survived

Nineteenth Century Reformer	Lifespan; Birthplace; Religion	Highest Educational Level[a]	Paid Work or Occupation
Tutwiler, Julia Strudwick	1841–1916 Tuscaloosa, Ala. Presbyterian	C	Teacher; principal; college president

Twentieth Century Reformer	Lifespan; Birthplace; Religion	Highest Educational Level[a]	Paid Work or Occupation
Barnard, Kate	1875–1930 Geneva, Neb. Catholic (?)	A	Teacher; stenographer
Barrett, Kate Harwood Waller	1857–1925 Falsmouth, Va. ?	G*	Physician
Barrows, Katherine Isabel Hayes (Chapin)	1845–1913 Irasburg, Vt. Presbyterian	G*	Stenographer; secretary; ophthalmologist
Booth, Maud Ballington	1865–1948 England Anglican	A	
Bryant, Louise Stevens	1886–1956 France (Amer. parents) ?	G†	Social worker

a. A = Academy, public school, Friends school; C = College, normal school; G = graduate degrees: *M.D., †Ph.D., ‡Ll.B.

Prison Reform Activities	Other Reform or Political Activities	Family[b]
Chair, WCTU prison reform committee (Ala.); opponent, convict lease system; religious instruction for prisoners	Tuscaloosa Benevolent Assoc.; vocational education for women; kindergarten movement	S

Prison Reform Activities	Other Reform or Political Activities	Family[b]
Prison visitor; opponent of contract labor; matron, Provident Assoc. (Okla. City)	Organizer, Federal Labor Union; Commissioner of Charities and Corrections (Okla.; elected office)	S
Pastoral work with prostitutes; home for unwed mothers (Ga.); pres., Florence Crittenton Mission	Pres. and sec., Natl Council of Women; delegate, Internatl. Council of Women; WCTU; DAR; Amer. Legion Auxiliary; woman suffrage; delegate, Democratic party	M (1876) W (1896) 7/6
Inspector, women's prisons; official stenographer for APA and NCCC; delegate, Internatl. Prison Congress	Foreign missionary	M (1863) W (1864) M (1867) W (1909) 1/1
Founder, Volunteer Prison League; pres., APA women's division	Salvation Army; cofounder, Volunteers of America; woman suffrage	M (1886) W (1940) 2/2
Director, Dept. of Statistics and Records, Municipal Court, Phila.	Phila. Conference on Illegitimacy; sec., Natl. Committee on Maternal Health; sec., U.S. Hospital Fund; War Industries Board; sec., Girl Scouts of America	M (1909) D (?)

b.   M = Married (date);   S = Single;   W = Widowed;   D = Divorced or separated (date); No. children born/No. children survived

Twentieth Century Reformer	Lifespan; Birthplace; Religion	Highest Educational Level[a]	Paid Work or Occupation
Davis, Katharine Bement	1860–1935 Buffalo, N.Y. Episcopalian	G†	Teacher; social worker; administrator; author
Doty, Madeline Zabriskie	1877–1963 Bayonne, N.J. ?	G†‡	Lawyer
Falconer, Martha	1862–1941 Delaware, Ohio Quaker/Episcopalian	A	Social worker
Fernald, Mabel Ruth	1883–1952 ? ?	G†	Psychologist; professor
Harris, Mary Belle	1868–1957 Pa. Baptist	G†	Administrator
Hodder, Jessie Donaldson	1867–1931 Cincinnati, Ohio Episcopalian	A	Social worker

a. A = Academy, public school, Friends school;   C = College, normal school;   G = graduate degrees: *M.D., †Ph.D., ‡Ll.B.

Prison Reform Activities	Other Reform or Political Activities	Family[b]
Superintendent, BH; Commissioner of Corrections, N.Y.C.; chair, N.Y.C. Parole Board	Project director, World's Columbian Exposition; Women's City Club (N.Y.); director, St. Mary's Street College Settlement (Phila.); emergency earthquake relief (Sicily); officer, Natl. Amer. Woman Suffrage Assoc.	S
N.Y. Prison Reform Commission	Lawyer, Manhattan Children's Court; sec., Children's Court Committee, Russell Sage Foundation; sec., Women's Internatl. League for Peace and Freedom	M (1919) D (1935)
Probation officer, Cook County Juvenile Court (Chicago); staff member, Ill. Children's Home and Aid Soc.; superintendent, girls' division, House of Refuge (Phila.); director, Committee on Prostitution and Delinquent Girls, WWI	Teacher, Chicago Commons Settlement House; Chicago Women's Club; New Century Club; organizer, Phila. Training School for Social Work; director, American Social Hygiene Soc.; exec. sec., Federation of Protestant Welfare Agencies	M (1885) D (?) 3/3
Psychologist, Laboratory of Social Hygiene, BH	Director, psychology lab, Cincinnati public schools	S
Penal committee, Women's City Club, N.Y.; superintendent, Blackwell's Island city penitentiary (N.Y.); superintendent, Clinton Farms (N.J.); asst., War Dept. section on training camps; superintendent, Federal Industrial Institution for Women (Alderson, W. Va.); Pa. Board of Parole	Director, boy's club, Hull House; Consumer's League (Md.); Women's City Club (N.Y.); Amer. Assoc. of University Women; woman suffrage	S
Superintendent, MRPW; translator, guide, Internatl. Prison Congress (D.C.); delegate, Internatl. Prison Congress (London); National Crime Commission; Wickersham Commission on Law Observance and Enforcement	Matron, Lancaster Girls' School; counselor, Mass. General Hospital (unwed mothers)	M (common law) D 2/1

b. M = Married (date); S = Single; W = Widowed; D = Divorced or separated (date); No. children born/No. children survived

Twentieth Century Reformer	Lifespan; Birthplace; Religion	Highest Educational Level[a]	Paid Work or Occupation
Kellor, Frances Alice	1873–1952 Columbus, Ohio ?	G†‡	Sociologist; author; lawyer
Menken, Alice Davis	1870–1936 New York City Jewish	A	Community worker
Monahan, Florence	? Chicago Catholic	G‡	Teacher; lawyer
O'Hare, Kate Richards (Cunningham)	1877–1948 Ada, Kans. Disciples of Christ	C	Machinist; teacher; author; editor; organizer
O'Reilly, Mary Boyle	1873–1939 Boston, Mass. Catholic	A	Journalist; social worker

a. A = Academy, public school, Friends school;   C = College, normal school;   G = graduate degrees: *M.D., †Ph.D., ‡Ll.B.

Prison Reform Activities	Other Reform or Political Activities	Family[b]
Research on women prisoners; sec., N.Y. Probation Commission; Committee of Fourteen on the Social Evil (N.Y.)	Investigator of employment agencies for College Settlement (Chicago); sec., North American Civic League for Immigrants; chief investigator, Bureau of Industries and Immigration (N.Y.); chair, Progressive Service, Progressive Party; Natl. League for the Protection of Colored Women; Collegiate Equal Suffrage League; official, Amer. Arbitration Assoc.	S
Organizer, probation officers' committee for Jewish women in Women's Night Court, N.Y., founder, Jewish Big Sisters; trustee, Florence Crittenton League; member, board of managers, BH; trustee, George Junior Republics	Jewish Board of Guardians; pres., Shearith Israel sisterhood; WWI ambulance and hospital service; Mayor's Committee on Women on Natl. Defence; Natl. Council of Jewish Women; DAR; N.Y.C. Federation of Women's Clubs; Progressive Party; Women's Org. for Natl. Prohib. Reform	M (1892) W (1930) 1/1
Superintendent, Minn. Women's Reformatory; state board of parole (Minn.)	Woman suffrage; Children's Bureau (Minn.); League of Women Voters	S
Florence Crittenton mission (Kans.); prisoner, Missouri State Penitentiary (Espionage Act conviction, later pardoned); organizer, Children's Crusade 1922 (to release wartime prisoners); opponent, contract labor; asst. director, Calif. Dept. of Penology	Temperance; socialist organizer, writer and editor; workers' education; End Poverty in Calif.	M (1902) D (1928) M (1928) 4/4
Mass. Prison Commission	Founder, St. Elizabeth Settlement House, Boston; trustee, Mass. Dept. of Children's Inst.; relief work, WWI: Child Labor Investigation	S(?)

b. M = Married (date);   S = Single;   W = Widowed;   D = Divorced or separated (date); No. children born/No. children survived

Twentieth Century Reformer	Lifespan; Birthplace; Religion	Highest Educational Level[a]	Paid Work or Occupation
Rogers, Helen Worthington	1869–? Connecticut ?	C	Social worker
Spaulding, Edith	1881–? ? ?	G*	Physician
Weidensall, Clara Jean	? Omaha, Neb. ?	G†	Psychologist; college professor
Wittpenn, Caroline Bayard Stevens (Alexander)	1859–1932 Hoboken, N.J. Episcopalian	A	

a. A = Academy, public school, Friends school; C = College, normal school; G = graduate degrees: *M.D., †Ph.D., ‡Ll.B.

Sources of Nineteenth Century Prison Reformers:

Barney: Frances E. Willard and Mary A. Livermore, *A Woman of the Century* (Detroit: Gale Research Co., 1967), p. 56; Susan Hammond Barney, "Care of the Criminal," in *Woman's Work in America*, ed. Annie Nathan Meyer (New York: Henry Holt, 1891), p. 359.

Barton: Edward T. James and Janet Wilson James, eds., *Notable American Women, 1607–1950: A Biographical Dictionary*, 3 vols. (Cambridge, Mass.: The Belknap Press, 1971), 1:103–108 (hereafter cited as *NAW*).

Chace: Lillie Buffum Chace Wyman and Arthur Crawford Wyman, *Elizabeth Buffum Chace, 1806–1899: Her Life and Its Environment* (Boston: W. B. Clarke Co., 1914); Allen Johnson and Dumas Malone, eds., *Dictionary of American Biography*, 22 vols. (New York: Charles Scribner's Sons, 1930), 3:584 (hereafter cited as *DAB*); *NAW* 1:317–19.

Chickering: Sarah E. Dexter, *Recollections of Hannah Chickering* (Cambridge, Mass.: Riverside Press, 1881).

Coffin: Mary C. Johnson, *Rhoda Coffin: Her Reminiscences, Addresses, Papers and Ancestry* (New York: Grafton Press, 1910); Mary Coffin Johnson and Percival Brooks Coffin, *Charles F. Coffin: A Quaker Pioneer* (Richmond, Ind.: Nicholson Printing Co., 1923); Papers of Charles R. and Rhoda M. Coffin, Earlham College, Richmond, Ind.

Collins: Negley K. Teeters, *They Were in Prison: A History of the Pennsylvania Prison Society, 1787–1937* (Chicago: Pennsylvania Prison Society, 1937).

Prison Reform Activities	Other Reform or Political Activities	Family[b]
Probation officer, juvenile court (Conn.); cofounder and trustee, Conn. State Reformatory for Women	Supervisor, Children's Aid Society; woman suffrage	M (?) ?
Physician, Juvenile Psychopathic Institute (Chicago), MRPW, and BH; director, Psychopathic Hospital, BH	?	?
Juvenile Psychopathic Institute (Chicago); director, Laboratory of Social Hygiene, BH	Woman suffrage	M (?) ?
Probation officer, Hudson, N.J.; Commission to establish a separate state women's reformatory (N.J.); pres., board of managers, Clinton Farms, N.J.; delegate, Internatl. Prison Commission	State Charities Aid Assoc.; cofounder, pres., N.J. Conference of Social Work; woman suffrage; Democratic Natl. Committeewoman (N.J.)	M D (1895) M (1915) W (1931) 1/1

b. M = Married (date); S = Single; W = Widowed; D = Divorced or separated (date);
No. children born/No. children survived

Comstock: *DAB*, 4:331–32; *NAW*, 1:369–70.

Daniel: *NAW*, 1:429–31.

Dix: Willard and Livermore, *Woman of the Century*, 1:245–46; *NAW*, 1:486–89; *DAB* 5:323–25.

Doremus: *DAB*, 5:377–78; *NAW*, 1:500–1; *The National Cyclopaedia of American Biography*, 51 vols. (New York: James White and Co., 1898–1973), 6:166.

Durant: Boston *Transcript*, 13 February 1917; Florence Morse Kingsley, *The Life of Henry Fowle Durant* (New York: The Century Co., 1924); *DAB*, 5:541.

Farnham: W. David Lewis, introduction to M. B. Sampson and E. W. Farnham, *Rationale of Crime* (1846; reprint ed., Montclair, N.J.: Patterson Smith, 1973); *DAB*, 6:282; New York *Times*, 18 December 1864; *NAW*, 1:598–600.

Felton: Willard and Livermore, *Woman of the Century*, 1:286–87; *DAB*, 6:318; *NAW*, 1:606–07; New York *Times*, 25 January 1930.

Fuller: *NAW*, 1:678–82; *DAB*, 7:63–66.

Gibbons: Sarah Hopper Emerson, ed., *Life of Abby Hopper Gibbons, Told Chiefly through Her Correspondence* (New York: The Knickerbocker Press, 1897); *NAW*, 2:28–29; *DAB*, 7:237–38.

Gilbert: Willard and Livermore, *Woman of the Century*, 1:318; *DAB*, 7:271; *NAW*, 2:31–32.

Hall: *NAW*, 2:119–20; Zebulon Reed Brockway, *Fifty Years of Prison Service: An Autobiography* (New York: Charities Publication Committee, 1912), pp. 409–16.

Hall-Brown: Howard A. Kelley and Walter L. Burrage, eds., *Dictionary of American Medical Biography* (1928; reprint Boston: Melford House, 1971), p. 514.

Homans: Boston Evening *Transcript*, 20 July 1914.

Johnson: *NAW*, 2:277–79; John Howard Brown, ed., *Lamb's Biographical Dictionary of the United States* (Boston: James H. Lamb, 1900), 4:397; *DAB*, 10:98–99.

Kirkland: *NAW*, 2:337–39; *DAB*, 10:430–31.

Leeds: Papers of Josiah Leeds, Haverford College, Haverford, Pa.

Leonard: *Woman's Journal*, 28 February 1874, p. 65.

Lowell: William Rhinelander Stewart, *The Philanthropic Work of Josephine Shaw Lowell* (New York: Macmillan Co., 1911); *NAW*, 2:437–39; *DAB*, 11:467–68; New York *Times*, 13 October 1905.

Mosher: Florence Hazzard, "Heart of the Oak," manuscript biography in the Papers of Eliza Mosher, Bentley Historical Library, University of Michigan, Ann Arbor, Mich.; "A Woman Doctor Who 'Stuck It Out'", *Literary Digest*, 4 April 1926, pp. 66–70; *NAW*, 2:587–89; Jessie Hubbell Bancroft, "Eliza M. Mosher, M.D.," *Medical Woman's Journal* 32 (1925): 123–27.

Palmer: *NAW*, 2:12–14.

Poor: Papers of the Poor Family, Schlesinger Library, Radcliffe College, Cambridge, Mass.; Alfred D. Chandler, Jr., *Henry Varnum Poor: Business Editor, Analyst and Reformer* (Cambridge, Mass.: Harvard University Press, 1956); Boston *Transcript* 13 August 1912.

Sedgewick: Mary E. Dewey, ed., *Life and Letters of Catherine M. Sedgewick* (New York: Harper and Brothers, 1871); Willard and Livermore, *Woman of the Century*, 2:639; *DAB*, 16:547–48; *NAW*, 3:256–58; New York *Times*, 1 August 1867.

Smith: Johnson, *Rhoda Coffin*.

Tutwiler: *NAW*, 3:488–90; *DAB*, 19:77–78; Hilda Jane Zimmerman, "Penal Systems and Penal Reforms in the South since the Civil War," (Ph.D. diss., University of North Carolina, 1947).

Sources of Twentieth Century Prison Reformers:

Barnard: *NAW*, 1:90–92.

Barrett: Otto Wilson, *Life of Dr. Kate Waller Barrett* (1933; reprint ed., New York: Arno Press, 1974); *NAW*, 1:97–99.

Barrows: Madeleine B. Stern, *So Much in a Lifetime: The Story of Dr. Isabel Barrows* (New York: Julian Messner, Inc., 1964).

Booth: *NAW*, 1:208–10.

Bryant: *Who Was Who in America*, 3:116; New York *Times*, 31 August 1956.

Davis: *NAW*, 1:439–41; Mabel Jacques Eichel, "Katharine Bement Davis," *Woman's Journal* 13 (1928): 20–21, 41; New York *Times*, 11 December 1935, p. 23.

Doty: Durand Howes, ed., *American Women, 1935–1936* (Los Angeles: Richard Blank Publishing Co., 1935), p. 50; Doty, *Society's Misfits* (New York: The Century Co., 1916); New York *Times*, 16 October 1963, p. 45.

Falconer: *NAW*, 1:594–96; New York *Times*, 28 November 1941, p. 23; Emma O. Lundberg, "Pathfinders of the Middle Years," *Social Service Review* 21 (1947): 1–34.

Fernald: New York *Times*, 10 October 1952, p. 25; *School and Society* 76 (1952): 255.

Harris: Mary Belle Harris, *I Knew Them in Prison* (New York: Viking Press, 1942); New York *Times*, 23 February 1957, p. 17; Howes, *American Women*, p. 236.

Hodder: Papers of Jessie D. Hodder and Papers of Elizabeth Glendower Evans, Schlesinger Library; *NAW*, 2:197–99; New York *Times*, 20 November 1931, p. 23.

Kellor: *National Cyclopaedia*, 15:248 s.v. "Kellar"; "New York State to Protect Aliens," *Survey* 25 (1910): 171–72; *Arbitration Journal* 6 (1951): 194–95; New York *Times*, 5 January 1952, p. 11.

Menken: Papers of Alice Davis Menken, American Jewish Historical Society, Waltham, Mass.; New York *Times*, 24 March 1936.

Monahan: Florence Monahan, *Women in Crime* (New York: I. Washburn, 1941); Howes, *American Women*, 383.

O'Hare: *NAW*, 1:417–20 s.v. "Cunningham"; Jack M. Holl, introduction to *In Prison*, by Kate Richards O'Hare (Seattle: University of Washington Press, 1976).

O'Reilly: New York *Times*, 22 October 1939, p. 40; *Who Was Who in America*, 1:918.

Rogers: Helen Worthington Rogers, "A History of the Movement to Establish a State Reformatory for Women in Connecticut," *Journal of Criminal Law and Criminology* 19 (1929): 518–41; John William Leonard, ed., *Woman's Who's Who in America, 1914–1915* (New York: The American Commonwealth Co., 1914).

Spaulding: Papers of Jessie D. Hodder; Edith R. Spaulding, *An Experimental Study of Psychopathic Delinquent Women* (New York: Rand McNally and Co., 1923).

Weidensall: Leonard, *Woman's Who's Who*; Clara Jean Weidensall, *Studies in Rhythm* (Cincinnati: Bohnett and Co., 1916).

Wittpen: *NAW*, 3: 638–39; New York *Times*, 5 December 1932; Mary Ann Stillman Quarles, "Organizational Analysis of the New Jersey Reformatory for Women," (Ph.D. diss., Boston University, 1966), pp. 40–41.

Abbreviations

APA—American Prison Association

BH—Bedford Hills, N.Y., Reformatory

DAR—Daughters of the American Revolution

IWP—Indiana Woman's Prison

Mass. Bd. Char.—Massachusetts Board of State Charities

Mass. Bd. CP—Massachusetts Board of Commissioners of Prisons

MPC—Massachusetts Prison Commission

MRPW—Massachusetts Reformatory Prison for Women

NCCC—National Conference of Charities and Corrections

NY Bd. Char.—New York Board of Charities

NYPC—New York Commission of Prisons

NYSS—New York Secretary of State

PANY—Prison Association of New York

WCTU—Women's Christian Temperance Union

WPA—Women's Prison Association, New York City

Note: The complete titles of annual reports and conference proceedings appear in the bibliography. In the notes, the first reference to an annual report or conference proceeding gives the place and date of publication. Thereafter, the abbreviated title includes the year covered by the volume.

Notes

Introduction

1. Recorded by Sweet Honey in the Rock, copyright Flying Fish Music, 1976.

2. Gerda Lerner, "The Lady and the Mill Girl," *Mid-Continent American Studies Journal* 10 (Spring 1969): 5–15; Mary P. Ryan, *Womanhood in America: From Colonial Times to the Present* (New York: Franklin Watts, 1975), pp. 106–7; Barbara J. Berg, *The Remembered Gate: Origins of American Feminism, the Woman and the City, 1800–1860* (New York: Oxford University Press, 1978), esp. chap. 3; Barbara Ehrenreich and Deirdre English, *For Her Own Good: 150 Years of the Experts' Advice to Women* (Garden City, N.Y.: Anchor Press, 1978), esp. p. 9. For a general review of the historiography, see Barbara Sicherman, "American History," *Signs* 1 (Winter 1975): 461–85.

3. Daniel Scott Smith, "Family Limitation, Sexual Control and Domestic Feminism in Victorian America," in *Clio's Consciousness Raised: New Perspectives on the History of Women*, ed. Mary Hartman and Lois W. Banner (New York: Harper and Row, 1974), pp. 119–36; Carl Degler, "Revolution Without Ideology: The Changing Place of Women in America," in *The Woman in America*, ed. Robert Jay Lifton (Boston: Beacon Press, 1964), pp. 193–210; Kathryn Kish Sklar, *Catharine Beecher: A Study in American Domesticity* (New Haven: Yale University Press, 1973); Ann Douglas, *The Feminization of American Culture* (New York: Alfred A. Knopf, 1977).

4. Barbara Welter, "The Cult of True Womanhood, 1820–1860," *American Quarterly* 18 (Summer 1966): 150–74.

5. Nancy Cott, *The Bonds of Womanhood: "Woman's Sphere" in New England, 1780–1835* (New Haven: Yale University Press, 1977); Carroll Smith-Rosenberg, "The Female World of Love and Ritual: Relations between Women in Nineteenth-Century America," *Signs* 1 (Autumn 1975): 1–29; Mary Beth Norton, "The Paradox of 'Women's Sphere'," in *Women of America: A History*, ed. Carol Ruth Berkin and Mary Beth Norton (Boston: Houghton Mifflin, 1979), pp. 139–49; Estelle Freedman, "Separatism as Strategy: Female Institution Building and American Feminism, 1870–1930," *Feminist Studies* 5 (Fall 1979): 512–29.

6. On abolitionism and feminism, see: Blanche Glassman Hersh, *The Slavery of Sex: Feminist-Abolitionists in America* (Urbana, Ill.: University of Illinois Press, 1978); Alice Rossi, ed., *The Feminist Papers: From Adams*

to de Beauvoir (New York: Bantam Books, 1974), pp. 282–96: Gerda Lerner, *The Grimké Sisters from South Carolina: Pioneers for Women's Rights and Abolition* (New York: Schocken Books, 1971); Ellen Carol DuBois, *Feminism and Suffrage: The Emergence of an Independent Women's Movement in America, 1848–1869* (Ithaca: Cornell University Press, 1978), pp. 31–40.

7. Orlando F. Lewis, *The Development of American Prisons and Prison Customs, 1776–1845, with special reference to early institutions in the State of New York* (Albany: Prison Association of New York, 1922), p. 11.

8. David J. Rothman, *The Discovery of the Asylum: Social Order and Disorder in the New Republic* (Boston: Little, Brown and Co., 1971), p. 295.

Chapter 1

1. Society for the Prevention of Pauperism in the City of New York, *Second Annual Report of the Managers* (New York, 1820), pp. 32–33.

2. On the punishment of men and women in preindustrial Europe and colonial America, see: Michel Foucault, *Discipline and Punish: The Birth of the Prison*, trans. Alan Sheridan (New York: Pantheon Books, 1977), pt. 1; Christopher Hibbert, *The Roots of Evil: A Social History of Crime and Punishment* (Boston: Little, Brown and Co., 1963), pp. 5, 20, 29–30; Ann D. Smith, *Women in Prison: A Study in Penal Methods* (London: Stevens, 1962), pp. 55–62; David J. Rothman, *The Discovery of the Asylum: Social Order and Disorder in the New Republic* (Boston: Little, Brown and Co., 1971), chap. 2; Raphael Semmes, *Crime and Punishment in Early Maryland* (Baltimore: Johns Hopkins Press, 1938), pp. 128, 181–82; Julia Cherry Spruill, *Woman's Life and Work in the Southern Colonies* (Chapel Hill, N.C.: University of North Carolina Press, 1938), pp. 314–25, 334–39; Eli Faber, "The Evil That Men Do: Crime and Transgression in Colonial Massachusetts" (Ph.D. diss., Columbia University, 1974); Hugh F. Rankin, *Criminal Trial Proceedings in the General Court of Colonial Virginia* (Williamsburg, Va.: Colonial Williamsburg, 1965), pp. 136–38, 206; Mary Sumner Benson, *Women in Eighteenth-Century America: A Study of Opinion and Social Usage* (New York: Columbia University Press, 1935), p. 229.

3. Rothman, *Discovery of the Asylum*, pp. 59–62; Foucault, *Discipline and Punish*, pp. 73–103; Harry Elmer Barnes, *The Evolution of Penology in Pennsylvania: A Study in American Social History* (Indianapolis: Bobbs-Merrill Co., 1927), pp. 76–77; Georg Rusche and Otto Kirchheimer, *Punishment and Social Structure* (New York: Russell and Russell, 1967).

4. Orlando F. Lewis, *The Development of American Prisons and Prison Customs, 1776–1845, with special reference to early institutions in the State of New York* (Albany: Prison Association of New York, 1922); Blake McKelvey, *American Prisons: A Study in American Social History prior to 1915* (Chicago: University of Chicago Press, 1936), chap. 1, 2; Rothman, *Discov-*

ery of the Asylum, pp. 105–7; W. David Lewis, *From Newgate to Danne-mora: The Rise of the Penitentiary in New York, 1796–1848* (Ithaca: Cornell University Press, 1965), chap. 4.

5. Rothman, *Discovery of the Asylum*; Gerald N. Grob, *Mental Institutions in America: Social Policy to 1875* (New York: Free Press, 1973). At the time of this writing, Rothman's study of the later period of American institutional history had not yet appeared.

6. Michael B. Katz, "Origins of the Institutional State," *Marxist Perspectives* 1 (Winter 1978): 6–22; idem, *The Irony of Early School Reform: Educational Innovation in Mid-Nineteenth-Century Massachusetts* (Cambridge, Mass.: Harvard University Press, 1968). See also Rusche and Kirchheimer, *Punishment and Social Structure*.

7. Foucault, *Discipline and Punish*.

8. J. J. Tobias, *Urban Crime in Victorian England* (New York: Schocken Books, 1967), pp. 22, 35–40, 92; Louis Chevalier, *The Laboring Classes and the Dangerous Classes in Paris during the First Half of the Nineteenth Century*, trans. Frank Jellinek (New York: Howard Fertig, 1973), esp. pp. 48, 49, 61, 78, 136; Michelle Perrot, "Delinquency and the Penitentiary System in Nineteenth-Century France," in *Deviants and the Abandoned in French Society: Selections from the Annales, Economies, Societés, Civilisations*, ed. Robert Forster and Orest Ranum, trans. Elborg Forster and Patricia M. Ranum (Baltimore: Johns Hopkins University Press, 1978), p. 220; V. A. C. Gatrell and T. B. Hadden, "Criminal Statistics and Their Interpretation," in *Nineteenth Century Societies*, ed. E. A. Wrigley (Cambridge, England: Cambridge University Press, 1972), p. 353. On perceptions of an American dangerous class, see: John K. Alexander, "The City of Brotherly Fear: The Poor in Late-Eighteenth Century Philadelphia," in *Cities in American History*, ed. Kenneth T. Jackson and Stanley K. Schultz (New York: Alfred Knopf, 1972), p. 84; Steven L. Schlossman, "The 'Culture of Poverty' in Ante-Bellum Social Thought," *Science and Society* 38 (June 1974): 153; Eric H. Monkennon, *The Dangerous Class: Crime and Poverty in Columbus, Ohio, 1860–1885* (Cambridge, Mass.: Harvard University Press, 1975); Roger Lane, "Crime and Criminal Statistics in Nineteenth Century Massachusetts," *Journal of Social History* 2 (Winter 1968): 156–63 and idem, "Crime and the Industrial Revolution: British and American Views," *Journal of Social History* 7 (Spring 1974): 287–303. Lane contends that "serious" crime was decreasing in the nineteenth century but that "the total crime rate was rising" ("Crime and Criminal Statistics," p. 160).

9. The 1779 bill to establish penitentiaries in England was intended to establish separate institutions for each sex, but only one was built (Foucault, *Discipline and Punish*, p. 123). Peel's reform measure of 1823 called for the separation of women within the prison under the supervision of matrons (Smith, *Women in Prison*, p. 89).

10. Christopher Lasch, *The World of Nations: Reflections on American History, Politics and Culture* (New York: Alfred A. Knopf, 1973), pp. 3–17; Foucault, *Discipline and Punish*; Perrot, "Delinquency and the Penitentiary System," p. 214.

11. Gustave de Beaumont and Alexis de Tocqueville, *On the Penitentiary System in the United States, and its Application in France* (Philadelphia: Carey, Lea and Blanchard, 1833), pp. 252–53. The average ratio for white prisoners was 37.88; for blacks, 6.96.

12. Calculated from tables in J. D. B. DeBow, *Statistical View of the United States* (Washington, D.C., 1854), pp. 165, 167.

13. New York Secretary of State, *Report in Relation to Convictions for Criminal Offenses* and *Abstracts of Convictions for Criminal Offenses* (Albany, 1838–1900) (hereafter cited as NYSS, *Convictions for Criminal Offenses*). All rates and ratios in the following discussion have been calculated for age-specific as well as sex-specific groups by subtracting the number of males and females under age fifteen from the population figures. Population figures come from the U.S. Censuses, 1830 to 1900 and the New York State Censuses of 1835, 1845, 1855, and 1865. For the 1875 and 1885 New York populations, for which there were no state censuses, interpolations were made from standard growth rates. New York State is used because it provides the longest series of conviction statistics for the nineteenth century and figured prominently in both prison reform and women's prison reform.

14. NYSS, *Convictions for Criminal Offenses, 1838*, pp. 11–12.

15. NYSS, *Convictions for Criminal Offenses, 1842*, p. 2.

16. NYSS, *Convictions for Criminal Offenses, 1840–1900*; Michael Hindus, "The Social Context of Crime in Massachusetts and South Carolina, 1760–1873: Theoretical and Quantitative Perspectives" (Paper delivered at the annual meeting of the American Historical Association, Chicago, December 1974), pp. 43–47. I would like to thank Professor Hindus for sharing with me his data and his observations on the New York rates.

17. Edith Abbott, "Civil War and the Crime Wave of 1865–1870," *Social Service Review* 1 (June 1927): 212–34; Elwin H. Powell, "Crime as a Function of Anomie," *Journal of Criminal Law, Criminology and Police Science* 57 (June 1966): 163; Theodore N. Ferdinand, "The Criminal Patterns of Boston since 1849," *American Journal of Sociology* 73 (July 1967): 87; Massachusetts Board of State Charities, *Annual Reports, 1865–1876* (hereafter cited as Mass. Bd. Char., *Annual Report*).

18. Prison Association of New York, *Twenty-first Annual Report of the Executive Committee* (New York, 1866), pp. 172–73 (hereafter cited as PANY, *Annual Report*). Data on property and person offenses appear in Estelle B. Freedman, "Their Sisters' Keepers: The Origins of Female Corrections in America" (Ph.D. diss., Columbia University, 1976), p. 35, n. 25. The Women's Prison Association and Home, *Twenty-first Annual Report* (New York, 1866), p. 7 (hereafter cited as WPA, *Annual Report*) found from one-

eighth to one-third more women in penal institutions in New York than in the previous year.

19. PANY, *Annual Report, 1865*, pp. 172–73. On abortion laws and enforcement, see James C. Mohr, *Abortion in America: The Origins and Evolution of National Policy* (New York: Oxford University Press, 1978). On women's serious crimes in Europe, see Mary S. Hartman, *Victorian Murderesses* (New York: Schocken Books, 1977).

20. Several contemporary male observers claimed that low wages led to the seduction of working women. See Matthew Carey, "Essays on the Public Charities of Philadelphia," in *Miscellaneous Essays* (Philadelphia: B. Franklin, 1830), p. 203 and William Sanger, *The History of Prostitution: Its Extent, Causes and Effects throughout the World* (New York: Medical Publishing Co., 1858), pp. 488–522. Recent historical analyses of the relationship of female crime, urbanization, and economic conditions appear in: J. M. Beattie, "The Pattern of Crime in England 1660–1800," *Past and Present* 62 (February 1974): 47–95; Monkennon, *Dangerous Class*; Harvey J. Graff, "Crime and Punishment in the Nineteenth Century: A New Look at the Criminal," *Journal of Interdisciplinary History* 7 (Winter 1977): 477–91; Frances Gouda, "Some Observations on Female Criminality in France, 1825–1913," (Paper delivered at Women's History and Quantitative Methodology Conference, the Newberry Library, Chicago, 5–7 July 1979).

21. Faber gives cases of women restored to good standing and marriage ("The Evil That Men Do," pp. 215, 371). The fictional Hester Prynne in Hawthorne's *Scarlet Letter* is not restored because she refuses to confess her partner. See also Wendy Martin, "Seduced and Abandoned in the New World: The Fallen Woman in American Fiction," in *The American Sisterhood: Writings of the Feminist Movement from Colonial Times to the Present*, ed. Wendy Martin (New York: Harper and Row, 1972), pp. 257–72.

22. PANY, *Annual Report, 1849*, p. 246. See below, chap. 2, for a discussion of the cause of woman's fall. For a personal account of how social ostracism led a fallen woman into a brothel, see Lucy Brewer, *The Adventures of Lucy Brewer* (Boston: N. Coverly, Jr., 1815). For a literary example of the condemnation of the fallen woman, see Louisa May Alcott, *Work: A Story of Experience* (New York: Schocken Books, 1977; originally published 1873), pp. 136–39.

23. W. D. Lewis, *From Newgate to Dannemora*, pp. 162, 163; O. F. Lewis, *Development of American Prisons*, pp. 96, 112.

24. Quoted in W. D. Lewis, *From Newgate to Dannemora*, p. 163.

25. Ibid., pp. 94–95; Philip Klein, *Prison Methods in New York State: A Contribution to the Study of the Theory and Practice of Correctional Institutions in New York State* (New York: Longmans, Green and Co., 1920), p. 69.

26. Harriet Martineau, *Retrospect of Western Travel* (New York, 1838), quoted in O. F. Lewis, *Development of American Prisons*, p. 97.

27. Quoted in W. D. Lewis, *From Newgate to Dannemora*, p. 164.

28. Clifford M. Young, *Women's Prisons Past and Present and Other New York State Prison History* (Elmira, N.Y., 1932), pp. 3, 4 and O. F. Lewis, *Development of American Prisons*, p. 284. Overcrowded conditions in the basements and attics that housed women prisoners are reported in other states as well.

29. Harold M. Helfman, "A History of Penal, Correctional and Reformatory Institutions in Michigan, 1839–1889" (Ph.D. diss., University of Michigan, 1947), pp. 166, 364.

30. Most accounts imply that the women became pregnant while imprisoned. When the term "illegitimate birth" is used, however, it is difficult to know whether the inmate was pregnant before incarceration.

31. Lucien V. Rule, *The City of Dead Souls, and How It Was Made Alive Again: A Hundred Years within the Walls* (Louisville, Ky.: Brighter Day League, 1920), pp. 77–95, based on an exposé by a former male prisoner. See below, chap. 3, on the investigation of these charges.

32. Joseph Ragen, "The Devil Stoned," Papers of Joseph Ragen, Illinois State Historical Library, Springfield, Ill., pp. 174–75; McKelvey, *American Prisons*, p. 78; Wiley Britton Sanders, "The History and Administration of the State Prisons of Illinois" (Ph.D. diss., University of Chicago School of Social Service Administration, 1929), pp. 34–42.

33. O. F. Lewis, *Development of American Prisons*, p. 112.

34. Massachusetts Prison Commissioner's [C. W. Bellows], *Report on the Subject of Matrons and Labor in the Common Jails* (Boston, 1854).

35. Helen W. Rogers, "A History of the Movement to Establish a State Reformatory for Women in Connecticut," *Journal of Criminal Law and Criminology* 19 (February 1929): 520–22.

36. W. D. Lewis, *From Newgate to Dannemora*, pp. 157, 159, 217.

37. Francis Lieber, introduction to de Beaumont and de Tocqueville, *On the Penitentiary System*, pp. xiv–xvi.

38. James B. Finley, *Memorial of Prison Life* (published in 1851), quoted in *Imprisoned in America: Prison Communications, 1776 to Attica*, ed. Cynthia Philip (New York: Harper and Row, 1973), p. 53.

39. Lieber, quoted in PANY, *Annual Report, 1855*, p. 73.

40. Henry W. Lord, "Dependent and Delinquent Children with Special Reference to Girls," *Proceedings of the Sixth Annual Conference of Charities* (Boston, 1879), pp. 184–85. The organization became the National Conference on Charities and Corrections and is hereafter cited as NCCC, *Proceedings*.

41. PANY, *Annual Report, 1855*, pp. 74–79. For fictional equivalents, see David Brion Davis, *Homicide in American Fiction, 1798–1860: A Study in Social Values* (Ithaca: Cornell University Press, 1957), esp. pp. 167, 205, 228.

42. Lord, "Delinquent Children," pp. 184–85. Cf. Charles Loring Brace,

The Dangerous Classes of New York (New York: Wynkoop and Hallenbeck, 1880), chap. 10: "Street Girls," esp. pp. 114–18. Brace, however, believed that fallen women never lost "some of the divine qualities of their sex."

43. On this sexual division and women's political and social function in the home, see: Mary P. Ryan, *Womanhood in America, From Colonial Times to the Present* (New York: Franklin Watts, 1979), chap. 3; Nancy R. Cott, *The Bonds of Womanhood: "Women's Sphere" in New England, 1780–1835* (New Haven: Yale University Press, 1977), p. 20; Gerda Lerner, "The Lady and the Mill Girl," *Mid-Continent American Studies Journal* 10 (Spring 1969): 5–15; Kathryn Kish Sklar, *Catharine Beecher: A Study in American Domesticity* (New Haven: Yale University Press, 1973); Linda Kerber, "Daughters of Columbia: Educating Women for the Republic, 1787–1805," in *Our American Sisters: Women in American Life and Thought*, ed. Jean E. Friedman and William Shade (Boston: Allyn and Bacon, 1976), pp. 76–92; Barbara Welter, "The Cult of True Womanhood, 1820–1860," *American Quarterly* 18 (Summer 1966): 150–74. On Jacksonian America and tensions in the male role, see: Douglas C. North, *The Economic Growth of the United States, 1790–1869* (Englewood Cliffs, N.J.: Prentice Hall, 1966), chap. 7; John William Ward, *Andrew Jackson: Symbol for an Age* (New York: Oxford University Press, 1955); Marvin Meyers, *The Jacksonian Persuasion: Politics and Belief* (Stanford: Stanford University Press, 1957).

44. Cooper, quoted in Meyers, *Jacksonian Persuasion*, p. 70. On moral guardianship as part of woman's domestic role, see: Sklar, *Catharine Beecher*, esp. pp. 158–63; Mary Patricia Ryan, "American Society and the Cult of Domesticity, 1830–1860" (Ph.D. diss., University of California, Santa Barbara, 1971), esp. pp. 66–70; Lawrence J. Friedman, *Inventors of the Promised Land* (New York: Alfred Knopf, 1975), chap. 1; Lerner, "The Lady and the Mill Girl"; Glenda Gates Riley, "The Subtle Subversion: Changes in the Traditionalist Image of the American Woman," *Historian* 32 (February 1970): 210–27. Both Riley and Sklar emphasize the power that women gained through domesticity.

45. On the ideology of female passionlessness, see: John S. Haller, Jr. and Robin M. Haller, *The Physician and Sexuality in Victorian America* (Urbana, Ill.: University of Illinois Press, 1974), pp. 91–97; Ben Barker-Benfield, "The Spermatic Economy: A Nineteenth-Century View of Sexuality," in *The American Family in Social-Historical Perspective*, ed. Michael Gordon (New York: St. Martins Press, 1973), pp. 348–49; David M. Kennedy, *Birth Control in America: The Career of Margaret Sanger* (New Haven: Yale University Press, 1970), pp. 56–57; Nancy Cott, "Passionlessness: An Interpretation of Victorian Sexual Ideology, 1790–1850," *Signs* 4 (Winter 1978): 219–36. On the relationship between ideology and practice, see Carl Degler, "What Ought to Be and What Was: Women's Sexuality in the Nineteenth Century," *American Historical Review* 79 (December 1974): 1467–90 and Carroll Smith-Rosenberg, "A Richer and a Gentler

Sex" (Paper delivered at the Berkshire Conference on Women's History, Bryn Mawr, Pa., June 1976).

46. Quoted in Davis, *Homicide in American Fiction*, p. 212.

47. Barker-Benfield, "The Spermatic Economy," pp. 338–46.

48. Carroll Smith-Rosenberg, "Sex as Symbol in Victorian Purity: An Ethnohistorical Analysis of Jacksonian America," in *Turning Points: Historical and Sociological Essays on the Family*, ed. John Demos and Sarane Spence Boocock (Chicago: University of Chicago Press, 1978), pp. S212–47. On the significance of antiprostitution in antebellum America, see also: Mary P. Ryan, "The Power of Women's Networks: A Case Study of Female Moral Reform in Antebellum America," *Feminist Studies* 5 (Spring 1979): 66–85; Barbara Berg, *The Remembered Gate: Origins of American Feminism, the Woman and the City, 1800–1860* (New York: Oxford University Press, 1978), p. 218; Barbara Hobson, "Seduced and Abandoned, a Tale of the Wicked City: The Response to Prostitution in Boston, 1820–1850" (Paper delivered at the Fourth Berkshire Conference on the History of Women, Mt. Holyoke College, 23 August 1978).

Chapter 2

1. Rhoda Coffin, "Women's Prisons," *Proceedings of the Annual Congress of the National Prison Association of the United States* (Detroit, 1885), p. 192.

2. Susan Hammond Barney, "Care of the Criminal," in *Woman's Work in America*, ed. Annie Nathan Meyer (New York: Henry Holt and Co., 1891), p. 359.

3. The summary of Elizabeth Fry's work draws on: John Kent, *Elizabeth Fry* (London: B. T. Batsford, Ltd., 1962); Ann D. Smith, *Women in Prison: A Study in Penal Methods* (London: Stevens, 1962), chap. 6; Enoch C. Wines, *The State of Prisons and Child-Saving Institutions in the Civilized World, 1880* (Cambridge, Mass.: University Press, 1880), pp. 16–17; Christopher Hibbert, *The Roots of Evil: A Social History of Crime and Punishment* (Boston: Little, Brown and Co., 1963), pp. 153–54. Fry's brother was the abolitionist John Gurney.

4. Kent, *Elizabeth Fry*, pp. 33, 97.

5. Elizabeth Fry, *Observations in Visiting, Superintendence and Government of Female Prisoners* (London: John and Arthur Arch, Cornhill, 1827), p. 8 (her emphasis). Fry's theories are discussed below in chap. 3.

6. Kent, *Elizabeth Fry*, pp. 100-121. Fry did not advocate women's rights; she thought that with courage and determination, any woman could achieve the influence she herself obtained.

7. E. C. Wines, *The State of Prisons*, p. 17; W. David Lewis, *From Newgate to Dannemora: The Rise of the Penitentiary in New York, 1796–1848* (Ithaca: Cornell University Press, 1965), p. 160; idem, "The Female Criminal and the Prisons of New York, 1825–1845," New York State Historical Association *Quarterly Journal* 42 (July 1961): 218; Frank Thistlewaite, *The Anglo-*

American Connection in the Early Nineteenth Century (Philadelphia: University of Pennsylvania Press, 1959), pp. 88–89.

8. See Blanche Glassman Hersh, *The Slavery of Sex: Feminist Abolitionists in America* (Urbana, Ill.: University of Illinois Press, 1978) and James M. McPherson, *The Abolitionist Legacy: From Reconstruction to the NAACP* (Princeton: Princeton University Press, 1975), app. 4. The prison reformers' lives are summarized in app. B. For brief biographies, see Estelle B. Freedman, "Their Sisters' Keepers: The Origins of Female Corrections in America" (Ph.D. diss., Columbia University, 1976), pp. 388–98.

9. Nancy Cott, *The Bonds of Womanhood: "Women's Sphere" in New England, 1780–1835* (New Haven: Yale University Press, 1976), esp. chap. 5.

10. Only an estimated 7 percent of all women worked in the paid labor force in 1830, and only an estimated 2.5 percent of married white women worked for pay as late as 1890 (Daniel Scott Smith, "Family Limitation, Sexual Control and Domestic Feminism in Victorian America," in *Clio's Consciousness Raised: New Perspectives on the History of Women*, ed. Mary S. Hartman and Lois Banner [New York: Harper and Row, 1974], table 2, p. 122).

11. Data on marriage in ibid., table 1, p. 121 and in John Modell, Frank F. Furstenberg, Jr., and Douglas Strong, "The Timing of Marriage in the Transition to Adulthood: Continuity and Change, 1860–1975," in *Turning Points: Historical and Sociological Essays on the Family*, ed. John Demos and Sarane Spence Boocock (Chicago: University of Chicago Press, 1978), pp. S122–24.

12. Antebellum revivals and reform are discussed in: David Brion Davis, ed., *Ante-Bellum Reform* (New York: Harper and Row, 1967), introduction; John L. Thomas, "Romantic Reform in America, 1815–1865," *American Quarterly* 17 (Winter 1965): 656–81; Timothy Smith, *Revivalism and Social Reform in Mid-Nineteenth Century America* (New York: Abingdon Press, 1957); Alice Felt Tyler, *Freedom's Ferment: Phases of American Social History to 1860* (New York: Harper and Row, 1962); Ronald Walters, *American Reformers, 1815–1860* (New York: Hill and Wang, 1978); Lois W. Banner, "Religious Benevolence as Social Control: A Critique of an Interpretation," *Journal of American History* 60 (June 1973): 23–41.

13. Mary Maples Dunn, "Women of Light," in *Women of America: A History*, ed. Carol Ruth Berkin and Mary Beth Norton (Boston: Houghton Mifflin, 1979), pp. 114–33; Nancy Cott, "Young Women in the Second Great Awakening in New England," *Feminist Studies* 3 (Fall 1975): 15–29; Keith Melder, "Ladies Bountiful: Organized Women's Benevolence in Early Nineteenth-Century America," *New York History* 48 (July 1967): 231–54.

14. Clifford S. Griffen, *Their Brothers' Keepers: Moral Stewardship in the United States, 1800–1865* (New Brunswick, N.J.: Rutgers University Press, 1960); Carroll Smith-Rosenberg, "Beauty, the Beast and the Militant Woman: A Case Study in Sex Roles and Social Stress in Jacksonian America," *American Quarterly* 23 (October 1971): 562–84; idem, *Religion*

and the Rise of the American City: The New York Mission Movement, 1812–1870 (Ithaca: Cornell University Press, 1971); Mary P. Ryan, "The Power of Women's Networks: A Case Study of Female Moral Reform in Antebellum America," *Feminist Studies* 5 (Spring 1979): 66–85; Barbara Berg, *The Remembered Gate: Origins of American Feminism, the Woman and the City, 1800–1860* (New York: Oxford University Press, 1978), chaps. 7–9.

15. Negley K. Teeters, *They Were in Prison: A History of the Pennsylvania Prison Society, 1787–1937* (Chicago: John C. Winston Co., 1937), pp. 249–50; Matilda Wrench, ed., *Visits to Female Prisoners at Home and Abroad* (London: Wertheim and Macintosh, 1852), pp. 305–7.

16. Smith, *Revivalism and Social Reform*, pp. 169–70; "Sarah Platt Doremus," *National Cyclopaedia of American Biography*, 51 vols. (New York: James White and Co., 1898–1973), 6:166; Barney, "Care of the Criminal," p. 360; "Phoebe Worrall Palmer," in Edward James and Janet Wilson James, eds., *Notable American Women, 1607–1950: A Biographical Dictionary*, 3 vols. (Cambridge, Mass.: Belknap Press of Harvard University Press, 1971), 2:12–14 (hereafter cited as *NAW*); Smith-Rosenberg, *Religion and the Rise of the American City*, pp. 98–120.

17. PANY, *Annual Report, 1845*, quoted in *Imprisoned in America: Prison Communications, 1776 to Attica*, ed. Cynthia Owen (New York: Harper and Row, 1973), p. 82.

18. Sarah Hopper Emerson, ed., *Life of Abby Hopper Gibbons, Told Chiefly Through Her Correspondence*, 2 vols. (New York: Knickerbocker Press, 1897), 1:2, 4, 26, 115, 132–34; W. D. Lewis, *From Newgate to Dannemora*, p. 224; Hersh, *Slavery of Sex*, pp. 128, 132.

19. Bell Gale Chevigny, *The Woman and the Myth: Margaret Fuller's Life and Writings* (Old Westbury, N.Y.: Feminist Press, 1976), pp. 335–36.

20. Margaret Fuller, "Our Cities Charities," New York *Tribune*, 19 March 1845.

21. Margaret Fuller, "Asylum for Discharged Female Convicts," New York *Tribune*, 19 June 1845.

22. WPA, *Annual Reports, 1855*, pp. 2, 5 and *1876*, p. 7; Mrs. James S. [Abby Hopper] Gibbons, "Sketch of Miss Sedgewick's Connection with the Women's Prison Association of New York," in *Life and Letters of Catherine M. Sedgewick*, ed. Mary E. Dewey (New York: Harper and Brothers, 1871), p. 422; WPA, *Annual Report, 1861–62*, pp. 5, 8.

23. Caroline M. Kirkland, *The Helping Hand: Comprising an Account of the Home for Discharged Female Convicts and an Appeal in Behalf of that Institution* (New York: Charles Scribner, 1853), pp. 99–100 (her emphasis). Figures for the Isaac Hopper Home in WPA, *Annual Report, 1863–64*, pp. 7, 8.

24. WPA, *Annual Report, 1863–64*, p. 10.

25. WPA, *Annual Report, 1849*, in PANY, *Annual Report, 1849*, pp. 246,

247; Kirkland, *The Helping Hand*, pp. 70–71; Wrench, *Visits to Female Prisoners*, pp. 311–12, quoting from WPA, *Annual Report, 1850–51*.

26. WPA, *Annual Report, 1849*, pp. 246–48.

27. Ibid., p. 247; Sedgewick to Mrs. K. S. Minot, 20 March 1853, in Dewey, *Letters of Catherine M. Sedgewick*, p. 346; Abby Hopper Gibbons to William Gibbons, 6 May 1854, in Emerson, *Abby Hopper Gibbons*, 1:186–87. Such thoughts were rarely expressed publicly.

28. Dewey, *Letters of Catherine M. Sedgewick*, p. 292; WPA, *Annual Report, 1863–64*, p. 7. In Philadelphia, prison visitors formed an Association of Women Friends and eventually established a home for released prisoners, the Howard Institution. Unlike New York reformers, they did not form an autonomous organization (Teeters, *They Were in Prison*, pp. 257–63).

29. WPA, *Annual Report, 1855*, p. 4; WPA, *Annual Report, 1861–62*, p. 5.

30. Kirkland, *The Helping Hand*, p. 51 (her emphasis).

31. Ellen DuBois, "The Radicalism of the Woman Suffrage Movement: Notes Toward the Reconstruction of Nineteenth Century Feminism," *Feminist Studies* 3 (Fall 1975): 63–71.

32. WPA, *Annual Report, 1855*, p. 5.

33. Emerson, *Abby Hopper Gibbons*, esp. 2:248.

34. William Rhinelander Stewart, *The Philanthropic Work of Josephine Shaw Lowell* (New York: Macmillan Co., 1911), pp. 95, 99; George M. Frederickson, *The Inner Civil War: Northern Intellectuals and the Crisis of the Union* (New York: Harper and Row, 1965), p. 212; *NAW*, 2:437–39.

35. "Ellen Cheney Johnson," *NAW*, 2:277; "A Separate Prison for Women," *Woman's Journal* 28 February 1874, p. 65; Isabel C. Barrows, "Ellen Johnson and the Sherborn Prison," *New England Magazine* 21 (January 1900): 628–29; Sarah Dexter, *Recollections of Hannah Chickering* (Cambridge, Mass.: Riverside Press, 1881); Papers of the Poor Family, Box 19, Schlesinger Library, Radcliffe College, Cambridge, Mass.

36. Mary C. Johnson, ed., *Rhoda Coffin: Her Reminiscences, Addresses, Papers, and Ancestry* (New York: Grafton Press, 1910), pp. 66–67, 85, 88, 137, 225, 145ff; Charles Coffin, "Influence of Friends in the Development of the Life of the State of Indiana," typescript in Papers of Charles F. and Rhoda M. Coffin, Earlham College, Richmond, Ind. The events leading up to the founding of the women's prison are discussed below in chap. 3.

37. William L. O'Neill, *The Woman Movement: Feminism in the United States and England* (Chicago: Quadrangle Books, 1969), pp. 23–24; Eleanor Flexner, *Century of Struggle: The Women's Rights Movement in the United States* (New York: Atheneum, 1970), pp. 105–8; Ann Douglas Wood, "The War Within a War: Women Nurses in the Union Army," *Civil War History* 18 (September 1972): 197–212; Ellen Langenheim Henle, "Clara Barton, Soldier or Pacifist?" *Civil War History* 24 (June 1978): 152–60.

38. Roy Lubove, *The Professional Altruist: The Emergence of Social Work*

as a Career, 1880–1930 (Cambridge, Mass.: Harvard University Press, 1965), p. 2. On the charities movement, social work, and women's involvement, see: Frank J. Bruno, *Trends in Social Work, 1874–1956* (New York: Columbia University Press, 1957), pp. 86–88; Robert H. Bremner, *From the Depths: The Discovery of Poverty in the United States* (New York: New York University Press, 1956), chap. 4, pp. 49–50.

39. Lillie Buffum Chace Wyman and Arthur Crawford Wyman, *Elizabeth Buffum Chace, 1806–1899: Her Life and Its Environment*, 2 vols. (Boston: W. B. Clarke Co., 1914), 1:312. The following account draws on sources in this work, esp. 1:219, 291, 303, 325–34; 2:65–76, 117–18 and Elizabeth Buffum Chace and Lucy Buffum Lovell, *Two Quaker Sisters* (New York: Liveright Publishing Corp., 1937), pp. xvii–xxv, 9ff. Chace had been a pacifist during the Civil War, but her energies were concentrated on gaining Negro and woman suffrage.

40. Lucy Stone to Elizabeth B. Chace, (n.d.), in Wyman and Wyman, *Elizabeth Buffum Chace*, 1:312.

41. "Memorial of Rhode Island Woman Suffrage Association," 24 March 1870, ibid., 1:322–30.

42. Chace to Governor Henry Lippitt, March 1876, ibid., 2:65–66.

43. Helen W. Rogers, "A History of the Movement to Establish a State Reformatory for Women in Connecticut," *Journal of Criminal Law and Criminology* 19 (February 1929): 523; Stewart, *Josephine Shaw Lowell*, pp. 87–88; Isabel C. Barrows, "The Massachusetts Reformatory Prison for Women," in *The Reformatory System in the United States*, ed. Samuel J. Barrows (Washington, D.C.: Government Printing Office, 1900), pp. 101–28; Norton Mezvinsky, "The White Ribbon Reform, 1874–1920" (Ph.D. diss., University of Wisconsin, 1959), p. 214.

44. Enoch C. Wines and Theodore Dwight, *Report on the Prisons and Reformatories of the United States and Canada* (Albany: Van Benthuysen and Sons, 1867); Blake McKelvey, *American Prisons: A Study in American Social History prior to 1915* (Chicago: University of Chicago Press, 1936), chaps. 3 and 4. Founders included Charles Coffin of Indiana, Zebulon Brockway of the Detroit House of Corrections, Franklin Sanborn of the Massachusetts Board of Charities, and Rutherford B. Hayes, then Governor of Ohio.

45. Enoch C. Wines, ed., *Transactions of the National Congress on Penitentiary and Reformatory Discipline* (Albany, 1871), p. 547. The organization became the American Prison Association; its proceedings are hereafter cited as APA, *Proceedings*. Women regularly contributed papers at annual meetings after 1871. From 1876 to 1900, the female proportion of the roll of annual conferences rose from 8 to 15 percent (APA, *Proceedings, 1876, 1885, 1886, 1888, 1894–1915*).

46. Jeanne M. Giovannoni and Margaret E. Purvine, "The Myth of the Social Work Matriarchy" (Paper delivered at the National Conference on Social Welfare, Atlantic City, N.J., 29 May 1973). Women presented three

times more papers in the 1880s than in the 1870s, and 12 percent of these papers were on prison methods.

47. The term appears in O'Neill, *The Woman Movement*, pp. 33–54.

48. Margaret Wyman, "The Rise of the Fallen Woman," *American Quarterly* 3 (Summer 1951): 167–77.

49. Josephine Shaw Lowell, "One Means of Preventing Pauperism," NCCC, *Proceedings, 1879*, pp. 187–99; Ellen C. Johnson, "Discipline in Female Prisons," APA, *Proceedings, 1891*, p. 137; "Memorial of the Indianapolis Board of Managers of the 'House for Friendless Women' in Behalf of the 'Indiana Reformatory Institution for Women and Girls,'" 4 May 1869, in Indiana House of Representatives *Journal*, Special Session, 1869, pp. 345–47.

50. Susan B. Anthony, "Social Purity," (1875), in *Up From the Pedestal: Selected Writings in the History of American Feminism*, ed. Aileen S. Kraditor (Chicago: Quadrangle Books, 1968), p. 161.

51. Ibid., p. 162.

52. Charlotte Perkins Gilman, *Women and Economics*, (1898; reprint, Boston: Small, Maynard and Co., 1900); Ellen M. Slocum, "The Causes of Prostitution," *Woman's Journal*, 18 January 1879, p. 22; Ellen Battelle Dietrick, "Rescuing Fallen Woman," *Woman's Journal*, 27 May 1893, p. 162; Indiana Reformatory Institution for Women and Girls, *Report of the Board of Managers to the Legislature* (Indianapolis, 1878), pp. 16–17 (hereafter cited as IWP, *Annual Report*).

53. WPA, *Annual Report, 1887*, p. 15.

54. Elizabeth Chace, "Prison for Women at Sherborn," *Woman's Journal*, 4 October 1879, p. 320; Dietrick, "Rescuing," p. 163; WPA, *Annual Report, 1897*, p. 26.

55. Dietrick, "Rescuing," p. 162.

56. "History of Inmates," Massachusetts Reformatory Prison for Women, Framingham, Mass. (hereafter cited as "History of Inmates," MRPW), particularly cases of inmates 3000, 2847, 4480, and 2845, which are quoted, and letters from attorneys, family, and prison commissioners attached to these cases. Of 153 inmate histories that cited parents and family, 40.5 percent mentioned good backgrounds, while only 21.16 percent faulted the parents and family. In contrast, of 133 cases that described inmates' husbands or lovers, only 8.3 percent gave positive evaluations, while 62.4 percent claimed that men's seductions or desertions, or unhappy marriages had contributed to the women's crimes. Indiana cases are cited in IWP, *Annual Report, 1878*, pp. 16–17 and "Indiana's Female Prison," Cincinnati *Gazette*, 6 December 187—, in Rhoda Coffin Scrapbook, Papers of Charles F. and Rhoda M. Coffin.

57. Massachusetts Reformatory Prison for Women, *Annual Report* (Boston, 1883), p. 48 (hereafter cited as MRPW, *Annual Report*); "History of Inmates," MRPW, cases 4480, 2845.

58. On deterministic criminology, see: Leon Radzinowicz, *Ideology and*

Crime: A Study of Crime in its Social and Historical Context (London: Heineman Educational Books, 1966), chap. 2, esp. pp. 29–58; Arthur E. Fink, *Causes of Crime: Biological Theories in the United States, 1800–1915* (Philadelphia: University of Pennsylvania Press, 1938), esp. p. 19; Charles Rosenberg, "The Bitter Fruit: Heredity, Disease and Social Thought in Nineteenth-Century America," *Perspectives in American History* 8 (1974): 189–235.

59. O'Neill, *The Woman Movement*, esp. pp. 40–42; Smith, "Domestic Feminism," pp. 119, 131–33.

60. Linda Gordon, "Voluntary Motherhood: The Beginnings of Feminist Birth Control Ideas in the United States," in *Clio's Consciousness Raised*, ed. Hartman and Banner, pp. 61–62; idem, *Woman's Body, Woman's Right: A Social History of Birth Control in America* (New York: Grossman, 1976).

Chapter 3

1. Estelle Freedman, "Separatism as Strategy: Female Institution Building and American Feminism, 1870–1930," *Feminist Studies* 5 (Fall 1979): 512–29.

2. Orlando F. Lewis, *The Development of American Prisons and Prison Customs, 1776–1845, with reference to early institutions in the State of New York* (Albany: Prison Association of New York, 1922), p. 16; Philip Klein, *Prison Methods in New York State: A Contribution to the Study of the Theory and Practice of Correctional Institutions in New York State* (New York: Longmans, Green and Co., 1920), p. 69. See above, chap. 1, on the first women's quarters.

3. Elizabeth Fry, *Observations in Visiting, Superintendence and Government of Female Prisoners* (London: John and Arthur Arch, Cornhill, 1827), pp. 26, 31, 34; John Kent, *Elizabeth Fry* (London: B. T. Batsford, Ltd., 1962), p. 46.

4. O. F. Lewis, *Development of American Prisons*, p. 112; Clifford Young, *Women's Prisons Past and Present and Other New York State Prison History* (Elmira, N.Y., 1932), p. 9; W. David Lewis, *From Newgate to Dannemora: The Rise of the Penitentiary in New York, 1796–1848* (Ithaca: Cornell University Press, 1965), pp. 162–77.

5. W. D. Lewis, *From Newgate to Dannemora*, pp. 234–50; Enoch C. Wines and Theodore Dwight, *Report on the Prisons and Reformatories of the United States and Canada* (Albany: Van Benthuysen and Sons, 1867), p. 111.

6. Suzanne Case, "Eliza Farnham: The Woman and Her Era, 1815–1864" (Honors thesis, History Department, Stanford University, 1979), pp. 65–72. On Farnham's contribution to phrenology, see W. David Lewis, "Eliza Farnham and Phrenological Contributions to American Penology," introduction to M. B. Sampson and E. W. Farnham, *Rationale of Crime* (Montclair, N.J.: Patterson Smith, 1973).

7. These included New Jersey; Cincinnati, Ohio; and the District of Columbia (Harry Elmer Barnes, *A History of the Penal, Reformatory and Correctional Institutions of the State of New Jersey: Analytical and Documentary* [Trenton, N.J.: MacCrellish and Quigley Co., 1918], pp. 159, 518; Wines and Dwight, *Report on the Prisons*, pp. 350–51; David K. Sullivan, "Behind Prison Walls: The Operation of the District Penitentiary, 1831–1862," in *Records of the Columbia Historical Society of Washington, D.C., 1971–1972*, ed. Francis Coleman Rosenberger [Washington, D.C.: Columbia Historical Society, 1973], pp. 243–66).

8. Elizabeth B. Chace to E. C. Wines, 1 October 1870, in APA, *Proceedings, 1871*, ed. E. C. Wines, p. 579.

9. William Rhinelander Stewart, *The Philanthropic Work of Josephine Shaw Lowell* (New York: Macmillan Co., 1911), p. 98.

10. Z. R. Brockway, "The Reformatory System," in *The Reformatory System in the United States: Reports Prepared for the International Prison Congress*, ed. Samuel J. Barrows (Washington, D.C.: Government Printing Office, 1900), pp. 17–27. British reform is discussed in Harry Elmer Barnes, "The Progress of American Penology as Exemplified by the Experience of the State of Pennsylvania, 1830–1920," *Journal of Criminal Law and Criminology* 13 (August 1922): 171ff; Christopher Hibbert, *The Roots of Evil: A Social History of Crime and Punishment* (Boston: Little, Brown and Co., 1963), pp. 138–56; Ann D. Smith, *Women in Prison: A Study in Penal Methods* (London: Stevens, 1962), pp. 93–94; Blake McKelvey, *American Prisons: A Study in American Social History prior to 1915* (Chicago: University of Chicago Press, 1936), pp. 60–61, 67–68.

11. *Our Convicts* (1864; reprint, Montclair, N.J.: Patterson Smith, 1969), pp. 204–69.

12. Massachusetts Board of State Charities, *Special Report on Prisons and Prison Discipline* (Boston, 1865), pp. 15–33; E. C. Wines, *Report on the International Penitentiary Congress of London, July 3–13, 1872* (Washington, D.C.: Government Printing Office, 1873), pp. 160–62; Lillie Buffum Chace Wyman and Arthur Crawford Wyman, *Elizabeth Buffum Chace, 1806–1899: Her Life and Its Environment*, 2 vols. (Boston: W. B. Clarke Co., 1914), 2:16–19.

13. G. S. Griffith, *Report on the International Prison Congress Held at London, July 3–13, 1872, to the Board of Managers of the Prisoners' Aid Association of Maryland* (Baltimore, 1873), p. 18.

14. "Notes on Prisons, Reformatories, Gaols through Ireland and Great Britain taken by Charles Coffin," p. 47, "St. Vincent's Reformatory for Women for Advanced Grade from Mt. Joy Female Prison," and "Reminiscences of Charles Coffin," pp. 107–11, in Papers of Charles F. and Rhoda M. Coffin, Earlham College, Richmond, Ind. In addition, Enoch Wines, Theodore Dwight, Samuel Gridley Howe, Franklin Sanborn, and members of the PANY all wrote favorably of the Mount Joy prison (Mass. Bd. Char., *Annual Report, 1866*, p. xliii; Wines and Dwight, *Report on the Prisons*, pp.

70–71; PANY, *Annual Report, 1876*, pp. 12–13).

15. Barbara Brenzel, "Lancaster Industrial School for Girls: A Social Portrait of a Nineteenth-Century Reform School for Girls," *Feminist Studies* 3 (Fall 1975): 40; Robert Mennel, *Thorns and Thistles: Juvenile Delinquents in the United States, 1825–1940* (Hanover, N.H.: University Press of New England, 1973), pp. 30, 49; Steven L. Schlossman, *Love and the American Delinquent: The Theory and Practice of "Progressive" Juvenile Justice, 1825–1920* (Chicago: University of Chicago Press, 1977), p. 40; Helen W. Rogers, "A History of the Movement to Establish a State Reformatory for Women in Connecticut," *Journal of Criminal Law and Criminology* 19 (February 1929): 522–23.

16. Harold M. Helfman, "A History of Penal, Correctional and Reformatory Institutions in Michigan, 1839–1889" (Ph.D. diss., University of Michigan, 1947), pp. 398–407. On the House of Shelter, see: Zebulon Brockway, *Fifty Years of Prison Service: An Autobiography* (New York: Charities Publication Committee, 1912), pp. 106–7, 110; Emma Hall, "To the Inspectors of the Detroit House of Corrections," (1873), Papers of Emma Hall, Bentley Historical Library, University of Michigan, Ann Arbor, Mich. *The Second Biennial Report of the Board of State Commissioners for the General Supervision of Charitable, Penal, Pauper, and Reformatory Institutions* (Lansing, Mich., 1875) shows that 46 percent of the state's women prisoners were in the Detroit facility.

17. Helen Wilson, *The Treatment of the Misdemeanant in Indiana, 1816–1936* (Chicago: University of Chicago Press, 1938), p. 27; Rhoda Coffin, "An Account of the Origin and Conduct of the Women's Prison and Girls' Reformatory at Indianapolis, Indiana," in *Rhoda Coffin: Her Reminiscences, Addresses, Papers and Ancestry*, ed. Mary C. Johnson (New York: Grafton Press, 1910), p. 153ff; Indiana House of Representatives *Journal*, 19 January 1869, p. 122, 9 February 1869, p. 140, Special Session, 5 May 1869, pp. 310–13 (Sarah Smith addressed the legislature at these times). The act was signed on 17 May 1869. Prison conditions in Indiana which precipitated the movement are discussed later in this chapter.

18. The original prison commission consisted of Dr. Estes Howe, the Reverend Daniel Noyes, Mr. Joseph Story, Hannah Chickering, Pauline Durant, and Clara Leonard (Massachusetts Board of Commissioners of Prisons, *Annual Report* [Boston, 1875], p. 60, hereafter cited as Mass. Bd. CP, *Annual Report*).

19. Mass. Bd. CP, *Annual Report, 1872*, pp. 4–5, 60.

20. Ibid., pp. 6, 8.

21. The House passed the measure in 1870, but state senators objected to the cost. Mass. Bd. CP, *Annual Report, 1876*, pp. 57–59; Sarah E. Dexter, *Recollections of Hannah Chickering* (Cambridge, Mass.: Riverside Press, 1881), pp. 35–36; Susan D. Nickerson, "A Five Year Fight for Humanity," *The Charity Review* 9 (October 1899): 330; Isabel Barrows, "The Massachu-

setts Reformatory Prison for Women," in S. Barrows, *The Reformatory System*, pp. 103–8; Massachusetts General Court and House *Journal*, 1870, p. 75; Massachusetts Senate *Journal*, 1873, pp. 247–305.

22. Mass. Bd. CP, *Annual Report, 1874*, pp. 16, 22–23.

23. "A League for the Establishment of a Separate Prison," Papers of the Poor Family, Box 19, Schlesinger Library, Radcliffe College, Cambridge, Mass.

24. Massachusetts General Court, House, and Senate *Journals*, January to March 1874, for names submitting petitions. Most supporters were historically anonymous, but included in the petitions were the signatures of former governors Washburn and Claflin; the Reverend Phillips Brooks; Bishop J. J. Williams; Civil War hero Robert C. Winthrop; feminist Sarah Grimké; Ralph Waldo Emerson; Samuel Bowles, editor of the Springfield (Mass.) *Republican*; Austin Phelps; "and 26 professors and students at the Andover Theological Seminary."

25. Chace to Wines, 1 October 1870, in APA, *Proceedings, 1871*, p. 579.

26. Mass. Bd. CP, *Annual Reports, 1872*, pp. 6, 26, 27–28 and *1875*, pp. 15–16.

27. Mass. Bd. CP, *Annual Report, 1872*, p. 29.

28. WPA, *Annual Report, 1888*, p. 11.

29. WPA, *Annual Report, 1855*, p. 9: "They are impressible [sic]; with the quick feeling of children—and adult children they are—they respond to our earnest appeals and Christian sympathy"; APA, *Proceedings, 1898*, p. 285; MRPW, *Annual Report, 1873*, cited in I. Barrow, "The Massachusetts Reformatory," p. 108. Steven Schlossman uses the term "affectional treatment" to describe what he sees as a post-Jacksonian form of treatment which emphasized affection, kindness, and persuasion rather than discipline and strict training (Schlossman, *Love and the American Delinquent*, pp. 49–53).

30. APA, *Proceedings, 1891*, p. 143.

31. Quoted in Stewart, *Josephine Shaw Lowell*, p. 99.

32. Caroline M. Kirkland, *The Helping Hand: Comprising an Account of the Home for Discharged Female Convicts and an Appeal in Behalf of that Institution* (New York: Charles Scribner, 1853), pp. 30, 31, 44, 74.

33. Quoted in Negley K. Teeters, *They Were in Prison: A History of the Pennsylvania Prison Society, 1787–1937* (Chicago: John C. Winston Co., 1937), p. 252.

34. See Hannah Chickering's statement to Massachusetts Legislative Committee on Prisons, 1864, quoted in Mass. Bd. CP, *Annual Report, 1875*, p. 55 and Warren Spalding, "Some Methods of Preventing Crime," NCCC, *Proceedings, 1880*, p. 73. Homes included those founded by the Magdalen Society; the House of Good Shepherd; the Florence Crittenton Homes; and the WCTU Rescue Homes. Several homes opened in New York City in the 1830s; the Massachusetts homes (Dedham and Springfield) opened in

the 1860s, as did Homes for the Friendless in Richmond, Ind.; East Haven, Conn.; Haverhill, Mass.; Hartford, Conn.; and Chicago, Ill. Baltimore had both a Female House of Refuge and an Industrial Home for Colored Girls by the 1880s (Klein, *Prison Methods*, p. 40; David J. Pivar, "The New Abolitionism: The Quest for Social Purity, 1876–1900" [Ph.D. diss., University of Pennsylvania, 1965], p. 27; Susan Hammond Barney, "Care of the Criminal," in *Woman's Work in America*, ed. Annie Nathan Meyer [New York: Henry Holt and Co., 1891], p. 363; Rogers, "A History of the Movement," p. 528; Chicago Woman's Club Minutes, 1915–16, p. 182, at Chicago Historical Society, Chicago, Ill.).

35. Kirkland, *The Helping Hand*, p. 15; *The Third Annual Report of the Home for the Friendless* (Richmond, Ind., 1871), pp. 2–3, described the moral force applied to women about to fall into prostitution: wake at 5 A.M., family worship, work training (in housework), three hours of school in the afternoon, prayer, and scripture lessons. The Florence Crittenton Homes, originally for rescuing prostitutes, searched inmates on entry, forbade profane or slang language and coarse jesting, required "family worship" morning and evening, censored letters and surveilled visitors, and taught "plain sewing and simple working," table setting, and orderly kitchen work. Bible readings required attendance, as did the "general work of the Home." (*The Florence Crittenton Magazine* 1 [May 1899]: 109).

36. Nathan Huggins, *Protestants Against Poverty: Boston's Charities, 1870–1900* (Westport, Conn.: Greenwood Publishing Corp., 1971), pp. 84–86; Mennel, *Thorns and Thistles*, pp. 36, 52–55; Schlossman, *Love and the American Delinquent*, chap. 3; Michael B. Katz, *The Irony of Early School Reform: Educational Innovation in Mid-Nineteenth-Century Massachusetts* (Cambridge, Mass.: Harvard University Press, 1968), pp. 188–92; Mass. Bd. Char., *Annual Report, 1866*, p. xlv; Gerald N. Grob, *Mental Institutions in America: Social Policy to 1875* (New York: Free Press, 1973), pp. 212–28.

37. Emma Hall, "Reformation of Criminal Girls," NCCC, *Proceedings, 1883*, p. 189. On the importance of the family in preventing women's crime, see Simeon Nash, *Crime and the Family* (Cincinnati: Robert Clark and Co., 1876), pp. 23–24.

38. "One Means of Preventing Pauperism," NCCC, *Proceedings, 1879*, p. 198.

39. Stewart, *Josephine Shaw Lowell*, p. 100.

40. Ibid., p. 102. Lowell cited Smith, Elizabeth Fry, and the reports of the Massachusetts women's reformatory prison to support her case, but she seemed to be unfamiliar with the work of Mary Carpenter.

41. New York Board of Charities, *Annual Reports, 1887*, pp. 54, 55 and *1888*, p. 329 (hereafter cited as NY Bd. Char., *Annual Report*). (Note the use of the term "girls." Inmates' ages ranged from fifteen to thirty.) Norma Vere Carson, "An Historical and Critical Study of New York State Reformatories for Women" (M.A. thesis, Columbia University, 1917), pp. 6–25.

See below, chaps. 4 and 5, for a comparison of the New York, Massachusetts, and Indiana institutions.

42. Stewart, *Josephine Shaw Lowell*, pp. 306–8; Sarah Hopper Emerson, ed., *Life of Abby Hopper Gibbons, Told Chiefly through Her Correspondence* (New York: Knickerbocker Press, 1897), pp. 270–73; *Report of the Western House of Refuge for Women* (Albany, 1893), p. 12 (hereafter cited as Western House of Refuge, *Annual Report*); McKelvey, *American Prisons*, p. 141.

43. Stewart, *Josephine Shaw Lowell*, pp. 308–12; WPA, *Annual Reports, 1892*, pp. 6–7; *1894*, p. 7; *1895*, pp. 7–8. On Bedford Hills, see below, chaps. 6 and 7. Although New York had three separate female reformatories by 1902, not all women criminals were committed to them. Felons and serious recidivists went to the Auburn women's department (Sing Sing had closed its women's building in 1877). Short-term sentences were served in local jails, and most New York City prostitutes and drunkards continued to serve at Blackwell's Island. The separate women's institutions never served the majority of female criminals, who remained in mixed jails and prisons.

44. Fry, *Observations in Visiting*, p. 26.

45. O. F. Lewis, *Development of American Prisons*, p. 205; W. D. Lewis, *From Newgate to Dannemora*, pp. 219–22; Dorothea Dix, *Remarks on Prisons and Prison Discipline in the United States* (Philadelphia: Joseph Kite and Co., 1845), pp. 107–8; Young, *Women's Prisons*, p. 14. That New Jersey, Ohio, Virginia, and Washington, D.C. had no matrons Dix attributed to the small number of female convicts in their institutions.

46. Irish women awaiting washing work, Jewish peddlers, or other unescorted women on the streets were subject to arrest for vagrancy, soliciting, or disorderly conduct, the WPA charged. At least one judge publicly condoned such arrests (WPA, *Annual Reports, 1888*, pp. 18–20; *1889*, pp. 17–18; *1897*, p. 26).

47. Wyman and Wyman, *Elizabeth Buffum Chace*, p. 108; Mrs. W. P. Lynde, "The Treatment of Erring and Criminal Women," NCCC, *Proceedings, 1880*, p. 250.

48. Dexter, *Hannah Chickering*, pp. 32–33; WPA, *Annual Reports, 1884*, p. 6; *1887*, p. 5; Barney, "Care of the Criminal," pp. 366–67; Rhoda Coffin, "Women's Prisons," APA, *Proceedings, 1885*, p. 193; Lowell, "One Means of Preventing Pauperism," p. 193.

49. Addie Irving to Mrs. E. C. Buchanan, reprinted in *Imprisoned in America: Prison Communications, 1776 to Attica*, ed. Cynthia Owen Philip (New York: Harper and Row, 1973), pp. 82–83.

50. Illegitimate births and sexual scandals in prison are mentioned in, e.g., "Pauperism and Crime in Michigan in 1874–75," appendix to *Second Biennial Report of State Commissioners*, p. 74; Lowell, "One Means of Preventing Pauperism," p. 193; Stewart, *Josephine Shaw Lowell*, pp. 323–25; Jane Zimmerman, "Penal Reform Movement in the South During the Progressive Era," *Journal of Southern History* 17 (November 1951): 259–62;

Rogers, "A History of the Movement," p. 519; New York *Times*, 24 January 1886, p. 1; Barnes, *Institutions of the State of New Jersey*, p. 518. See below on Indiana.

51. Coffin, "Women's Prisons," p. 189. The exposé was authored by Harry Youngerman (possibly a pseudonym) and called "State Prison Life, by One Who Has Been There"; it is summarized and quoted in Lucien V. Rule, *The City of Dead Souls, and How it was Made Alive Again: A Hundred Years within the Walls* (Louisville: Brighter Day League, 1920), pp. 77–95.

52. Barney, "Care of the Criminal," pp. 365–66.

53. Sarah W. Devall, "The Results of the Employment of a Police Matron in the City of Portland, Maine," NCCC, *Proceedings, 1881*, pp. 309–10; Mrs. E. R. Cobb, APA, *Proceedings, 1902*, pp. 344–48; Teeters, *They Were in Prison*, pp. 271–72; Chlöe Owings, *Women Police: A Study of the Development and Status of the Women Police Movement* (New York: Frederick H. Hitchcock, 1925), pp. 98–101.

54. Stewart, *Josephine Shaw Lowell*, pp. 320–23.

55. "Police Matrons Bill—Report of Special Committee" (to the Executive Committee of the PANY), in PANY *Annual Report, 1884*, pp. 62–66.

56. WPA, *Annual Reports, 1887*, p. 11; *1888*, p. 5; Mrs. J. K. (Susan) Barney, "Prison and Police Matrons," APA, *Proceedings, 1886*, p. 303. Mrs. J. B. Hobbs of Chicago said of the matrons movement: "It is natural that a Christian motherly heart should have more influence with these girls than a man would have. . . . I assure you that many have been drawn by the matrons's influence from the downward path into which their feet have entered, into the straight and narrow path. . . ." (APA, *Proceedings, 1885*, p. 289).

57. Statements in favor of women's employment appear in: *Prison Reform in the United States*, Proceedings of a Conference held at Newport, R.I., (1877), p. 44; Emory Washburn, *Reasons for a Separate State Prison for Women* (Boston, 1874), p. 4; Wines and Dwight, *Report on the Prisons*, p. 123. On the "feminization" of juvenile corrections, see Katz, *Irony of Early School Reform*, p. 193.

58. APA, *Proceedings, 1876*, p. 43ff.

59. "Report of the Indiana Board of Visitors," APA, *Proceedings, 1874*, p. 305; Elizabeth Comstock to Governor Thomas Hendricks, 21 December 1875, Papers of Thomas A. Hendricks, Box 21, Indiana State Archives, Indianapolis, Ind.; "Visitor's reports," IWP, *Annual Report, 1876*, pp. 52–54; Coffin, "An Account of the Origin," pp. 158, 161; NCCC, *Proceedings, 1878*, p. 21; MRPW, *Annual Report, 1878*, p. 13.

60. NCCC, *Proceedings, 1881*, p. 269.

61. Ibid.

62. J. J. Milligan, "Control of Vicious and Criminally Inclined Females," NCCC, *Proceedings, 1882*, p. 181 (emphasis added).

63. "Resolutions," APA, *Proceedings, 1885*, p. 319; "Address by President Hayes," APA, *Proceedings, 1887*, p. 54.

64. NCCC, *Proceedings, 1891*, p. 241.

65. Milligan, "Control," p. 184 (his emphasis).

Chapter 4

1. Eliza Mosher to her sister Hannah, 12 September 1877. Papers of Eliza Mosher, Bentley Historical Library, University of Michigan, Ann Arbor, Mich. All Mosher correspondence cited below is in this collection.

2. Harry Elmer Barnes, *The Evolution of Penology in Pennsylvania: A Study in American Social History* (Indianapolis: Bobbs-Merrill Co., 1927), pp. 78, 139; Michel Foucault, *Discipline and Punish: The Birth of the Prison*, trans. Alan Sheridan (New York: Pantheon Books, 1977), pp. 200–9; David J. Rothman, *The Discovery of the Asylum: Social Order and Disorder in the New Republic* (Boston: Little, Brown and Co., 1971), pp. 83–84; Norman Johnston, *The Human Cage: A Brief History of Prison Architecture* (New York: The American Foundation, Inc., Institute of Corrections, 1973); Z. R. Brockway, "The Reformatory System," in *The Reformatory System in the United States*, ed. Samuel J. Barrows (Washington, D.C.: Government Printing Office, 1900), pp. 17–27, esp. plan facing p. 24; Franklin B. Sanborn, "The Elmira Reformatory," in *The Reformatory System in the United States*, pp. 28–47.

3. Mass. Bd. CP, *Annual Report, 1875*, p. 63; Joseph Burnett, "The Proper Construction of Prisons for Women," APA, *Proceedings, 1876*, pp. 450–51; WPA, *Annual Reports, 1889*, p. 5 and *1891*, p. 5.

4. Frederick H. Wines, *The Massachusetts Reformatory Prison for Women* (Worcester, Mass., n.d.), pp. 2, 12; Isabel C. Barrows, "Ellen Cheney Johnson and the Sherborn Prison," *New England Magazine* 21 (January 1900): 616; Mass. Bd. Char., *Annual Report, 1877–78*, p. 217; Eugenia Lekkerker, *Reformatories for Women in the United States* (The Hague: J. B. Wolters, 1931), p. 94. The Framingham structure had a capacity of 500 inmates. The building, which consisted of three stories and a basement, cost over $300,000 to construct, or over $600 per inmate (Mass. Bd. Char., *Annual Report, 1877–78*, pp. 217–18). Cottages were built in the 1950s.

5. Western House of Refuge, *Annual Report, 1893*, p. 8; NY Bd. Char., *Annual Report, 1887*, p. 170; Minutes of Board of Managers, Hudson House of Refuge, 13 June 1903, in New York State Executive Department, Boards of Officers of State Institutions, New York State Library, Albany.

6. IWP, *Annual Report, 1908*, p. 5; *Reasons for Asking for the Separation of the Woman's Prison from the Reform School for Girls* (Pamphlet in Indiana State Library, c. 1901), p. 6. The institution cost $100,000, twice the initial appropriation, or $500 per inmate.

7. Isabel Barrows, "The Reformatory Treatment of Women in the United States," in *Penal and Reformatory Institutions*, ed. Charles Richmond Henderson (New York: Russell Sage Foundation, 1910), pp. 145, 154, 163. Infants born at the Indiana Women's Prison were removed as soon as they

could leave their mothers (IWP, *Annual Report, 1888*). At the Hudson House of Refuge, infants remained until age two and then went to orphan asylums in Albany, unless the mother was released or a relative could take the child (New York Commission of Prisons, *Annual Report, 1902*, p. 38 [hereafter cited as NYPC, *Annual Report*]).

8. F. H. Wines, *Massachusetts Reformatory Prison*, p. 7, noted the lack of architectural precedents and the inadequate appropriations.

9. The favorable comment on Framingham's design appeared in Lekker-kerker, *Reformatories for Women*, p. 94; the critical remark is by Lucy Rap-perport, "The Massachusetts Reformatory for Women, Framingham, Mas-sachusetts" (B. Arch. thesis, Harvard University Graduate School of Design, 1954). On Indiana's features, see IWP, *Annual Reports, 1871*, pp. 6–10 and *1874*, p. 5; and NCCC, *Proceedings, 1876*, pp. 25–27.

10. Western House of Refuge, *Second Annual Report*, pp. 11, 22; NY Bd. Char., *Annual Reports, 1892*, p. 48 and *1893*, p. liii; Papers of the Indiana State Board of Charities, Box MM, Indiana State Library, Indianapolis, Ind.; MRPW, *Annual Report, 1878*, pp. 12, 18; NCCC, *Proceedings, 1876*, p. 30.

11. APA, *Proceedings, 1876*, pp. 450–51.

12. Norma Vere Carson, "An Historical and Critical Study of New York State Reformatories for Women" (M.A. thesis, Columbia University, 1917), p. 53; Mass. Bd. CP, *Annual Report, 1877*, p. 65; NCCC, *Proceedings, 1876*, p. 28. Problems with male employees are discussed in "Correspondence," Box Q, Papers of the Indiana State Board of Charities.

13. Mass. Bd. CP, *Annual Reports, 1879*, p. 3, and *1880*, p. 14.

14. On inadequate staff and salaries, see: Carson, "New York State Re-formatories," pp. 67–70; Massachusetts General Court, Committee on Pris-ons, "Report on Penal Institutions," 24 April 1879, Senate Document no. 272, p. 9; Mass. Bd. CP, *Annual Report, 1887*, p. 165; Minutes of Board of Managers, Hudson House of Refuge, May 1902; NYPC, *Annual Report, 1900*, p. 104.

15. MRPW, *Annual Report, 1883*, p. 6; IWP, *Annual Report, 1883*, p. 14; Carson, "New York State Reformatories," pp. 150–53. Women physicians did not reside at the New York reformatories until 1900 (Hudson) and 1907 (Albion). Indiana's officer corps became completely female with the addition of a woman doctor in 1885. Nightwatchwoman was first sug-gested in "Investigation by State Board of Charities Committee on Penal and Reformatory Institutions, February 1896," Box Q, Papers of Indiana State Board of Charities, after the watchman was accused of impregnat-ing reformatory girls.

16. Warren Spalding, "Reformatory Prisons for Women," APA, *Proceed-ings, 1886*, p. 299; Sarah F. Keely, NCCC, *Proceedings, 1888*, pp. 207–8. See also NCCC, *Proceedings, 1876*, p. 28 and "The Best Woman's Prison," New York *Times*, 31 March 1895, pt. 4, p. 30.

17. Mosher to Hannah, 12 September 1877; Florence Woolsey Hazzard,

"Heart of the Oak: The Story of Eliza Mosher," pp. 3–4, in Papers of Eliza Mosher.

18. Mosher to family, 17 March and 4 August 1879; Hazzard, "Heart of the Oak," pp. 5–6.

19. Mosher to family, 4 August 1879.

20. Mosher to Hannah, January 1878 and 17 February 1879; Hazzard, "Heart of the Oak," pp. 7, 10.

21. Mosher, 3 December 1882 and 17 October 1881; Hazzard, "Heart of the Oak," pp. 7, 10; Massachusetts General Court, Committee on Prisons, "Report on Penal Institutions," 1881, House Document no. 421.

22. Hazzard, "Heart of the Oak," pp. 13–14; MRPW, *Annual Report, 1881*, p. 37; Alice Freeman to Clara Barton, 28 November 1883, Box 19, Papers of Clara Barton, Library of Congress, Washington, D.C. All Barton correspondence cited below is in this collection. I am grateful to Ellen Langenheim Henle, who is writing a career biography of Barton, for directing me to Barton's letters.

23. Mosher to Satie, 15 January 1881 and 6 November 1881.

24. Mosher to sister (?), 12 November 1882; Hazzard, "Heart of the Oak," pp. 35–37. Mosher returned to private practice and later became Dean of Women at the University of Michigan, as well as an inventor and the editor of the *Women's Medical Journal*. Mosher's ties to the prison were not entirely broken, however, for she had adopted a young Irish inmate whose family had rejected her. She secured nurse's training for the girl and made her one of her heirs (Hazzard, "Heart of the Oak," p. 34).

25. Letters to Clara Barton concerning her commission, Papers of Clara Barton; "The Best Woman's Prison," New York *Times*, 30 March 1895 pt. 4, p. 30.

26. Lucy Hall to Barton, 5 June 1883; Ellen Johnson to Barton, 22 May 1883. Inmate letters to Barton are full of personal communications, expressions of affection, and gratitude for her help.

27. A clipping from the Framingham (Mass.) *Gazette* (10 August 1883) anticipated that Barton would give free service at the prison because she had volunteered on the battlefield (Papers of Clara Barton).

28. Benjamin Butler to Barton, n.d.

29. Barton to Mr. Dwight, 8 February 1884, in response to his question, "Who has the worst time the jailer or the birds?"

30. Quoted in I. Barrows, "Ellen Cheney Johnson," p. 630.

31. (Her emphasis.) Johnson to Barton, 22 May, 5 and 6 June, and 1, 7, 18, and 30 September 1883, and esp. 19 December 1883.

32. Ellen Cheney Johnson, *Modern Prison Management: The Underlying Principles of Prison Reform, as Applied in the Reformatory Prison for Women at Sherborn, Massachusetts* (Boston: Massachusetts Prison Association, 1899), p. 4; Ellen Cheney Johnson, "Prison Discipline," APA, *Proceedings, 1897*, p. 345.

33. Former staff members to Barton, 28 March and 8 May 1884.

34. Massachusetts General Court, Committee on Prisons, "Report on Penal Institutions," 1884, Senate Document no. 369, p. 6.

35. Carson, "New York State Reformatories," p. 58; Western House of Refuge, *Seventh Annual Report*, pp. 6–7; NYPC, *Annual Report, 1902*, p. 46.

36. E. Johnson to Rhoda Coffin, 22 March 1892, in Papers of Charles F. and Rhoda M. Coffin, Earlham College, Richmond, Ind. The comments on the decline of the institution were made after a fire broke out at the prison while "Miss Keely was away as usual."

37. Letter to Governor Mount, 7 January 1901, Box Q: "Report of Investigation of Industrial School for Girls and Women's Prison Held December 31, 1900 to January 3, 1901," Box MM; "Investigations of Complaints," Box Q, (1908, 1913); "Investigations, 1913–1932," all in Papers of Indiana State Board of Charities; Indianapolis *Star*, 19 December 1905.

38. In 1890, the inmates of the Indiana, New York, and Massachusetts women's prisons constituted 28 percent of all female prisoners in state institutions in the United States, but this figure did not include those in county and local jails. In 1910, with all correctional facilities included, the women's prisons held only 1.2 percent of all female prisoners in America. U.S. Department of the Interior, Census Office, *Report on Crime, Pauperism and Benevolence in the United States at the Eleventh Census: 1890, Pt. 2* (Washington, D.C., 1895), table 10, pp. 21–24; Department of Commerce, Bureau of the Census, *Prisoners and Juvenile Delinquents in the United States, 1910* (Washington, D.C., 1918), table 60, p. 79.

39. *Reasons for Asking*, pp. 4–5; NCCC, *Proceedings, 1876*, p. 29.

40. Carson, "New York State Reformatories," pp. 105–7; Letter from Josephine Shaw Lowell, 17 February 1892, New York State Board of Charities Correspondence, New York State Library, Albany. Felons could also serve after 1896 if they had sentences of under one year. The original age range had been twelve to twenty-five; it was changed in 1899.

41. Mass. Bd. Char., *Annual Report, 1877–78*, p. 218; MRPW, *Annual Report, 1879*, p. 4.

42. Because changes over time were relatively slight, the mean for each category is presented to summarize the entire prison population over the period. For time series of annual percentages for inmate characteristics, see Estelle Freedman, "Their Sisters' Keepers" (Ph.D. diss., Columbia University, 1976), pp. 190–91, 403–7.

43. MRPW, *Annual Report, 1880*, p. 14.

44. These comparisons are based on the United States Prisoner Censuses for 1880, 1890, and 1910 for those categories in which the tables give data by state. The percentages of the female prison population in each category are displayed in table 5. The Massachusetts recidivism rates appear in Mass. Bd. CP, *Annual Reports, 1871*, p. 368 and *1873*. The recommitment rate for all Massachusetts institutions between 1864 and 1871 averaged 57 percent of all prisoners; for female inmates the average in 1873 was 57.6 percent recidivists.

45. The inmate sample of 640 cases drawn from every twelfth record for the years 1877–1883, 1887–1893, 1897–1903, and 1907–1913 was taken from the "History of Inmates" volumes at the Massachusetts Correctional Institution at Framingham. The cases consisted of relatively short, often abbreviated and inconsistent entries.

46. See Freedman, "Their Sisters' Keepers," (1976), table 10, for the means of annual statistics on all prisoners, broken down for drunkenness, prostitution, and larceny offenders, 1880 to 1901; and table 11, ibid., for the results of the sample of 640 inmate records at the MRPW, 1877 to 1913. Mosher's data appear in "Health of Criminal Women," *Boston Medical and Surgical Journal* 107 (October 1882): 316–17.

47. All cases discussed below come from the "History of Inmates." Inmates' names have been modified.

48. MRPW, *Annual Reports, 1895, 1896, 1898, 1900*. The average recidivism rates for these years were: public order, 72 percent; chastity, 16 percent; person or property, 12 percent. Of recidivists, 72 percent had only one previous conviction.

49. The longest sentences included: eighty-four months for attempted poisoning; seventy-eight months for abortion; thirty-six months for adultery.

Chapter 5

1. Rhoda Coffin, "An Account of the Origin and Conduct of the Women's Prison and Girl's Reformatory at Indianapolis, Indiana," in *Rhoda Coffin: Her Reminiscences, Addresses, Papers and Ancestry*, ed. Mary C. Johnson (New York: Grafton Press, 1910), pp. 156–57.

2. MRPW, *Annual Report, 1878*, p. 17.

3. NY Bd. Char., *Annual Report, 1888*, pp. 326–27.

4. Michael B. Katz, *The Irony of Early School Reform: Educational Innovation in Mid-Nineteenth-Century Massachusetts* (Cambridge, Mass.: Harvard University Press, 1968), pp. 191–92, 199.

5. For a description of classes, see Estelle Freedman, "Their Sisters' Keepers" (Ph.D. diss., Columbia University, 1976), pp. 226–29.

6. On the contract labor controversy, see Blake McKelvey, *American Prisons: A Study in American Social History prior to 1915* (Chicago: University of Chicago Press, 1936), chap. 5. "Domestic servants," "servants," and "other servants" were the top ranking female occupations from 1870 to 1950. Agricultural laborers ranked second until 1920 (Rosalyn Baxandall, Linda Gordon, and Susan Reverby, comps. and eds., *America's Working Women: A Documentary History, 1600 to the Present* [New York: Vintage Books, 1976], pp. 406–7).

7. Chace to E. C. Wines, APA, *Proceedings, 1870*, p. 580.

8. APA, *Proceedings, 1876*, p. 426.

9. IWP, *Annual Report, 1876*, pp. 15–16, 17, 45.

10. Rhoda Coffin, "Female Criminals and Convicts—Their Relation to the Labor Problem," Chicago *Daily News*, 9 April 1886; idem, "Convict Labor Issues," in *Rhoda Coffin*, p. 195.

11. IWP, *Annual Reports, 1877*, pp. 9–10; *1882*, p. 11; *1895*, p. 14; *1896*, p. 17; *1899*, p. 14; APA, *Proceedings, 1898*, p. 280.

12. Sarah Keely, "The Organization and Discipline of the Indiana Woman's Prison," APA, *Proceedings, 1898*, p. 280; IWP, *Annual Reports, 1911*, p. 8; *1912*, p. 7; *1914*, p. 6; *1915*, p. 5; "Visitors' Report," 22 April 1913, Box MM, Papers of the Indiana State Board of Charities, Indiana State Library, Indianapolis, Ind. Other prisons had a similar pattern. The Hudson refuge called for industrial training, but domestic work prevailed. The Western House of Refuge had "supervised housework," dressmaking, sewing, cooking, and a steam laundry. However an industrial building opened in 1910, and typing and stenography courses began after 1899 (NY Bd. Char., *Annual Report, 1890*, p. 44; Norma Vere Carson, "An Historical and Critical Study of New York State Reformatories for Women" [M.A. thesis, Columbia University, 1917], pp. 175–78; Philip Klein, *Prison Methods in New York State: A Contribution to the Study of the Theory and Practice of Correctional Institutions in New York State* [New York: Longmans, Green and Co., 1920], p. 266; NYPC, *Annual Report, 1901*, p. 38; Eugenia C. Lekkerkerker, *Reformatories for Women in the United States* [The Hague: J. B. Wolters, 1931], p. 103).

13. MRPW, *Annual Reports, 1879*, p. 40; *1883*, pp. 44–46; *1884*, p. 31; *1885*, p. 29; *1888*, p. 102; *1891*, p. 95; *1898*, p. 81; *1909*, p. 52; Isabel Barrows, "The Reformatory Treatment of Women in the United States," in *Penal and Reformatory Institutions*, ed. Charles Richmond Henderson (New York: Charities Publication Committee, 1910), p. 145.

14. MRPW, *Annual Report, 1893*, p. 83.

15. MRPW, *Annual Report, 1879*, pp. 18–19; Warren Spalding, "Some Methods of Preventing Crime," NCCC, *Proceedings, 1880*, pp. 67–68. (The 1879 law followed the precedent of both juvenile reformatories and a little-used statute that permitted the indenture of reformed nightwalkers.) Figures on indenture and returns to the prison were compiled from the list of indentures at the Framingham reformatory. From 1877 to 1913, 1,460 women went to service and 129 returned to the prison without completing their indentures, about 8.9 percent. A sample for the period 1878–1883 showed that prisoners served about three-fourths of their sentences before indenture, regardless of the crimes for which they had been imprisoned.

16. Ellen Cheney Johnson, APA, *Proceedings, 1887*, p. 170; Letters in reference to indenture, esp. 30 March 1881, 22 June 1881, and 15 June 1881, Letterbook of Warren Spalding, vol. 1, Massachusetts State Library, Boston, Mass.; Ellen C. Pratt to Mrs. Johnson, 22 November 1884, "History of Inmates," MRPW.

17. MRPW, *Annual Reports, 1879*, p. 19; *1885*, p. 4; Letterbook of Warren

Spalding. Want ads in Boston newspapers in the 1880s offered from $2 to $4 a week for domestics and $6 to $8 a week for mill workers.

18. Carrie W. to Clara Barton, 23 September 1883, Box 19, Papers of Clara Barton, Library of Congress, Washington, D.C.; Letters to Mrs. Johnson, 10 December 1886, 7 August 1886 in "History of Inmates," MRPW.

19. Letters to Mrs. Johnson, 10 December 1886 and 7 August 1886, in "History of Inmates," MRPW and letters to Johnson dated 7 May 1885, and 16 July 1886, Framingham, Mass.; letter to Mosher, 1 October 1882, in "History of Inmates," MRPW. After 1900, the New York House of Refuge at Albion also paroled women to homes and expected that employers would continue inmates' training (Minutes of the Managers of the New York State House of Refuge for Women at Albion, 1906, in New York State Executive Department, Boards of Officers of State Institutions, New York State Library, Albany [hereafter cited as "Albion Minutes"].

20. Letter to Johnson, 16 July 1886, in "History of Inmates," MRPW; MRPW, *Annual Report, 1888*, p. 99.

21. The proportion of household workers among all working women declined from 50.1 percent in 1870 to 29.4 percent in 1900 to 16.2 percent in 1920 (David Katzman, *Seven Days a Week* [New York: Oxford University Press, 1978]). On the increase in white collar jobs for women, see W. Elliot Brownlee and Mary M. Brownlee, *Women in the American Economy: A Documentary History, 1675–1929* (New Haven: Yale University Press, 1976), pp. 32–37.

22. Sarah Smith to E. C. Wines, March 1874, in APA, *Proceedings, 1874*, p. 306; "Reports of the Board of Visitors to the Indiana Woman's Prison," in IWP, *Annual Reports, 1874*, p. 26; *1875*, p. 14; *1876*, p. 26.

23. MRPW, *Annual Report, 1885*, p. 27.

24. Ellen Cheney Johnson, *Modern Prison Management: The Underlying Principles of Prison Reform, as Applied in the Reformatory Prison for Women at Sherborn, Massachusetts* (Boston: Massachusetts Prison Association, 1899), p. 5; idem, APA, *Proceedings, 1887*, pp. 80–81; "Albion Minutes," May 1907.

25. "The Best Woman's Prison," New York *Times*, 31 March 1895, pt. 4, p. 30.

26. Quoted in Edna Cheyney, *Louisa May Alcott: Her Life, Letters, and Journals* (Boston: Roberts Brothers, 1889), p. 322.

27. The story was often recalled, e.g., Smith in APA, *Proceedings, 1874*, p. 305.

28. E. Johnson, *Modern Prison Management*, p. 8; idem, "Prison Recreation," APA, *Proceedings, 1889*, pp. 209–15.

29. Morton, comment in APA, *Proceedings, 1900*, p. 270; idem, "Methods of Reform in Prisons for Women and Girls," APA, *Proceedings, 1905*, p. 90; idem, "The Treatment of Women Prisoners," APA, *Proceedings, 1906*, p. 282; and MRPW, *Annual Report, 1902*, p. 32.

30. MRPW, *Annual Reports, 1879*, p. 20; *1880*, pp. 10, 30; *1881*, p. 27;

1896, pp. 87–90; Ellen Cheney Johnson, "Prison Discipline," APA, *Proceedings, 1897*, p. 340; idem, "Prison Recreation," p. 213; Frederick Wines, *Massachusetts Reformatory Prison for Women* (Worcester, Mass., n.d.), p. 20; E. Johnson, *Modern Prison Management*, p. 5; IWP, *Annual Report, 1896*, p. 19; Carson, "New York State Reformatories," p. 207; Western House of Refuge, *Annual Report, 1898*, pp. 16–17; "Albion Minutes," 12 October 1909; Indianapolis *News*, 2 December 1903; Keely, "Indiana Woman's Prison," p. 280. Indiana prison privileges included butter on Sunday morning, tea for dinner every winter day, and immediate delivery of prisoner's mail.

31. MRPW, *Annual Report, 1903*, p. xii; MRPW, "Rules and Regulations," (1909), pp. 19–20, citing the Acts of 1903. New York and Indiana also instituted the indeterminant sentence in the early twentieth century.

32. IWP, *Annual Reports, 1879*, p. 6; *1884*, p. 20; *1888*, p. 16; *1882*, p. 10; *1885*, p. 10; Keely, "Indiana Woman's Prison," p. 281; MRPW, *Annual Report, 1883*, pp. 48–49.

33. MRPW, *Annual Report, 1896*, p. 91.

34. Smith to E. C. Wines, APA, *Proceedings, 1874*, p. 306; Keely, "Indiana Woman's Prison," p. 281; IWP, *Annual Reports, 1879*, p. 6; *1884*, p. 20; *1888*, p. 16; *1885*, p. 10; "Visitors' Report," 17 February 1910, Box MM, Papers of the Indiana State Board of Charities. The 1884 Indiana *Annual Report* noted solitary confinement might be required for up to several weeks to secure submission. According to a New York *Times* report in 1887, women were "cruelly whipped and made to stand in uncomfortable positions for long periods of time" (*Times*, 29 November 1887, p. 2). In 1881 in Massachusetts, one lawyer accused the prison of long solitary confinement (nineteen days), poor medical treatment, and the cropping of an inmate's hair for attempted escape (Letterbook of Warren Spalding, p. 168).

35. NYPC, *Annual Report, 1900*, p. 104; NY Bd. Char., *Annual Report, 1888*, pp. 330–31; Klein, *Prison Methods*, pp. 226–27; "The Hudson House of Refuge for Women," *Charities Review* 9 (December 1899): 369, 429–31; Carson, "New York State Reformatories," pp. 207–12.

36. New York Prison Commission, *Investigation of the State Prisons and Report Thereon, 1876* (Albany, 1877), p. 374. A black woman who had been punished was found dead in her cell.

37. Massachusetts General Court, Committee on Prisons, "Report on Penal Institutions," 1888, Senate Document no. 287, p. 9; MRPW, *Annual Report, 1888*, p. 81. On Hudson, see n. 35 above.

38. Indianapolis *News*, 2 February 1903.

39. F. Wines, *Massachusetts Reformatory*, pp. 18–19; also cited in I. Barrows, "The Reformatory Treatment of Women," p. 149.

40. I. Barrows, "The Reformatory Treatment of Women," p. 153.

41. On "total institutions," see Erving Goffman, *Asylums: Essays on the Social Situation of Mental Patients and Other Inmates* (Garden City, N.Y.: Doubleday and Co., 1961), p. 4.

42. Mina B. to Clara Barton, 18 June 1883, Papers of Clara Barton. For a discussion of the process of "mortification" on entry into total institutions, see Goffman, *Asylums*, pp. 23ff.

43. Quoted in Isabel Barrows, "The Massachusetts Reformatory Prison for Women," in *The Reformatory System in the United States*, ed. Samuel J. Barrows (Washington, D.C.: Government Printing Office, 1900), pp. 125–26. Goffman describes a similar process of "conversion" in which "the inmate appears to take over the official or staff view of himself and tries to act out the role of the perfect inmate" (*Asylums*, p. 63). Bruno Bettleheim's study of the concentration camp experience is the classic analysis of prisoners' identification with guards. See "Individual and Mass Behavior in Extreme Situations," *Journal of Abnormal Psychology* 38 (October 1943): 447.

44. Massachusetts Governor and Council, "Investigations of State Departments and Institutions" vol. 3, (1911), Massachusetts State Library, Boston, Mass. The following excerpts are taken from various points in prisoner testimony.

45. Elizabeth F. to Clara Barton, 26 June 1883, Papers of Clara Barton.

46. Reports cited are from I. Barrows, "The Massachusetts Reformatory," pp. 112, 125 and letters inserted into the "History of Inmates," MRPW. Former inmates did return to visit; one wrote thanking Clara Barton for allowing her to call: "You are my only friend I have to visit" (Carrie to Barton, 13 December 1883, Papers of Clara Barton).

47. MRPW, *Annual Report, 1902*, p. 31.

48. E.g., Edward Grubb, *Methods of Penal Administration in the United States: Notes of a Personal Inquiry, February and March 1904* (London: Wertheimer, Lea and Co., 1904), p. 25.

49. For an historical analysis of one female institution, Mt. Holyoke, that does raise questions about hierarchy and power, see Louise Knauer, "Mothers in Israel, Daughters of Zion: Recruitment of Evangelical Missionaries, 1840–1890" (Paper delivered at the Fourth Berkshire Conference on the History of Women, Mt. Holyoke College, 25 August 1978).

Chapter 6

1. Gibbons died in 1893 at age 92; Chace and Ellen Cheney Johnson in 1899 at ages 93 and 70, respectively; Lowell in 1905 at age 62; and Coffin in 1909 at age 83.

2. The proportion of American women who did not marry peaked at 10 to 11 percent for the generation born between 1860 and 1880. The total fertility rate for white women declined from 6.73 in 1820 to 3.17 in 1920. Labor force participation expanded from approximately 10 percent of all women in 1860 to 24 percent in 1920 (Daniel Scott Smith, "Family Limitation, Sexual Control and Domestic Feminism in Victorian America," in *Clio's Consciousness Raised: New Perspectives on the History of Women*, ed.

Mary S. Hartman and Lois Banner [New York: Harper and Row, 1974], tables 1, 2, 3, pp. 121–23 and W. Elliot Brownlee and Mary M. Brownlee, *Women in the American Economy: A Documentary History, 1675–1929* [New Haven: Yale University Press, 1976], pp. 24–29).

3. Leon Radzinowicz, *In Search of Criminology* (Cambridge, Mass.: Harvard University Press, 1962), pp. 114–18; Arthur E. Fink, *Causes of Crime: Biological Theories in the United States, 1880–1915* (Philadelphia: University of Pennsylvania Press, 1938); Mark H. Haller, *Eugenics: Hereditarian Attitudes in American Thought* (New Brunswick, N.J.: Rutgers University Press, 1963), pp. 40–44.

4. Peter Tyor, "Segregation or Surgery: The Mentally Retarded in America, 1850–1920" (Ph.D. diss., Northwestern University, 1972), pp. 134, 195–97, 201; George Stocking, *Race, Culture, and Evolution* (New York: Free Press, 1968), chap. 10; Stanley Powell Davies, *Social Control of the Mentally Deficient* (New York: Thomas Crowell Co., 1930), pp. 66, 67. After 1900, the rediscovery of Mendel's laws of inheritance replaced the Lamarkian theory of the inheritance of acquired traits which had previously tempered strict biological determinism.

5. The eugenicists claimed that they could alleviate the problems of crime, pauperism, and insanity by controlling weaker biological strains in the population through sterilization, permanent institutionalization of the feebleminded, and immigration restriction. See Haller, *Eugenics*, pp. 6, 15 and Seymour Halleck, "American Psychiatry and the Criminal: A Historical Review," *American Journal of Psychiatry* 121 (March 1965): iv–v. On racial thought, see Oscar Handlin, *Race and Nationality in American Life* (Boston: Little, Brown and Co., 1957) and John Higham, *Strangers in the Land: Patterns of American Nativism, 1860–1925* (New Brunswick, N.J.: Rutgers University Press, 1955).

6. Anthropologist Franz Boas presented evidence of environmental influences on immigrants; French sociologist Gabriel Tarde influenced Americans with his critique of biological determinism; American sociologist William I. Thomas repudiated his earlier biological interpretations for a cultural explanation of abnormal behavior. See Rosalind Rosenberg, "The Dissent from Darwin, 1890–1930: The New View of Woman among American Social Scientists" (Ph.D. diss., Stanford University, 1974), pp. 79–80, 136, 145.

7. The Juvenile Psychopathic Institute, directed between 1909 and 1917 by William Healy, was founded and staffed primarily by women Progressives. Many of the psychologists who worked with Healy contributed to the literature discussed in this chapter, including Jean Weidensall, Edith Spaulding, Mary Hayes, and Augusta Bronner (who married Healy in 1932). James Angell, chairman of the University of Chicago psychology department, where most of these women trained, was a member of the Institute's Advisory Council. Julia Lathrop was the president of the Institute. (William Healy, *The Individual Delinquent: A Textbook of Diagnosis*

and Prognosis for All Concerned in Understanding Offenders [Boston: Little, Brown and Co., 1915], app. B.)

8. "Frances Kellar" [*sic*], *National Cyclopaedia of American Biography*, 51 vols. (New York: James White and Co., 1898–1973), 15:248; "New York State to Protect Aliens," *Survey* 25 (November 1919): 171–72; *The Arbitration Journal* 6 (1951): 194–95; New York *Times*, 5 January 1952, p. 11.

9. On the proliferation of Lombroso's theories in America in the 1890s, see Anthony Platt's discussion of "The Natural Criminal," in *The Child Savers: The Invention of Delinquency* (Chicago: University of Chicago Press, 1969), pp. 18–28. Although Lombroso's later works also credited environmental origins of criminality, his major legacy was the theory of the born criminal type. See: Walter Reckless, *Criminal Behavior* (New York: McGraw-Hill Book Co., 1940), pp. 164, 401–3; Christopher Hibbert, *The Roots of Evil: A Social History of Crime and Punishment* (Boston: Little, Brown and Co., 1963), pp. 194–95, 225; Leon Radzinowicz, *Ideology and Crime: A Study of Crime in its Social and Historical Context* (London: Heineman Educational Books, 1966), pp. 46–57; Carol Smart, *Women, Crime and Criminology: A Feminist Critique* (London: Routledge and Kegan Paul, 1977), pp. 31–37.

10. Cesare Lombroso and William Ferrero, *The Female Offender* (New York: D. Appleton and Co., 1900; originally published in English, 1895), chaps. 1–4, esp. pp. 152, 187.

11. Ibid., pp. 147–51.

12. Ibid., p. 152. Americans echoed his theories in, e.g., August Drahms, *The Criminal: His Personnel and Environment, a Scientific Study* (New York: Macmillan Co., 1900) and H. Harrell, "Women as Criminals," *Arena* 24 (July 1900): 108–12.

13. Franz Boas, for example, criticized Lombroso's methodology and conclusions in his review of the *Female Offender* in the March 1897 issue of *Psychological Review* (cited in Rosenberg, "Dissent from Darwin," p. 78).

14. Frances Kellor, "Criminal Sociology: The American vs. the Latin School," *Arena* 23 (March 1900): 303–4; idem, "Psychological and Environmental Study of Women Criminals," *American Journal of Sociology* 5 (January 1900): 528.

15. Kellor, "Psychological and Environmental Study," pp. 528–30; idem, "Criminal Sociology: Criminality Among Women," *Arena* 23 (May 1900): esp. pp. 516, 524.

16. Kellor, "Psychological and Environmental Study," p. 531.

17. Ibid., pp. 533–43. She did note that prostitutes scored poorly on the tests and were mentally and physically weaker than other women criminals.

18. Ibid. In a separate article on psychological tests of black women criminals, Kellor again stressed environment over heredity: "There are no defects among the negroes which show idiocy or degeneracy so much as they show diverted and undeveloped capabilities" (Frances Kellor, "The

Criminal Negro: A Sociological Study," *Arena* 25–26 [January–November 1901]: 66).

19. Kellor, "Psychological and Environmental Study," pp. 519, 675.

20. Ibid., pp. 680–81.

21. Kellor, "Criminality Among Women," pp. 516, 521 and "Psychological and Environmental Study," p. 679.

22. Kellor, "Criminality Among Women," p. 521.

23. Ibid., p. 517.

24. Linda Gordon makes this important differentiation between an environmentalism that cites influences on the individual and one that cites influences on the basis of sex or class (Gordon, *Woman's Body, Woman's Right: A Social History of Birth Control in America* [New York: Grossman, 1976], p. 303).

25. Tyor, "Segregation or Surgery," p. 214. Henry Goddard, who introduced intelligence tests to the United States and wrote *The Criminal Imbecile* (1915) and *The Kallikak Family* (1912), presented this view to the APA (*Proceedings, 1912*, pp. 353–57) and in "Relation of Feeblemindedness to Crime," *Bulletin of the American Academy of Medicine* 15 (April 1914): 105–12.

26. European writers who linked mental capacity and criminality included Charles Goring, Havelock Ellis, and Gustav Aschaffenburg. In America, Dr. Walter S. Fernald, of the Massachusetts School for the Feeble Minded, urged the term "defective delinquent" and claimed that 25 percent of all prisoners were mentally defective. Even William Healy's *The Individual Delinquent* (1915) cited mentality as a "causative factor" (p. 30). For an uncritical summary of the studies on mentality and crime and a bibliographic guide to them, see James Burt Miner, *Deficiency and Delinquency: An Interpretation of Mental Testing* (Baltimore: Warwick and York, Inc., 1918). See also: Tyor, "Segregation or Surgery," p. 195; Corrine Bacon, *Prison Reform* (New York: H. W. Wilson Co., 1917), p. 417; Davies, *Social Control*.

27. Frank Tannenbaum, *Crime and the Community* (Boston: Ginn and Company, 1938), pp. 203, 206.

28. "Katharine Bement Davis," *NAW*, 1:439–41; Mabel Jacques Eichel, "Katharine Bement Davis," *Woman's Journal* 13 (April 1928): 20–21, 41; Obituary, New York *Times*, 11 December 1935, p. 23. Davis's methods at Bedford Hills are discussed in the next chapter.

29. Katharine Davis, introduction to Mabel Ruth Fernald et al., *A Study of Women Delinquents in New York State* (1920; reprint Montclair, N.J.: Patterson Smith, 1968), p. vii; idem, "Moral Imbeciles," APA, *Proceedings, 1906*, pp. 345–46; idem, "The New York State Reformatory for Women," *Survey* 25 (February 1911): 851–54; idem, "A Study of Prostitutes Committed from New York City to the State Reformatory for Women, Bedford Hills," in George Kneeland, *Commercialized Prostitution in New York City* (New York: Century Co., 1913), chap. 8.

30. Davis, "Reformation of Women: Modern Methods of Dealing With Offenders," *Annals of the American Academy of Political and Social Science* 36 (July 1910): 38.

31. Rowland, "Report of Experiments at the State Reformatory for Women at Bedford, New York," *Psychological Review* 20 (May 1913): 245–48; Katharine Davis, introduction to Jean Weidensall, *The Mentality of the Criminal Woman: A Comparative Study of the Criminal Woman, the Working Girl and the Efficient Working Woman in a Series of Mental and Physical Tests* (Baltimore: Warwick and York, 1916).

32. New York State Reformatory for Women, Bedford Hills, New York, *Annual Report, 1911–1912*, pp. 10, 11, 20 (hereafter cited as BH, *Annual Report*); Davis, introduction to *The Mentality of the Criminal Woman*, pp. xi, xii. The directors of the Bureau of Social Hygiene were Rockefeller, Davis, stockbroker Paul M. Warburg, and attorney Starr J. Murphy. On the white slave scare and investigations of prostitution, see: Roy Lubove, "The Progressives and the Prostitute," *Historian* 24 (May 1962): 308–30; Egal Feldman, "Prostitution, the Alien Woman, and the Progressive Imagination, 1910–1915," *American Quarterly* 19 (Summer 1967): 192–206; and Jeremy P. Felt, "Vice Reform as a Political Technique: The Committee of Fifteen in New York, 1900–1901," *New York History* 54 (January 1973): 24–51. On shifting interpretations, see, Robert Riegel, "Changing American Attitudes toward Prostitution," *Journal of the History of Ideas* 29 (July–September 1968): 437–52.

33. BH, *Annual Report, 1911–1912*, p. 21. Total costs for building, equipment, and maintenance for five years were over $100,000. Members of the staff of the laboratory included, at various times, Spaulding, Weidensall, Mabel Fernald, Mary Hayes, Buford Johnson, Jessie Taft, Margaret Cobb, Almena Dawley, Virginia Robinson, Vida Elvin, Marie Lawrence, Grace Massoneau, Maude Moore, Mary B. Clark, Agnes Crowley, Christine Brigham, Helen Towey, Marjorie Taft, and Louise Russell. On Rockefeller's support for medical research, see Barbara Ehrenreich and Deirdre English, *For Her Own Good: 150 Years of the Experts' Advice to Women* (Garden City, N.Y.: Anchor Press, 1978), pp. 74–77.

34. "Clara Jean Weidensall," in *Woman's Who's Who of America*, ed. John William Leonard (New York: American Commonwealth Co., 1914), p. 863.

35. Weidensall, "The Woman Offender," New York City Conference of Charities and Corrections, *Proceedings, 1914* (Albany, 1914), p. 199.

36. Weidensall, *Mentality of the Criminal Woman*, pp. 250, 268, 246, 249. The comparative data came from another woman social scientist, Helen Wooley Thompson, in Cincinnati. Weidensall's results confirmed the findings of Augusta Bronner, whose study of 500 criminals showed that only 10 percent were feebleminded (Bronner, "A Research on the Proportion of Mental Defectives Among Delinquents," cited in Davies, *Social Control*, p. 174).

37. Alberta S. Guibord, "Are the Disciplinary Cases in a Reformatory

Identical with Psychopathic Cases?" APA, *Proceedings, 1915*, pp. 122–24.

38. The hospital for psychopathic delinquent women operated at Bedford Hills between 1916 and 1918. An average of eighteen patients resided at any one time, for approximately seven months each. The selection was based on symptoms of personality disorders, not on IQ scores. Nurses who had been trained in mental hospitals offered occupational therapy, recreation, and physical exercise. The hospital also provided hydrotherapy and treatment for venereal disease. The staff encouraged patients to assume some institutional responsibilities, and at least a dozen inmates served on the hospital staff. (Edith R. Spaulding, *An Experimental Study of Psychopathic Delinquent Women* [New York: Rand McNally and Co., 1923].)

39. Edith R. Spaulding and William Healy, "Inheritance as a Factor in Criminality," *Bulletin of the American Academy of Medicine* 15 (February 1914): 4–27.

40. MRPW, *Annual Reports, 1911*, pp. 50, 51; *1913*, p. 55; *1914*, pp. xii, 45; Edith M. Burleigh, "New Use of a Clinic in a Woman's Reformatory," *Survey* 31 (November 1913): 155; Edith R. Spaulding, "The Results of Mental and Physical Examinations of 400 Women Offenders: with particular reference to their treatment during commitment," *Journal of Criminal Law and Criminology* 5 (January 1915): 704–18.

41. Spaulding, *An Experimental Study*, pp. 101, 102, 117.

42. Ibid., p. 109.

43. Ibid., pp. 14–17, 48, 99, 137. Cf. other recommendations for separate treatment of psychopathic women prisoners: Louise Ordahl and George Ordahl, "A Study of 49 Female Convicts," *Journal of Delinquency* 2 (November 1917): 331–51; Louise Stevens Bryant, "The Women at the House of Correction in Homesburg, Pennsylvania," *Journal of Criminal Law and Criminology* 8 (March 1918): 844–89; Clinton P. McCord, "One Hundred Female Offenders: A Study of the Mentality of Prostitutes and 'Wayward' Girls," *Journal of Criminal Law and Criminology* 6 (September 1915): 385–87, 407.

44. Miner, *Deficiency and Delinquency*, pp. 140–41.

45. The most radical critique appeared in Emma Goldman, "The Traffic in Women," in *Anarchism and Other Essays* (New York: Mother Earth Publishing Co., 1910). On radicals' views of prostitution see Leslie Fishbein, "Righteousness, Romance, Sex Drives, Hard Cash: Changing Views of Prostitution, 1870–1920" (Paper delivered at the Organization of American Historians, Atlanta, Ga., 1977). I am appreciative of correspondence from Dorie Klein that emphasized this point.

46. Gabriel Tarde, *Penal Philosophy* (Boston: Little, Brown and Co., 1912; originally published 1900); Healy, *Individual Delinquent*; William Adrian Bonger, *Criminality and Economic Conditions*, trans. Henry P. Horton (Boston: Little, Brown and Co., 1916).

47. Goldman, "Traffic in Women"; Charlotte Perkins Gilman, *Women*

and Economics (Boston, 1900: Small, Maynard and Co.; originally published 1898).

48. For instance, in "The Woman and the Law: A View of the Proper Judicial Treatment of the Female Lawbreaker," John J. Freschi wrote: "And at the bottom of this is the shifting of woman's sphere from the home to the outside world; the lowering of the bars of conventionality ... " (*Harper's Weekly* 55 [September 1911]: 7–8). See Mary Conyngton, *Relation Between Occupation and Criminality of Women* (Washington, D.C.: Government Printing Office, 1911), p. 11. For a contemporary revival of this theory, see Freda Adler, *Sisters in Crime: The Rise of the New Female Criminal* (New York: McGraw-Hill, 1975). Reactions to her views appear in *Proceedings of the National Conference on Women and Crime*, Washington, D.C., 26–27 February 1976 (sponsored by the National League of Cities and the U.S. Conference of Mayors), esp. pp. 3–21.

49. Conyngton, *Criminality of Women*, esp. pp. 15, 29, 57, 65–68.

50. Ibid., p. 71.

51. Fernald, *Women Delinquents in New York State*, pp. 434, 527–29. All mental tests excluded non-English speaking cases and controlled for race. Each institutional group had IQ scores comparable to the male groups for those institutions. Correlations between test scores and recidivism, types of offense, age at first conviction, and length of term served all produced coefficients under .20. Fernald's critique of the methods of mental testing and explanation of her methodology appear on pp. 413–14.

52. Fernald, *Women Delinquents in New York State*, pp. 5, 6.

53. Ibid., p. 525. The "poorer" the home, the earlier the age of first conviction; the larger the family, the more likely it was to produce a criminal. "Defective strains" that might be inherited affected a significant minority of the families: 20 percent included alcoholics; 16 percent had epilepsy, feeblemindedness, insanity, or neurosis; 19 percent had tuberculosis. The study devoted only two pages to hereditary defects.

54. Ibid., p. 527.

55. Jeanne Robert, "The Care of Women in State Prisons," *Review of Reviews* 44 (July 1911): 83–84.

56. O'Reilly quoted in ibid., p. 83; Kate Richards O'Hare, *In Prison* (New York: Alfred A. Knopf, 1923; originally published 1920; reprint ed., Seattle: University of Washington Press, 1976), p. 73.

57. These pamphlets are in the Louise de Koven Bowen Scrapbook, vol. 1, Chicago Historical Society, Chicago, Ill.

58. Menken was a member of the Jewish Board of Guardians and an organizer of New York City's Jewish "Big Sisters" (Alice Davis Menken, interview in *Jewish Chronicle*, December 1916, in Menken Scrapbook 1, Box 6, Papers of Alice Davis Menken, American Jewish Historical Society, Waltham, Massachusetts).

59. Maude E. Miner, "The Woman Delinquent," *Proceedings of the Second*

New York City Conference of Charities and Corrections (Albany, 1911), p. 163.

60. E. R. A. Seligman, *The Social Evil, with Special Reference to Conditions Existing in the City of New York* (New York: G. P. Putnam's Sons, 1902), pp. 173–74. Lubove, "The Progressives and the Prostitute"; Joseph Mayer, "The Passing of the Red Light District," cited in Howard B. Woolston, *Prostitution in the United States, Volume 1: Prior to the Entrance of the United States into the World War* (New York: Century Company, 1921), p. 266.

61. M. Miner, "Woman Delinquent," p. 163; Menken, *Can We Help Our Unfortunate Sister, and How?* pamphlet in Scrapbook, Papers of Alice Davis Menken.

62. See Davies, *Social Control*, p. 148ff.

63. On pragmatism, see Richard Hofstadter, *Social Darwinism in American Thought* (Boston: Beacon Press, 1971), pp. 49, 123, 167, 169 and John Burnham, "Psychiatry, Psychology and the Progressive Movement," *American Quarterly* 12 (Winter 1960): 457–65. On professionals' status interests, see: Platt, *The Child Savers*, pp. 19–29 and Roy Lubove, *The Professional Altruist: The Emergence of Social Work as a Career: 1880–1930* (Cambridge, Mass.: Harvard University Press, 1965), pp. 220–21.

Chapter 7

1. On the Progressive era concern over prostitution, see Ruth Rosen, "Prostitution: Symbol of an Age" (Paper presented at the American Historical Association Meeting, San Francisco, 29 December 1978) and Robert Riegel, "Changing American Attitudes Toward Prostitution," *Journal of History of Ideas* 29 (July–September, 1968): 437–52.

2. Roy Lubove, "The Progressives and the Prostitute," *Historian* 24 (May 1962): 308–30, and Egal Feldman, "Prostitution, the Alien Woman, and the Progressive Imagination, 1910–1915," *American Quarterly* 19 (Summer 1967): 192–206.

3. Feldman, "Prostitution," pp. 201–3.

4. Katherine Hattendorf, "The Big Sister Movement," APA, *Proceedings, 1922*, p. 141.

5. Otto Wilson, *Fifty Years Work With Girls, 1883–1933: A Story of the Florence Crittenton Homes* (Alexandria, Va.: The National Florence Crittenton Mission, 1933), p. 8. Other rescue homes operating in this period include: the Magdalen Home, the Catholic Protective Society, the Empire Friendly Shelter (for black women), and the Salvation Army Rescue Homes (Alice Menken, "Survey of Reformatory and Correctional Institutions," 1919, Box 6, Papers of Alice Davis Menken, American Jewish Historical Society, Waltham, Mass., pp. 20–35).

6. Chlöe Owings, *Women Police: A Study of the Development and Status*

of the Women Police Movement (New York: Frederick H. Hitchcock, 1925), app. 1; Eleonore L. Hutzel, "The Work of a Policewoman," APA, *Proceedings, 1922*, pp. 73–75; Maude E. Miner, "The Policewoman and the Girl Problem," NCCC, *Proceedings, 1919*, pp. 134–38; Helen D. Pigeon, "Policewomen in the United States," *Journal of Criminal Law and Criminology* 18 (November 1927): 373.

7. Martha Falconer, *The Jail as a Perverter of Womanhood* (New York: Russell Sage Foundation, 1922), pp. 3–5. For a similar complaint, see "Some Difficulties in Reformatory Work Among Women," APA, *Proceedings, 1907*, pp. 235–39.

8. On Massachusetts, Elizabeth L. Tuttle, "Probation," APA, *Proceedings, 1901*, pp. 229–33; on Chicago, Adena Miller Rich, "Detention of the Woman Offender," in *Reports Comprising the Survey of the Cook County Jail made by the Chicago Community Trust at the request of the Board of Commissioners of Cook County, Ill.* (Chicago, n.d.), pp. 114–18.

9. George E. Worthington and Ruth Topping, *Specialized Courts Dealing with Sex Delinquency* (New York: Frederick H. Hitchcock, 1921).

10. Frederick H. Whitin, "The Women's Night Court in New York City," *Annals of the American Academy of Political and Social Sciences* 52 (March 1914): 181–82; Worthington and Topping, *Specialized Courts*, pp. 274–79, 345; Irving W. Halpern, *A Decade of Probation* (1939; reprint, Montclair, N.J.: Patterson Smith, 1969), p. 16.

11. On other reformers who wanted to reserve institutionalization for the "notoriously debauched" or feebleminded, see E. R. A. Seligman, *The Social Evil, with Special Reference to Conditions Existing in the City of New York* (New York: G. P. Putnam's Sons, 1902), p. 176.

12. Worthington and Topping, *Specialized Courts*, pp. 345, 360; Menken, "Survey of Reformatory and Correctional Institutions," Papers of Alice Davis Menken, p. 3; Maude E. Miner, "Treatment of Women Offenders," NCCC, *Proceedings, 1912*, p. 311; Charles Richmond Henderson, *Preventive Agencies and Methods* (New York: Charities Publication Committee, 1910), pp. 190–98. Of those convicted in the New York Women's Court, 9 percent were sentenced to the reformatory and 78 percent served at the workhouse on Blackwell's Island (Whitin, "The Women's Night Court," p. 184).

13. Worthington and Topping, *Specialized Courts*, pp. 4, 26–29, 31, 83–91, 111, 395–97; Whitin, "The Women's Night Court, p. 182. In Chicago, a Women's Protective Association, founded in 1916, followed the cases of women offenders through the court proceedings.

14. Whitin, "The Women's Night Court," p. 182.

15. Recommendations of vice commission reports are one indication of this response. Of twenty-five reports summarized in a 1918 survey, as many recommended rescue work with women as called for establishing reformatories (Joseph Mayer, "The Passing of the Red Light District," cited in Howard B. Woolston, *Prostitution in the United States, Volume 1: Prior*

to the Entrance of the United States into the World War [New York: Century Company, 1921], pp. 266–67).

16. Jack M. Holl, *Juvenile Reform in the Progressive Era: William R. George and the Junior Republic Movement* (Ithaca: Cornell University Press, 1971), esp. introduction. Holl noted that women's clubs and organizations were responsible for founding five of the seven Junior Republics in America (pp. 14–15).

17. "Sing Sing and Warden Osborne," in Corinne Bacon, *Prison Reform* (New York: H. W. Wilson Co., 1917), pp. 109–46; Thomas Mott Osborne, "New Methods at Sing Sing Prison," ibid., p. 120.

18. WPA, *Annual Report, 1892*; Abby Hopper Gibbons to D. N. Carvalho, 2 August 1892, in *Life of Abby Hopper Gibbons, Told Chiefly through Her Correspondence*, ed. Sarah Hopper Emerson (New York: Knickerbocker Press, 1897), p. 307; William Rhinelander Stewart, *The Philanthropic Work of Josephine Shaw Lowell* (New York: Macmillan Co., 1911), pp. 308–12, 317–19.

19. NYPC, *Annual Report, 1901*, p. 36; WPA, *Annual Report, 1901*, p. 25; "Data on Classification of Inmates," typescript from superintendent's reports, New York State Reformatory for Women, Bedford Hills, N.Y., p. 1. These excerpts and summaries of Katharine Davis' reports for the years 1901 to 1911 will hereafter be cited as BH, "Reports."

20. BH, "Reports," 1907.

21. BH, "Reports," 1906; Minutes of the meetings of the Board of Managers, New York State Reformatory for Women at Bedford, 19 March 1903, in New York State Executive Department, Boards of Officers of State Institutions, New York State Library, Albany. These minutes, which run from 1902 to 1911, hereafter will be cited as BH, "Minutes of Managers."

22. BH, "Reports," 1902–1905; BH, "Minutes of Managers," 12 June 1903.

23. BH, "Reports," 1901–1903, 1905, 1907, 1909; BH, *Annual Reports, 1911–12*, p. 13; *1914–1915*, p. 28.

24. Ida M. Tarbell, "Good Will to Woman," *American Magazine* 75 (December 1912): 49; BH, "Reports, 1903–1906.

25. BH, "Reports," 1903.

26. Ibid., 1902–1905, 1908; BH, "Minutes of Managers," 8 May 1903.

27. BH, "Reports," 1903; NYPC, *Annual Report, 1906*, p. 129; BH, "Reports," 1909.

28. Two other sources influenced her. Progressives often depicted residents of the large cities as the victims of insufficient light, air, and exercise. In addition, many Progressive women, and a few of their predecessors (like Drs. Eliza and Clelia Mosher), promoted physical exercise as a feminist reform.

29. Katharine B. Davis, "The Fresh Air Treatment for Moral Disease,"

APA, *Proceedings, 1905*, pp. 205–12 and "Outdoor Work for Women," NCCC, *Proceedings, 1909*, pp. 289–94.

30. BH, "Reports," 1901, 1905; BH, *Annual Reports, 1911–1912*, pp. 7, 24; *1914–1915*, pp. 22–23.

31. Tarbell, "Good Will," p. 50; "Heavy Work for Women," New York *Daily Tribune*, 4 June 1905, pt. 2, p. 5; William McAdoo, "Women Offenders in New York," NCCC, *Proceedings, 1912*, p. 229.

32. "Jessie Donaldson Hodder," *NAW*, 2:197–99; Obituary, New York *Times*, 20 November 1931, p. 23; Correspondence with Elizabeth Glendower Evans in Papers of Elizabeth Glendower Evans, Box 1, Schlesinger Library, Radcliffe College, Cambridge, Mass. Alfred Hodder married Mary Gwyn, an associate of M. Carey Thomas' at Bryn Mawr. He died, probably a suicide, before Jessie Hodder could conclude her bigamy case against him. Their daughter had died in Switzerland and Jessie raised their son alone.

33. MRPW, *Annual Report, 1911*, pp. 48–49.

34. MRPW, *Annual Report, 1913*, p. 52. Some reformers had already abandoned it. In 1911, Massachusetts Prison Commissioner Mary Boyle O'Reilly resigned from her position "in disgust" at the failures of the reformatory.

35. MRPW, *Annual Reports, 1911*, pp. 52–53; *1913*, pp. 52, 55–56; Massachusetts Governor and Council, "Investigations of State Departments and Institutions" vol. 3, n. 11, (1911), Massachusetts State Library, Boston, Mass.

36. MRPW, *Annual Report, 1914*, p. 45; Jessie Hodder to Julia C. Lathrop, 18 August 1912, folder 591, Papers of Ethel Sturges Dummer, Schlesinger Library, Radcliffe College, Cambridge, Mass.

37. MRPW, *Annual Report, 1911*, p. 53; "History of Framingham," typescript covering the years 1919–1926, p. 19, Massachusetts Correctional Institution, Framingham, Mass.

38. Massachusetts "Investigations of State Departments and Institutions"; MRPW, *Annual Reports, 1911*, p. 168; *1912*, p. 162; *1913*, p. 53. Herndon still wanted to cultivate prisoners' sentiments through nature and domesticity. Hodder had the support of prison physician Frances Potter in arguing for vocational training.

39. *Annual Report* of the Board of Directors of the Connecticut State Farm for Women to the Governor, 1 July 1917 to 30 September 1918, pp. 7, 9.

40. Harry Elmer Barnes, *A History of the Penal, Reformatory and Correctional Institutions of the State of New Jersey: Analytical and Documentary* (Trenton, N.J.: MacCrellish and Quigley Co., 1918), p. 306; James Leiby, *Charity and Correction in New Jersey: A History of State Welfare Institutions* (New Brunswick, N.J.: Rutgers University Press, 1967), p. 138; Mary Ann Stillman Quarles, "Organizational Analysis of the New Jersey Reforma-

tory for Women in Relation to Stated Principles of Corrections, 1913–1963: A Case Study in Institutional Change" (Ph.D. diss., Boston University, 1966); Mary Belle Harris, *I Knew Them in Prison* (New York: Viking Press, 1942), p. 100.

41. Quarles, "Organizational Analysis of the New Jersey Reformatory," pp. 76, 151–53, 164–65, 259; Harris, *I Knew Them in Prison*, p. 100ff.

42. See W. Elliot Brownlee and Mary M. Brownlee, *Women in the American Economy: A Documentary History, 1675–1929* (New Haven: Yale University Press, 1976), pp. 35, 37.

43. BH, "Minutes of Managers," 10 July 1903 and 11 January 1902, asking for transfer of those "who give no promise of improvement"; NYPC, *Annual Reports, 1907*, pp. 74, 89; *1910*, pp. 63–65. Both the WPA and the state prison commissioners worked for the establishment of the state farm, which opened after 1912.

44. BH, "Reports," 1904; BH, "Reports," 1906; BH, "Minutes of Managers," 13 July 1906 and February 1911; BH, *Annual Report, 1911–1912*, p. 32. The proportion of Jewish women in the total reformatory population increased from 11.3 percent in 1911 to 18.8 percent in 1912. No explicitly anti-Semitic statements appeared in the record. Over the next decade special religious and social services were established for Jewish inmates, and Alice Davis Menken of the Jewish Big Sisters became a member of the prison Board of Managers in the 1920s.

45. BH, "Reports," 1910, discusses the reduction of appropriations; BH, "Minutes of Managers," November 1904; BH, *Annual Report, 1912–1913*, p. 6, mentions the need for funds to alleviate overcrowding. The period from 1909 to 1913 appears to be that of the most stringent finances, while overcrowding seems worst after 1911. At one point, Lawrence Vieller and the Charity Organization Society waged a public campaign to restore Bedford's appropriations and succeeded in gaining a legislative allotment of over $400,000 (BH, *Annual Report, 1912–1913*, p. 6). "Abnormal attachments" are mentioned in BH, "Minutes of Managers," April 1908 and February 1911.

46. BH, "Minutes of Managers," November 1904.

47. According to former staff members, Davis had stimulated high morale in the face of difficulties, but her successor could not do the same (Virginia Robinson, *Jessie Taft: Therapist and Social Work Educator, a Professional Biography* [Philadelphia: University of Pennsylvania Press, 1962], pp. 43–44).

48. New York Board of Charities, *Report of the Special Committee appointed to Investigate charges made against the New York State Reformatory for Women at Bedford Hills, New York* (Albany, 1915), pp. 4, 10, 25 (hereafter cited as *Bedford Investigation, 1915*).

49. *Bedford Investigation, 1915*, p. 10.

50. Ibid., pp. 7, 17–18. Cf. Margaret Otis, "A Perversion Not Commonly

Noted," *Journal of Abnormal Psychology* 8 (June–July 1913): 112–16 on interracial sex in prison.

51. *Bedford Investigation, 1915*, pp. 5, 8, 9, 18, 21.

52. Several historians have suggested that tolerance for women's homoerotic and homosexual relationships declined in the early twentieth century. See: Carroll Smith-Rosenberg, "The Female World of Love and Ritual: Relations between Women in Nineteenth-Century America," *Signs* 1 (Autumn 1975): 1–29 and Nancy Sahli, "Smashing: Women's Relationships Before the Fall," *Chrysalis* 8 (Summer 1979): 17–27.

53. BH, "Minutes of Managers," April 1908 and February 1911.

54. Ibid., p. 26; BH, *Annual Report, 1916–1917*, p. 16.

55. *Bedford Investigation, 1915*, pp. 25–28. By 1917, four new cottages had been built.

56. New York Commission of Prisons, *Report to the Governor Relative to the Investigation and Inquiry into Allegations of Cruelty to Prisoners in the New York State Reformatory for Women, Bedford Hills* (Albany, 1920), p. 28 (hereafter cited as *Bedford Investigation, 1920*); BH, *Annual Report, 1916–1917*, pp. 8, 62. Rockefeller had established the laboratory for a five-year period, indicating that the state could then take it over. He extended its support for a year, but subsequent appeals to both the state and the philanthropist failed to procure funds.

57. *Bedford Investigation, 1920*, pp. 5–6, 19–20.

58. Ibid., p. 6.

59. Eugenia C. Lekkerkerker, *Reformatories for Women in the United States* (The Hague: J. B. Wolters, 1931), p. 110.

Chapter 8

1. MRPW, *Annual Report, 1918*, p. 66.

2. Committee on Penal and Correctional Institutions, *What Should Be Done for Chicago's Women Offenders? Recommendations and Report of the City Council Crime Commission* (Chicago: Hale-Crossley, 1916); Janie M. Coggeshall and Alice D. Menken, "A Woman's Reformatory in the Making: Minimum Standards," *Journal of Criminal Law and Criminology* 23 (January 1933): 819–28; Committee on the Care and Training of Delinquent Women and Girls of the National Committee on Prisons and Prison Labor, *Industries for Correctional Institutions for Women* (New York, 1927); New York State Department of Prisons, *Report of the Prison Survey Committee* (Albany, 1920), chap. 19, esp. p. 372; Jack M. Holl, introduction to *In Prison*, by Kate Richards O'Hare (Seattle: University of Washington Press, 1976). Holl notes that Frank Tannenbaum was the exception; Tannenbaum would have abolished the institutions, while other reformers of the 1920s believed in improving their staffs, training programs, and classification systems.

3. *Journal of the American Institute of Criminal Law* 12 (November 1921): 440–42; Megan Graves, "The Creation and Development of the Federal Reformatory for Women" (Research paper, University of Washington, 1973); Mary Belle Harris, *I Knew Them in Prison* (New York: Viking Press, 1942), esp. pp. 260–68; Rose Giallombardo, *Society of Women: A Study of a Women's Prison* (New York: John Wiley and Sons, Inc., 1966), p. 27.

4. For example, in 1921 members of the American Bar Association law enforcement committee blamed "women banded together as prison reformers" for creating crime waves by their sentiment for criminals, and called for "real punishment" (Hartford [Conn.] *Times*, 2 November 1921); Dr. Ellen Potter in 1934 suggested selective sterilization as an alternative to committing prostitutes to prison (Potter, "The Problem of Women in Penal and Correctional Institutions," *Journal of Criminal Law and Criminology* 25 [May 1934]: 65–75). Even women like O'Hare, who served at the Missouri State Penitentiary herself, or Madeleine Zabriskie Doty, who could withstand less than one week of her voluntary commitment to the Auburn, N.Y., women's prison, campaigned for *better* women's reformatories, rather than for abolition of the institutions. See Kate Richards O'Hare, *In Prison* (New York: Alfred A. Knopf, 1923; originally published 1920; reprint ed., Seattle: University of Washington Press, 1976); Madeleine Z. Doty, *Society's Misfits* (New York: Century Co., 1916).

5. Jessie Hodder, "The Problems of Discipline of the Troublesome and Disorderly Prisoner," APA, *Proceedings, 1920*, pp. 206–16.

6. O'Hare, *In Prison*, p. 178.

7. Mary Macey Dietzler, *Detention Houses and Reformatories as Protective Social Agencies in the Campaign of the United States Government Against Venereal Diseases* (Washington, D.C.: Government Printing Office, 1922); Harris, *I Knew Them in Prison*, p. 310. Between 1918 and 1931, fourteen states enacted penal provisions which made it easier to convict prostitutes by not requiring proof of soliciting. See Max Grunhut, *Penal Reform* (1948; reprint, Montclair, N.J.: Patterson Smith, 1972), p. 407.

8. Helen W. Rogers, "A Digest of Laws Establishing Reformatories for Women in the United States," *Journal of Criminal Law and Criminology* 13 (November 1922): 384.

9. Allison T. French, "The Need for Industrial Homes for Women," *Social Hygiene* 5 (January 1919): 11–12.

10. Dietzler, *Detention Houses*, pp. 1, 3, 28. These ranged from new state reformatories in the South to local detention centers within hospitals.

11. Martha Falconer, "Work of the Section on Reformatories and Houses of Detention," NCCC, *Proceedings, 1918*, p. 668; idem, "The Part of the Reformatory Institution in the Elimination of Prostitution," *Social Hygiene* 5 (January 1919): 1–9.

12. Dietzler, *Detention Houses*, pp. 3–5.

13. Ibid., p. 64.

14. Ralph R. Arditi et al., "The Sexual Segregation of American Prisons,"

Yale Law Journal 82 (May 1973): 1229–73. I am grateful to the authors for offering me access to their sources and in particular to Fred Goldberg for first asking me about the history of women's prisons.

15. Ibid., p. 1245, n. 92, n. 94.

16. Harris, *I Knew Them in Prison*, p. 285.

17. Arditi et al., "Sexual Segregation," 1237–43; Miriam Van Waters, "Specialized Treatment of the Women Offenders in America and the Reasons for the Success of This Movement," *Bulletin of the International Penal and Penitentiary Commission* 13 (November 1948): 3–5.

18. New York *Prison Survey*, 1920, pp. 382–83.

19. Ibid., pp. 382–85.

20. Committee on the Care and Training of Delinquent Women and Girls, *Industries for Correctional Institutions for Women*, esp. pp. 8–9.

21. E.g., Austin H. MacCormick *The Education of Adult Prisoners: A Survey and a Program* (New York: National Society of Penal Information, 1931), p. 296 (MacCormick was then Assistant Director of the United States Bureau of Prisons); New York State Commission to Investigate Prison Administration and Construction, *The Correctional Institutions for Women* (Albany, 1932), which suggested clerical and commercial courses as well as industrial training for traditional women's work, such as sewing, canning, and knitting (p. 15ff); *A United States System of Correction: Final Report of the Prison Study Committee* (Hartford, Conn., 1957), cited in Sasha Harman, "Attitudes toward Women in the Criminal Process" (Research paper, Yale University Law School, 1972), p. 34.

22. Heber H. Votaw, quoted in Graves, "Federal Reformatory for Women," p. 7. The hearings were on HR 13927, 67th Congress, 4th Session.

23. Ibid., pp. 39–40.

24. On the overt and subtle pressures undermining feminism and women's careers after 1920, see: Mary P. Ryan, *Womanhood in America: From Colonial Times to the Present*, rev. ed., (New York: Franklin Watts, 1979), chap. 5; Estelle B. Freedman, "The New Woman: Changing Views of Women in the 1920's," *Journal of American History* 61 (September 1974): 372–93; and William H. Chafe, *The American Woman: Her Changing Social, Economic, and Political Roles, 1920–1970* (New York: Oxford University Press, 1972), esp. chap. 4.

25. Chafe, *The American Woman*, chap. 4.

26. The outstanding exceptions for the period after 1930 were Miriam Van Waters, a juvenile reformer who succeeded Jessie Hodder at Framingham and gained national renown, and Eleanor Glueck, who coauthored with Sheldon Glueck, *Five Hundred Delinquent Women* (New York: Alfred A. Knopf, 1934). Even Van Waters, however, came under attack in the 1940s; she successfully defended herself from an attempt to remove her as superintendent.

27. Sinclair Lewis, *Ann Vickers* (Garden City, N.Y.: Doubleday Doran and Co., Inc., 1933), p. 562.

28. The incidents of sexual assault by women which have been reported in women's institutions do not occur routinely, as they do in men's or mixed prisons. The cases cited by Brownmiller in her study of rape, for instance, occurred in mental institutions or juvenile centers, and boys were often involved in them (Susan Brownmiller, *Against Our Will: Men, Women, and Rape* [New York: Simon and Schuster, 1975], pp. 267–68).

29. O'Hare, *In Prison*, p. 64.

30. Jessie Hodder, "The Treatment of Delinquent Women," APA, *Proceedings, 1922*, p. 16.

31. O'Hare, *In Prison*, p. 160.

32. E.g., Bedford Hills (see chap. 7 above). The Federal Industrial Institution for Women at Alderson suffered a similar fate in the 1930s; overcrowding peaked in 1937 and 1938 and necessitated the establishment of a second federal women's reformatory in Texas in 1940. After World War II, however, the additional institution was converted to a men's prison (Harris, *I Knew Them in Prison*, p. 306; Graves, "Federal Reformatory for Women," pp. 47–49).

33. Arditi et al., "Sexual Segregation," app. 2 and 3, pp. 1269–73.

34. Kathryn W. Burkhart, *Women in Prison* (Garden City, N.Y.: Doubleday and Co., 1973), p. 128 and chap. 5.

35. One male convict summarized his impressions after having served time at both a men's and a newly integrated women's institution: "Men are treated as adults, even in prison; women are treated as children, out there and in prison" (Interview with author, 9 May 1973, Framingham, Mass.). On the social roles of women in contemporary prisons, see Giallombardo, *Society of Women*, esp. chaps. 8 and 9; and David A. Ward and Gene G. Kassebaum, *Women's Prison: Sex and Social Structure* (Chicago: Aldine, 1965).

36. See, for example, "Women Locked Up," issue of *Women: A Journal of Liberation* 3:3, esp. Susan Atkins, "Karlene: On Prisons," pp. 30–32; Burkhart, *Women in Prison*; "Women against Prisons," *Off Our Backs*, June 1978, p. 7; "Close Down Alderson," *No More Cages* 4 (August 1979): 7.

37. Radical criminologists share these views. See Dorie Klein and June Kress, "Any Woman's Blues: A Critical Overview of Women, Crime, and the Criminal Justice System," *Crime and Social Justice* 5 (Spring-Summer 1976): 34–49 for an important critical review of women and criminal justice.

38. "Statement of Purpose," *No More Cages* 1 (August 1979): n.p. On decriminalization, see, e.g., Edwin M. Schur, *Crimes without Victims: Deviant Behavior and Public Policy: Abortion, Homosexuality, Drug Addiction* (Englewood Cliffs, N.J.: Prentice-Hall, Inc., 1965); Women Endorsing Decriminalization, "Prostitution: A Non-Victim Crime?" *Issues in Criminology* 8 (Fall 1973): 137–62.

39. The best national coverage of women prisoners has appeared in *Off Our Backs*, the Washington, D.C. feminist monthly paper. Newsletters

which cover specific prisons include: "Through the Looking Glass: A Women's and Children's Prison Newsletter" (Seattle, Wash.); "No More Cages" (West Nyack, N.Y.); "Rose in a Cage" (San Francisco City Jail); "Free Flight" (Federal Correctional Institution at Pleasanton, Calif.). Local projects of the 1960s and 1970s included: Women Free Women in Prison (New York); Women Against Prisons (San Francisco); Santa Cruz (Calif.) Women's Prison Project; Women's Prison Project (Bedford Hills, N.Y.); Legal Services for Prisoners with Children (San Francisco). I am grateful to Ellen Barry for information on these projects.

40. "Framingham's Co-Ed Prison," Boston *Globe*, 28 May 1973; "Connecticut is Going Co-Ed," New York *Times*, 27 May 1973, p. E 10; Arditi et al., "Sexual Segregation," p. 1232, n. 4; "Plan for Women Guards in Men's Prisons Opposed," New York *Times*, 2 September 1973, p. 28; "Men's Prison Gets a Woman Warden," New York *Times*, 22 August 1975, p. 33; "Sheriff Fights Back After Control of Jail is Shifted to a Woman," New York *Times*, 31 August 1975, p. 30.

41. New York *Times*, 26 November 1978, p. 56.

42. Alderson inmates also rioted in September 1971 (Frieda Adler, *Sisters in Crime: The Rise of the New Female Criminal* [New York: McGraw-Hill, 1975], pp. 178, 181).

Selected Bibliography

Manuscripts and Typescripts

American Jewish Historical Society, Waltham, Mass.
  Alice Davis Menken Papers
Chicago Historical Society, Chicago, Ill.
  Chicago Woman's Club Papers
  Louise de Koven Bowen Papers
Earlham College, Archives, Richmond, Ind.
  Charles F. Coffin and Rhoda M. Coffin Papers
Haverford Quaker Collection, Haverford College, Haverford, Pa.
  Josiah Leeds Papers
Illinois State Historical Library, Springfield, Ill.
  Joseph Ragen Papers
Indiana State Library, Indiana Division, Indianapolis, Ind.
  Thomas A. Hendricks Papers
  Indiana State Board of Charities Papers
Library of Congress, Manuscript Division, Washington, D.C.
  Clara Barton Papers
Massachusetts Correctional Institution, Framingham, Mass.
  History of Framingham, 1919–26
  History of Inmates, 1877–1915
  Record of Indentures
  Records of Births, 1877–91
Massachusetts State Library, Boston, Mass.
  Massachusetts Governor and Council Investigation of State Departments and Institutions
  Warren F. Spalding Letter Book
New York State Library, Manuscripts and History, Albany, N.Y.
  New York State Board of Charities Correspondence
  New York State Executive Department Papers
New York State Reformatory for Women, Bedford Hills, N.Y.
  Superintendent's Reports, 1901–11
Radcliffe College, Arthur and Elizabeth Schlesinger Library, Cambridge, Mass.
  Ethel Sturgis Dummer Papers
  Elizabeth Glendower Evans Papers
  Jessie Donaldson Hodder Papers
  Poor Family Papers

227

University of Chicago, Regenstein Library, Chicago, Ill.
  Grace and Edith Abbott Papers
University of Illinois, Chicago Circle Campus Library, Chicago, Ill.
  Chicago Women's Aid Papers
University of Michigan, Bentley Historical Library, Ann Arbor, Mich.
  Emma Hall Papers
  Eliza Mosher Papers

Unpublished Secondary Sources

Carson, Norma Vere. "An Historical and Critical Study of New York State Reformatories for Women." Master's thesis, Columbia University, 1917.

Case, Suzanne. "Eliza Farnham: The Woman and Her Era, 1815–1864." Senior honors thesis, Department of History, Stanford University, 1979.

Faber, Eli. "The Evil That Men Do: Crime and Transgression in Colonial Massachusetts." Ph.D. dissertation, Columbia University, 1974.

Fishbein, Leslie. "Righteousness, Romance, Sex Drives, Hard Cash: Changing Views of Prostitution, 1870–1920." Paper delivered at the Annual Meeting of the Organization of American Historians, Atlanta, Ga., 1977.

Freedman, Estelle B. "Their Sisters' Keepers: The Origins of Female Corrections in America." Ph.D. dissertation, Columbia University, 1976.

Giovannoni, Jeanne M., and Purvine, Margaret E. "The Myth of the Social Work Matriarchy." Paper presented at the National Conference on Social Welfare, Atlantic City, N.J., 29 May 1973.

Graves, Megan. "The Creation and Development of the Federal Reformatory for Women." Research paper, University of Washington, 1973.

Harman, Sasha. "Attitudes towards Women in the Criminal Process." Research paper, Yale University Law School, 1972.

Hazzard, Florence Woolsey. "Heart of the Oak: The Story of Eliza Mosher." Manuscript biography. Eliza Mosher Papers, Bentley Historical Library, University of Michigan, Ann Arbor.

Helfman, Harold M. "A History of Penal, Correctional and Reformatory Institutions in Michigan, 1839–1889." Ph.D. dissertation, University of Michigan, 1947.

Hindus, Michael S. "The Social Context of Crime in Massachusetts and South Carolina, 1760–1873: Theoretical and Quantitative Perspectives." Paper presented at the annual meeting of the American Historical Association, Chicago, December 1974.

Hobson, Barbara. "Seduced and Abandoned, a Tale of the Wicked City: The Response to Prostitution in Boston, 1820–1850." Paper delivered at the Fourth Berkshire Conference on the History of Women, Mt. Holyoke College, 23 August 1978.

Knauer, Louise. "Mothers in Israel, Daughters of Zion: Recruitment of Evangelical Missionaries, 1840–1890." Paper delivered at the Fourth

Berkshire Conference on the History of Women, Mt. Holyoke College, 25 August 1978.

Menken, Alice Davis. "Survey of Reformatory and Correctional Institutions and Agencies as Related to the Problem of Commercialized Vice." Mimeographed copy of report for the Special Sub-Committee of the Committee of Fourteen, August 1919. Menken Papers, American Jewish Historical Society, Waltham, Mass.

Mezvinsky, Norton. "The White-Ribbon Reform, 1874–1920." Ph.D. dissertation, University of Wisconsin, 1959.

Pivar, David Jay. "The New Abolitionism: The Quest for Social Purity, 1876–1900." Ph.D. dissertation, University of Pennsylvania, 1965.

Quarles, Mary Ann Stillman. "Organizational Analysis of the New Jersey Reformatory for Women in Relation to Stated Principles of Corrections, 1913–1963: A Case Study in Institutional Change." Ph.D. dissertation, Boston University, 1966.

Rapperport, Lucy. "The Massachusetts Reformatory for Women, Framingham, Massachusetts." B. Arch. thesis, Graduate School of Design, Harvard University, 1954.

Rosen, Ruth. "Prostitution: Symbol of an Age." Paper presented at the American Historical Association Meeting, San Francisco, Calif., 29 December 1978.

Rosenberg, Rosalind. "The Dissent from Darwin, 1890–1930: The New View of Woman among American Social Scientists." Ph.D. dissertation, Stanford University, 1974.

Sanders, Wiley Britton. "The History and Administration of the State Prisons of Illinois." Ph.D. dissertation, University of Chicago, 1929.

Smith-Rosenberg, Carroll. "A Richer and Gentler Sex." Paper delivered at the Berkshire Conference on Women's History, Bryn Mawr College, June 1976.

Tyor, Peter. "Segregation or Surgery: The Mentally Retarded in America, 1850–1920." Ph.D. dissertation, Northwestern University, 1972.

Zimmerman, Hilda Jane. "Penal Systems and Penal Reforms in the South since the Civil War." Ph.D. dissertation, University of North Carolina, 1947.

Official Records

Chicago Crime Commission, Committee on Penal and Correctional Institutions. *What Should Be Done for Chicago's Women Offenders? Recommendations and Report of the City Council Crime Commission.* Chicago: Hale-Crossley, 1916.

Connecticut. Commission on a Reformatory for Women. *Report of the Commission on a Reformatory for Women to the General Assembly, 1915.* Hartford: 1915.

———. State Farm for Women. *Annual Report of Directors of the Connecti-*

cut State Farm for Women to the Governor for the Period between July 1, 1917 and September 30, 1918. Hartford: 1918.

Indiana. Department of Statistics and Geology. *Annual Report of the Department of Statistics and Geology, 1879–1880.* Indianapolis: 1880.

———. General Assembly. House of Representatives. Committee on Prisons. *Report of the Southern Prison.* Indianapolis: 1869.

———. General Assembly. House of Representatives. *Journal.* Indianapolis: 1869.

———. General Assembly. Senate. *Journal.* Indianapolis: 1869.

———. Industrial School for Girls and Indiana Woman's Prison. *Report.* Indiana: 1899–1907.

———. Reformatory Institution for Women and Girls. *Report of the Board of Managers.* Indianapolis: 1870–88.

———. Reform School for Girls and Woman's Prison. *Report.* Indianapolis: 1889–98.

———. State Board of Charities. *Annual Report.* Indianapolis: 1890–1903.

———. Woman's Prison. *Annual Report of the Board of Trustees.* Indianapolis: 1908.

Massachusetts. *Annual Report of the Board of Prison Commissioners, 1901–1914/15.* Boston: 1902–16.

———. Board of Commissioners of Prisons. *Annual Report of the Commissioners of Prisons of Massachusetts, 1871–1900.* Boston: 1872–1901.

———. Board of Commissioners of Prisons. *Rules and Regulations for the Government of the State Prison.* Boston: 1892.

———. Board of Commissioners of Prisons. *Special Report Covering the Period from October 4, 1870 to February 9, 1871.* House Document no. 84, 1871.

———. Board of State Charities. *Annual Report of the Board of State Charities, 1864–1878.* Boston: 1865–79.

———. Board of State Charities. *Special Report on Prisons and Prison Discipline.* Boston: 1865.

———. Bureau of Statistics of Labor. *The Census of Massachusetts: 1875.* Boston: 1876–77.

———. Bureau of Statistics of Labor. *The Census of Massachusetts: 1880.* Boston: 1883.

———. Bureau of Statistics of Labor. *Census of the Commonwealth of Massachusetts: 1895.* Boston: 1896–1900.

———. General Court. House of Representatives. Committee on Prisons. *Report on Penal Institutions.* Legislative Documents no. 388, 1880; no. 421, 1881. Boston: 1880, 1881.

———. General Court. House of Representatives. *Journal.* Boston: 1870–75.

———. General Court. Senate. Committee on Prisons. *Report on Penal Institutions.* Legislative Documents no. 272, 1879; no. 369, 1884; no. 287, 1888; no. 335, 1889. Boston: 1879, 1884, 1888, 1889.

———. General Court. Senate. *Journal.* Boston: 1870–75.

———. Prison Commissioner. *Report on the Subject of Matrons and Labor in the Common Jails.* Boston: 1884.

———. Reformatory Prison for Women. *Annual Report, 1878–1922.* Boston: 1878–1922. (In Massachusetts Board of Commissioners of Prisons. *Annual Report, 1878–1900.*)

Michigan. *Second Biennial Report of the Board of State Commissioners for the General Supervision of Charitable, Penal, Pauper, and Reformatory Institutions.* Lansing: 1875.

New York. Board of Charities. *Annual Report, 1867–1916.* Albany: 1868–1916.

———. Board of Charities. *Report of the Special Committee appointed to investigate charges made against the New York State Reformatory for Women at Bedford Hills, New York.* Albany: 1915.

———. Commission of Prisons. *Annual Report, 1894–1920.* Albany: 1895–1921.

———. Commission of Prisons. *Report to the Governor Relative to the Investigation and Inquiry into Allegations of Cruelty to Prisoners in the New York State Reformatory for Women, Bedford Hills.* Albany: 1920.

———. Commission on Prison Administration and Construction. *The Correctional Institutions for Women. Special Report by the Commission to Investigate Prison Administration and Construction.* Albany: 1932.

———. Legislature. Assembly. *Journal.* Albany: 1887, 1891, 1892.

———. Legislature. Assembly. *Report of the Western House of Refuge for Women.* Legislative Documents no. 67, 1895; no. 35, 1896; no. 12, 1897; no. 38, 1898; no. 25, 1899; no. 51, 1900; no. 48, 1901. Albany: 1895–1901.

———. Legislature. Senate. *Report of the Inspectors of State Prisons.* Legislative Documents no. 99, 1856, no. 22, 1870. Albany: 1856, 1870.

———. Prison Commission. *Investigation of the State Prisons and Report Thereon, 1876.* Albany: 1877.

———. Prison Department. *Annual Report of the Superintendent of State Prisons, 1887.* Albany: 1888.

———. Prison Reform Commission. *Preliminary Report.* Albany: 1914.

———. Prison Survey Committee. *Report of the Prison Survey Committee.* Albany: 1920.

———. Reformatory for Women, Bedford Hills. *Annual Report, 1911/12–1929.*

———. Secretary of State. *Census of New York State, 1835, 1845, 1855, 1865, 1875.* Albany: 1836, 1846, 1857, 1867, 1877.

———. Secretary of State. *Report in Relation to Convictions for Criminal Offences,* and *Abstracts of Convictions for Criminal Offences.* Legislative Documents, 1838–1900. Albany: 1838–1900.

United States. Department of Commerce. Bureau of the Census. *Prisoners and Juvenile Delinquents in the United States, 1910.* Washington, D.C.: 1918.

———. Department of the Interior. Census Office. *Compendium of Tenth Census, June 1, 1880, Part II*. Washington, D.C.: 1883.

———. Department of the Interior. Census Office. *Report on Crime, Pauperism and Benevolence in the United States at the Eleventh Census: 1890, Part II*. Washington, D.C.: 1895.

———. Department of the Interior. Census Office. *Report on the Defective, Dependent, and Delinquent Classes of the Population of the United States*. Washington, D.C.: 1888.

———. Immigration Commission. Reports of the Immigration Commission. Vol. 26. *Immigration and Crime*. Washington, D.C.: 1911.

Organizational Reports

American Prison Association. *Proceedings of the Annual Congress of the American Prison Association*, 1909–25.

Conference of Charities. *Proceedings of the Conference of Charities*, 1875–79.

Conference of Charities and Corrections. *Proceedings of the Conference of Charities and Corrections*, 1880–81.

Dedham Temporary Asylum for Discharged Female Prisoners. *Annual Report*. Dedham: 1864.

Home for the Friendless. *Third Annual Report*. Richmond, Ind.: 1871.

National Conference of Charities and Corrections. *Proceedings of the National Conference of Charities and Corrections*, 1882–1916.

National Conference of Social Work. *Proceedings of the National Conference of Social Work*, 1917–22.

National Prison Association. *Proceedings of the Annual Congresses of the National Prison Association*, 1884–1908.

National Prison Association. *Transactions of the National Prison Association*, 1874–76.

Prison Association of New York. *Annual Reports*. New York and Albany: 1844–95.

Society for the Prevention of Pauperism in the City of New York. *Second Annual Report of the Managers*. New York: 1820.

Women's Prison Association and Home of New York. *Annual Report*. New York: 1844–1907.

Newspapers

Boston *Transcript*, 1912, 1914, 1917.

Indianapolis *Journal*, 1860–89.

Indianapolis *News*, 1898–1907.

Indianapolis *Sentinel*, 1860–89.

Indianapolis *Star*, 1905.

New York *Times*, 1872–79, 1886–89, 1894–96, 1899, 1905.

New York *Tribune*, 1844, 1845, 1888, 1905.

Woman's Journal, 1874–89, 1891, 1893–97, 1900–1902, 1911–13, 1928.

Selected Books and Articles

Abbott, Edith. "The Civil War and the Crime Wave of 1865–1870." *Social Service Review* 1 (1927): 212–34.

Arditi, Ralph R.; Goldberg, Frederick, Jr.; Hartle, M. Martha; Peters, John H.; and Phelps, William R. "The Sexual Segregation of American Prisons." *Yale Law Journal* 82 (1973): 1229–73.

Barrows, Isabel C. "The Massachusetts Reformatory Prison for Women." In *The Reformatory System in the United States*, edited by Samuel J. Barrows. Washington, D.C.: Government Printing Office, 1900.

———. "The Reformatory Treatment of Women in the United States." In *Penal and Reformatory Institutions*, edited by Charles Richmond Henderson. New York: Russell Sage Foundation, 1910.

Beaumont, Gustave de, and Toqueville, Alexis de. *On the Penitentiary System in the United States, and Its Application in France*. Translated by Francis Lieber. Philadelphia: Carey, Lea and Blanchard, 1833.

Carpenter, Mary. *Our Convicts*. 1864. Reprint. Montclair, N.J.: Patterson Smith, 1969.

Conyngton, Mary. *Relation Between Occupation and Criminality of Women*. Washington, D.C.: Government Printing Office, 1911.

Davis, Katharine Bement. "The New York State Reformatory for Women." *Survey* 25 (1911): 851–54.

Dietzler, Mary Macey. *Detention Houses and Reformatories as Protective Social Agencies in the Campaign of the United States Government Against Venereal Diseases*. The United States Interdepartmental Social Hygiene Board. Washington, D.C.: Government Printing Office, 1922.

Emerson, Sarah Hopper, ed. *Life of Abby Hopper Gibbons, Told Chiefly through Her Correspondence*. New York: Knickerbocker Press, 1897.

Fernald, Mabel Ruth; Hayes, Mary; and Dawley, Almena. *A Study of Women Delinquents in New York State*. 1920. Reprint. Montclair, N.J.: Patterson Smith, 1968.

Foucault, Michel. *Discipline and Punish: The Birth of the Prison*. Translated by Alan Sheridan. New York: Pantheon Books, 1977.

Freedman, Estelle. "Separatism as Strategy: Female Institution Building and American Feminism, 1870–1930." *Feminist Studies* 5 (1979): 512–29.

Fry, Elizabeth. *Observations in Visiting, Superintendence and Government of Female Prisoners*. London: John and Arthur Arch, Cornhill, 1827.

Henderson, Charles Richmond, ed. *Penal and Reformatory Institutions*. Vol. II, *Corrections and Prevention*. New York: Charities Publication Committee, 1910.

Holl, Jack M. *Juvenile Reform in the Progressive Era: William R. George and the Junior Republic Movement*. Ithaca: Cornell University Press, 1971.

Johnson, Ellen Cheney. *Modern Prison Management: The Underlying Principles of Prison Reform, as Applied in the Reformatory Prison for Women at Sherborn, Massachusetts*. Boston: Massachusetts Prison Association, 1899.

Johnson, Mary C. *Rhoda Coffin: Her Reminiscences, Addresses, Papers and Ancestry.* New York: The Grafton Press, 1910.

Kellor, Frances Alice. "Psychological and Environmental Study of Women Criminals." *American Journal of Sociology* 5 (1900): 527–43, 671–82.

Kent, John. *Elizabeth Fry.* London: B. T. Batsford, Ltd., 1962.

Kirkland, Caroline M. *The Helping Hand: Comprising an Account of the Home for Discharged Female Convicts and an Appeal in behalf of that Institution.* New York: Charles Scribner, 1853.

Lekkerkerker, Eugenia C. *Reformatories for Women in the United States.* The Hague: J. B. Wolters, 1931.

Lewis, Orlando F. *The Development of American Prisons and Prison Customs, 1776–1845, with special reference to institutions in the State of New York.* Albany: Prison Association of New York, 1922.

Lewis, W. David. *From Newgate to Dannemora: The Rise of the Penitentiary in New York, 1796–1848.* Ithaca: Cornell University Press, 1965.

Lombroso, Cesare, and Ferrero, William. *The Female Offender.* New York: D. Appleton and Company, 1900. Originally published in English in 1895.

McKelvey, Blake. *American Prisons: A Study in American Social History prior to 1915.* Chicago: University of Chicago Press, 1936.

Mosher, Eliza M. "Health of Criminal Women." *Boston Medical and Surgical Journal,* 5 October 1882, pp. 316–17.

O'Hare, Kate Richards. *In Prison.* New York: Alfred A. Knopf, 1923. Originally published in 1920. Reprint. Seattle: University of Washington Press, 1976.

Rogers, Helen W. "A Digest of Laws Establishing Reformatories for Women in the United States." *Journal of Criminal Law and Criminology* 13 (1922): 382–437.

Rothman, David J. *The Discovery of the Asylum: Social Order and Disorder in the New Republic.* Boston: Little, Brown and Co., 1971.

Smith, Ann. D. *Women in Prison: A Study in Penal Methods.* London: Stevens, 1962.

Smith-Rosenberg, Carroll. "Beauty, the Beast and the Militant Woman: A Case Study in Sex Roles and Social Stress in Jacksonian America." *American Quarterly 23 (1971):* 562–84.

———. *Religion and the Rise of the American City: The New York Mission Movement, 1812–1870.* Ithaca: Cornell University Press, 1971.

Stewart, William Rhinelander. *The Philanthropic Work of Josephine Shaw Lowell.* New York: Macmillan Company, 1911.

Wines, Enoch C., and Dwight, Theodore. *Report on the Prisons and Reformatories of the United States and Canada.* Albany: Van Benthuysen and Sons, 1867.

———. *The State of Prisons and Child-Saving Institutions in the Civilized World, 1880.* Cambridge, Mass.: University Press, 1880.

Worthington, George E., and Topping, Ruth. *Specialized Courts Dealing with Sex Delinquency*. New York: Frederick H. Hitchcock, 1921.

Wyman, Lillie Buffum Chace, and Wyman, Arthur Crawford. *Elizabeth Buffum Chace, 1806–1899: Her Life and Its Environment*. Boston: W. B. Clarke Co., 1914.

Index